CHRIS SCOTT is best known guides including the *Adve Overland, Australia Rough* His early Saharan visits are

not writing books or kayaking in Scotland, he leads tours to Morocco and beyond with camels, 4x4s or bikes.

[Desert Biking is] *not the obvious choice for a holiday, but you can see the appeal.* **Loaded**

[Sahara Overland] *is the essential Sahara guide.* **Sunday Times**

Gets right to the heart of desert travel. **Michael Palin**

[Adventure Motorcycling Handbook] *does for adventure riding books what* Saving Private Ryan *does for war movies.* **Motorcycle Consumer News**

you must read this book… Chris Scott's a veteran of serious travel. **Bike**

[AMH] *is the book that I can say, without exaggeration, helped change my life.* **Lois Pryce, Overland Journal**

The first thing we did was buy the Adventure Motorcycling Handbook. **Ewan McGregor, Long Way Round**

Fortunately, I had Chris Scott's indispensible Adventure Motorcycling Handbook up my sleeve, which clearly outlines the unwritten rules. **Dan Walsh, Bike magazine 500th issue**

That rare and best sort of travel book, where the journey is one of growth and personal development… Desert Travels comes high up on our list of best books. **Classic Bike**

Light-hearted and readable account… as the author graduates from apprentice to desert connoisseur. **Lonely Planet**

I cannot recommend [Overlanders Handbook] *highly enough. It is the first… last and middle word on overlanding.* **4x4 SA**

[OLH is] *one of the most comprehensive travel books I have ever read.* **Getaway**

Morocco Overland is the bible… **Wanderlust**

The Street Riding Years

Despatching through 80s London

Chris Scott

Published by Chris Scott

Copyright © Chris Scott; fourth reprint 2018

Originally published in 2015 as *Adventures in Motorcycling*.

A CIP catalogue record of this book is available from the British Library.

978-0-9930465-2-0

Printed in Poland

Do we really want to travel in hermetically sealed popemobiles through the rural provinces of France, Mexico and the Far East, eating only in Hard Rock Cafes and McDonalds? Or do we want to eat without fear, tearing into the local stew, the humble taqueria's mystery meat, the sincerely offered gift of a lightly grilled fish head? I know what I want. I want it all. I want to try everything once.

Anthony Bourdain, Kitchen Confidential.

Most accidents happen within three miles of home.

Walker (Lee Marvin), *Point Blank*, 1967.

1

TERRA INCOGNITA

Honda SS50

It was the perfect night for a small accident. For two weeks I'd been prowling the neighbourhood's avenues on my new moped, perfecting my moves, exploring the limits. The time had now come for juvenile confidence to overtake experience – on the inside, head down and without a cautionary glance in the mirrors.

That chilly winter's night I was encased in my mountaineering duvet jacket under a NATO-patterned shooting coat and a pair of huge, AA patrolman's gauntlets. Snugly camouflaged for north European warfare, I felt invulnerable, if slightly on the hot side. The moment had come to see just what my little Honda SS50 could do. It was time to go for the big Four Zero.

Ahead of me there was no shimmering salt lake, no deserted runway with paramedics on standby. I was at the summit of Norbury Court Road, with a fire station down on the corner of the busy A23 Brighton Road. If, like Steve Austin in the opening sequence of the *Six Million Dollar Man*, the atmospheric friction of hitting Mach 0.0525 saw me burst into flames on re-entry, I was sure the brigade would be on hand to hose me down. That's if they weren't on strike.

It was January 1977 and, then as now, Norbury was a nondescript south London suburb that is still best described as 'between Streatham and Croydon'. If Norbury had any claim to fame it was the rumour that Deryck Guyler, the caretaker from the ITV schoolyard sitcom *Please Sir!* lived up on the airy heights of Pollards Hill.

The previous summer's heatwave had passed and with it went my interest in schooling. A few weeks after dutifully trotting into the sixth form, it dawned on me I didn't *have* to be there any more. So I made my excuses, cleared my desk and strode down the hill singing The Who's 'I'm Free', and actually meaning it. My school tie – two halves stapled together and pockmarked with magnifying-glass burns – was scrunched in my pocket, never to be worn again. I felt exhilarated. While it may not have suffered a catastrophic explosion, for me on that October day, School – Was – Out – For – Ever.

The Saturday job at Sainsbury's became full-time and, as I was still living at home, my £19.50 weekly wage meant that by the new year I could afford not only a flash duvet jacket and a Chouinard ice axe, but a hundred and twenty quid's worth of moped as well. Looking back, £120 seems extravagant. Was I bike mad? Not really. At that time the classic climbing routes of Chamonix held more interest than Brands Hatch or the Isle of Man TT. Barry Sheene may have just become world champion, but I didn't know him from Barry Humphries, nor a Yamaha Fizzie from a bottle of Corona cherryade. Instead, like most sixteen-year-olds I was bored of pedalling myself around these last ten years and saw motorbikes as a natural progression. I assumed I'd eventually migrate to cars, but right

now I was ready for the excitement and adventure of motorbikes. I imagine I felt the same when I learned to walk fifteen
years earlier.

I was a player in the finale of the brief sports moped era,
when a manly, full-power, leg-over mini motorcycle came with
an actual kickstart, actual gears and a saddle for two – we all
knew what that suggested. Until just five years earlier, sixteen-
year-olds on a learner's licence had been free to ride a 250 with
no training or even a helmet (though by then the majority did
wear lids). Most 250s weren't that fast, but, as ever, teenagers were. Recreational motorcycling was booming in the UK
and casualties soared with it, so in 1972 under-seventeens
got limited to riding mopeds. In those days that meant 50cc
'pedal-and-go' stick insects like Puchs or Mobylettes, flat-out
at 30mph and with a wire basket on the front. Such harmless
mopeds weren't subject to restrictions on horsepower or top
speeds, so canny manufacturers soon fell over themselves to
design the fastest, flashiest and most furious fifty – with pedals. Accident rates for under-seventeens went off the graph
again and by 1975 manufacturers agreed to limit sports mopeds to 40mph. Meanwhile, a hard-hitting 'Think Bike' campaign started in the media to alert drivers and new riders to
the 'Sorry, mate, I didn't see you' syndrome.

Among these Sixteener Specials, Yamaha's two-stroke
FSIE 'Fizzie' was by far the most popular and one of the
fastest, along with the Italian Fantic 50 and the Garelli. In
the last weeks of school, a rich kid had come in on a Garelli
Tiger Cross. 'Flash bastard,' we all agreed. Lucky flash bastard, though. As soon as you got your hands on your two-
stroke sports moped you set about adapting it to scream up to
52mph, to the intense annoyance of anyone in earshot. "Oo
does 'e think 'e is, Barry Sheene?'

Like on the Fizzie, the Honda's engine was suspended from
its pressed-steel frame. What I later deduced was a carburettor

protruded from somewhere and disappeared into the engine, which thrust forward like Bruce Lee's slab-smashing fist. A high-level silencer was clad in a perforated chrome guard to suggest heat, power and melted PVC overtrousers.

The only flies in the SS ointment were the pedals-cum-footrests. Like others, Honda had found a way to get one pedal crank to disengage and rotate through 180° then lock in place to become a matching flimsy footrest. Even I could see it was still all a bit crap. Put any weight on either and the pedal cranks would shear for sure. Out of curiosity I disengaged the crank once and tried pedalling the Honda. It was like running through cold porridge with an SS50 under your arm.

The reason I'd settled on the Honda was that the only person I knew with a sports moped – ex-schoolmate Phil – let me have a go on his. I wasn't bothered about not getting the fastest fifty – I wasn't going to be riding it one minute past my seventeenth birthday, which was only a few months away. At that point I'd get a proper 250cc motorbike. All I needed to do was learn how to ride. The idea of being taught by experts in a safe car park full of cones never occurred to me or my mum. Instead, Phil came round and showed me how to spur his SS into life with the awkwardly articulated kickstarter. The motor ran with a muted purr, so much more refined than a Fizzie's ear-grating din. I turned the throttle and the purring became more insistent. I did it again. Vrrroooom… vroom-vrooooom.

'Yeah, all right, steady on, Chris. You'll bend a valve.'

Phil patiently explained the launch procedure. First pull in the clutch lever on the left handlebar, then click down to select first gear with the left foot. Now the tricky bit: synchronise the release of the clutch with the turning of the throttle on the right bar, while balancing and steering. I listened without really taking any of it in.

With my right foot on the ground steadying me, I pulled in

the clutch, trod down on the gear lever and turned the throttle. Then, once the engine was making a good noise, I released the clutch like a bowstring. The little bike shot out from under my legs, ran on, then tipped over and scraped down the road. Wondering what had just happened, I stood there, legs apart and slightly bent, hands resting on handlebars that were no longer there. Phil rushed over to attend to his moped, an instinct ingrained in any biker, as I'd soon learn. No matter how crippled you were, guts spilling down the road like wet tagliatelle, the first thing you did was right the bike and make sure it was OK. Only then was it safe to pass out.

Watching Phil's SS50 catapult away from me, I was beginning to see what they meant by 'sports mopeds'. These were clearly highly strung beasts, snarling petrol-fed leopards that would require some taming. We tried again and eventually I got the bike to move off with me still on it.

Once I had my own black four-speed SS50 mastering the coordination of the controls was child's play. Cornering, braking and even timing the gear changes with a dip in power delivery were much the same as on pushbikes and now the night had come to give my onyx leopard its head.

I set off down Norbury Court Road, shuffled a little, then hunkered down purposefully, just like those ski jumpers on *Ski Sunday*. I was focused not on a jump but on the speedo needle calibrating a similar leap into the abyss. I had to reach thirty well before halfway. Any later and I'd blow it or shoot into the Brighton Road and plant myself like a dozy crow in the side of a 109 bus.

The 2.5 horsepower motor screeched beneath me, aided by the lethal gradient. The needle crept around the dial, 34mph... 35... into top gear ... 36... 37... 37.5... the junction wasn't so far ahead now. I tucked in a bit more... 38... I'm running out of road... 38.5... The motor screamed. Sod it! I'm not going to make it.

11

'Houston, I can't hold her. She's breaking up. She's breaking—'

I snatched at the brakes as if I was pruning a gnarly shrub, and the combination of wet road and seventies-era tyres saw the bike flip in an instant. The Honda and I slid helplessly down the road towards the junction, until the friction of our assorted extremities slowed us to a stop.

Luckily my timing was better than my braking technique and we came to rest below the Give Way sign. I'd had my first 'prang'. In my over-padded get-up I was unharmed, but the Honda's headlamp, indicators and ungainly pedals were never to regain their factory-perfect alignment. Mach 0.0525 would have to wait for another day.

A few weeks earlier the postman had delivered a beautifully produced thirty-two-page brochure showcasing Honda's vast range of motorcycles. In it each succulent model was allotted a full page comprising a studio photo, technical data in two neat columns, and a colour illustration of you (possibly your lady) and your Honda in an idealised setting. The ST70 minibike rested by a village pond where Angler Man was hauling in a prize carp. Opposite was the CF70 Chaly, another dinky runabout, but a step-thru and clearly pitched at the demurer sex. Its mise en scène was a fairground where a coven of nymphs clad in miniskirts appeared to be rehearsing their routine. Over the page the smart CB200 twin was assisting at a hot air balloon event. I'd seen CB200s around and with their distinctive vinyl tank patches I thought them extremely handsome machines. A few pages on, the CB360K6 watched over two enraptured lovers enjoying a Mediterranean sunset. And who could miss the sensational CB400F. It was featured, cranked over, on the front cover, all the better to 'present' its sensuously contoured four-into-one downpipes like a sexed-up baboon. Below it ran Honda's pithy mission statement: 'More Sense, More Style'. It summed up my own teenage aspirations.

Even before that brochure arrived I'd become infatuated with my first motorcycle. It sat in the window of a tiny shop on Mitcham Lane in Streatham, a black and chrome apparition hovering gently behind the glass. Back then it was just One Sexy-Looking Motorbike – a Triumph – but the shiny chrome features have stayed with me: a perforated round air-filter housing and a tank-top grill on which to lash your oilskins. It was probably a mid-sixties T100SS with clip-ons and rear-sets. So my early taste wasn't so bad, even if it was already a decade behind the times. At least it wasn't a chopper or some horrible 175cc CZ breadbin.

Before I discovered bikes I'd taken up rock climbing. Unfortunately I was living in the wrong end of the country to make the most of that. I'd climbed everything going inside the house and the doorframes were beginning to show the strain. The artificial climbing wall up at the Sobell Sports Centre in Finsbury Park, north London, was the next best thing. With my EB rock shoes stuffed in a knapsack, I undertook my first motorcycling adventure one February evening after work: a bold traverse from Norbury, SW16 to Finsbury Park, N7, to be done *direttissima*, in the spirit of climbing legend Walter Bonatti. From SW16 down to SW1 and all the way back up to N7 would mean covering no less than twenty-three postal zones – something I wasn't sure I could manage without porters and extra oxygen. I studied the family *A-Z* closely and soon became baffled by the arrangement of London's postal zones. N7 was in fact adjacent to N1, which was above riverside EC4. Not so far then. The Sherpas were recalled to Namche Bazaar.

I set off up the A23 to negotiate the bandit-ridden badlands of the Elephant and Castle, then forded the Thames by means of the Blackfriars Bridge. Beyond lay terra incognita, which the most recent maps identified as 'north London'.

I buzzed warily over Ludgate Circus and below the ornate Holborn Viaduct. Just beyond, Topham Street EC1 remains ingrained in my memory as the very first time I breathlessly married a street name with the index and page of an *A-Z* – 'ground to map' as navigators call it. With my position re-affirmed, I established that the snowy peak of Mount Pleasant lay just ahead. Here, I needed to follow Rosebery Avenue uphill, deeper into the Death Zone, then bear north for the Angel Islington. I knew that one! It was a £100 cheapie from Monopoly. From Islington it was a short traverse along Upper Street then left at Highbury Corner and along Holloway Road for the Sobell.

After spending the evening clawing my way along a brick-lined corridor fixed with limestone knobs and chalk dust, I had to admit my inaugural expedition had been a triumphant success. The principles of thorough research and planning, adequate provisions and meticulous navigation had been proven and were all to stand me in good stead in years to come.

Before long my SS50 and I began making trips deep into the Weald of Sussex, where I'd mess about on the dank excuse of an outcrop called Harrison's Rocks, the southeast's answer to the Peak District's airy gritstone edges. In a matter of weeks I was ready to undertake my first full-scale, multi-day international overland expedition. Destination: the Snowdonia massif in North Wales, 250 miles from Norbury.

The previous December, just before buying the moped and while a traumatised nation was tutting over the Sex Pistols' sweary tirade on early-evening TV, I'd discovered the peaks of Snowdonia. The overnight train had arrived in Bangor early in the morning, but there was no prospect of putting up in a hotel or getting a taxi onwards – that was clearly only for spoiled film stars. Instead, I walked the eleven miles to Llanberis, dozing in a bus shelter on the way. That afternoon I ran out of daylight trying to get to the summit of Snowdon itself but was thrilled to have passed the hallowed ramparts of Clogwyn Du'r Arddu. 'Cloggy' was where the cream of British rock-climbing talent went, pulling off radical new routes. When darkness fell, I ended up digging a snow hole below Snowdon's summit, alongside the mountain lake of Glaslyn. Under the twinkling starlight I dared myself to walk onto the middle of the frozen tarn. Still in the mountains a couple of days later, I actually hid from an RAF helicopter hovering over Tryfan, ridiculously thinking I might get into trouble for tackling the Carnedd Horseshoe ridge walk alone. Dodging the deadly snow cornices that hung over the crests, I ended that perfect winter's day with a textbook ice-axe arrest after stumbling on a snow slope on the way down. I returned to the Idwal Valley with a good idea of where I wanted to spend my spare time in future.

Now that I was independently mobile, there would be no need to walk half the night to a bus shelter. I could simply ride to North Wales and, if I was quick, get in some more snowy mountain action before the thaw. I scanned the *Reader's Digest Atlas of Great Britain* my dad had bought me as a kid and saw that one road, the A5, led magically all the way from central London to the heart of Snowdonia. All I had to do was memorise the letter 'A' and the number '5'. I might have failed my Maths and English exams, but even I could manage that.

Originally built by the Romans and once known as Watling Street, the A5 ends at Holyhead on Anglesey; in the 1800s it was the main coaching road linking London with Ireland. For me too, the A5 has a historical significance: it evokes the overland adventure of getting to North Wales, being there and getting back. As I was to find in the Sahara years later, accomplishing those three things without incident takes some practice.

The A5 starts in London at Marble Arch at the end of Oxford Street. With over 190 miles to cover to the Welsh border post, I had to get a move on. In a haze of naive confidence I bored resolutely up the Edgware Road and into the dreary late-winter counties north of London at the speed of a trotting Roman legion. Every two minutes a mile clicked on the odometer of my SS50, the weather held off and the passing traffic tolerated my presence. But as I neared Nuneaton the engine began to falter; then it picked up only to die again. I stopped for some petrol. Perhaps the engine needed the 'weight' of fuel pressing down on it. It made a slight difference but even so, with the afternoon drawing in and barely halfway to the Welsh border, I pulled off the A5 to look for lodgings.

Like most people, I'd never heard of Coalville, nor have I come across any reference to it since. But that's where the day ended, in a place with a name like an Outback mining town. With the bike playing up, carrying on deeper into the unknown was unwise. I accepted that for the first but certainly not the last time, I'd bitten off more than I could chew and decided to tactically retreat next morning.

When that time came it wasn't made easy. The snows of Snowdonia had taken pity on me and reached out to carpet the lanes and roofs of Leicestershire. Feet stuck out as outriggers, I slithered back towards the A5, retraced my route along Watling Street to London and was home for tea. To paraphrase the guy out of *Jaws*, I was going to need a bigger bike.

2

A Year in Zschopau

MZ TS250 and TS150

Not long after returning from Wales, the Honda's health deteriorated and the intrepid fifty fell into a deep coma. Diagnosis: broken camshaft. 'What's a camshaft?' I wondered. 'What's a cam?' I pushed the moped back to the dealer's in Streatham, bent over on the special stool provided, and received my first shafting at the hands of a motorbike workshop over a repair that baffled me.

'Whole new top end, mate. We'll 'ave to get the parts in from Japayn. Could take a couple a months.'

By the time the SS50 was running again I was seventeen and could ride anything up to a 250. It was obviously going to be a 250 – why waste time with 125s or 175s? There were many comparatively great 250s around because, as with the sports mopeds, the merciless Japanese made sure any spotty learner who survived their sports moped got the full monty all over again from their 250. Yamaha's RD250 and Suzuki's

GT250 were thirty-horse screamers that were said to be good for 100mph. Within a year the lighter Suzuki X7 and the RD250LC were even more demented and would help bring about another change in the law.

And the law was just not keeping up. Incredibly, as a learner I could ride a bike of *any* capacity just as long as it was safely attached to a sidecar (with L-plates). A sidecar rigidly clamped to something like the 100hp Van Veen OCR 1000, or maybe just a Kawasaki 750 H2 triple, would have been a truly lethal contraption. So it didn't take long for someone to find a way of crapping on the spirit of the outdated law, just as they had with the Sixteener Specials. The Sidewinder was a notional sidecar that was actually little more than an articulated plastic tray with a wheel on a pivoting frame which retracted as you leant either way through bends. Even seventeen-year-olds desperate to outdo their peers could see that attaching a 'chair' – pivoting or otherwise – to anything faster than a picnic table would end in tears and maybe a funeral.

Even so, was all this a good enough excuse for getting an MZ, East Germany's two-wheeled answer to the Trabant? At the supermarket I'd got chummy with a fellow biker called Vic, a guy I knew from my time in the Scouts. I hadn't liked him much then, as when other guys were around he'd rag me for various failings, which could be summed up as not being a beery, smoky, sweary 'one of the lads'. But when it was just Vic, he behaved normally. As I'd never been picked on in school I put it down to adolescent antler bashing. Following many outdoor escapades in the far-flung corners of Britain, I left the Scouts to do my own thing, and my recent adventures in North Wales proved I was on the right track.

One night in the supermarket while tidying the Ski yoghurts on the dairy counter, Vic explained why they didn't like me back then and I could see he had a point: I wouldn't be part of the gang but was too timid to make my mark. That settled, we got on to bikes and, just as I'd followed schoolmate Phil on to a Honda fifty, so Vic, my former campfire tormentor, turned me on to MZs. I nearly got away with it, though. Steve, another part-timing student working the meat counter, was selling his early-seventies BSA 250 Starfire. Later, Steve and I became climbing mates, but at the time I didn't move fast enough on the Starfire, which was probably a blessing.

Vic rode a particularly striking example of the East German marque: the MZ ES 250 Trophy, one of the world's uglier motorcycles. The Brits and Japs had produced a few turkeys of their own in the preceding decade, but with the ES Trophy you thought: jeez, can't they make that Iron Curtain a bit higher? Today, like a lot of shite from that era, the toucan-beaked Trophy is probably a highly prized classic.

To his credit, having the guts to ride that quarter-litre Commie Quasimodo put Vic a lot further down Rebellion Road than me. But MZ – or Motorradwerk [of] Zschopau, near Dresden as I soon learned – were actually iconoclastic innovators unmoved by the simpering aesthetics of the decadent Free World. Most M-Zeders could confidently blurt out that in the late fifties it was MZ engineer Walter Kaaden who developed the expansion chamber. This was the now familiar bulging two-stroke exhaust pipe which enabled pulses of purged gases to bounce back as a pressure wave to create a kind of supercharging effect, so greatly increasing the power and efficiency of the engine. Say all that quickly and most of your Belstaff-clad comrades would believe you. You were then ready to deliver your knockout moto-nugget: in 1961 an MZ factory racer poised to win the championship for MZ had sabotaged his bike, swiftly defected, then handed Kaaden's secrets to Suzuki. The Japs never looked back and dominated two-stroke racing for decades until strokers fell from favour. Furthermore, under the marginally less obscure DKW badge, in the late 1920s MZ had been the world's biggest motorcycle manufacturer. After the war DKW's RT125 had been handed over to the West as a patent-free reparation, reappearing in the UK as the cock-a-doodling BSA Bantam.

It goes on. Despite that costly defection and the fact that the Russians obstructed Zschopau's efforts in order to protect their own infinitely more primitive motorcycle industry, in the sixties MZ won their class in the International Six Days Trial dirt 'motathlon' no less than six times. And in the early seventies a Trophy Sport similar to Vic's had been the millionth MZ to slither off the Zschopau production line, like something out of *Doctor Who*. By that time each MZ sported a chunky alloy filler cap commemorating their numerous ISDT victories.

All that must have sounded impressive if you'd spent your life queuing for bread and believing there was only one type of cheese. But seen from the West, Vic's bike was the product of a bunker-bound mentality that, bereft of sunlight and fresh air, had strayed into a mutant branch of design that led only to Neanderthal graves. Its slabby, collectivist profile was dominated by an all-in-one tank-headlight cowling, ahead of which the sickle-like front mudguard was better served by the American word 'fender'. Cheap metal was clearly not in short supply in the GDR and at 330lb, including a drainpipe silencer from a refinery scrap heap, the Trophy was built to last longer than you'd wish.

Clued-up bikers like Vic weren't bothered by such trivial jibes and took comfort in the many functional features that were standard on an MZ motorcycle. The Earles-type fork might have looked like it came off a Heinkel 111's undercarriage, but it didn't dive under hard braking, an inherent flaw of regular telescopic forks which survives to this day. Just over the border, BMW, purveyor of the 'Finest Motorcycles in the World', ran such forks for many years until fashion and costs dictated tubes. An MZ's rear chain was made of compressed vodka bottle tops but was fully enclosed in a chunky rubber casing. In these pre-O-ring-chain days that greatly reduced wear. The rear shocks had a lever cast into their bodies to allow you to raise or lower the pre-load without having to resort to knuckle-scraping tools. And just like BMWs, MZs came with a tyre pump under the seat, plus a set of tools that made the Japanese equivalent look like something that fell out of a Christmas cracker. The aforementioned fuel cap even had an integrated cup on its underside to measure out the pre-mix oil. Who cared if it all came in a package that made bystanders chuckle? More fool them – they were at a bus stop, you were astride the Wingless Toucan of Achilles.

At some vulnerable juncture Vic must have let me loose on his Trophy and clearly I was too much of a two-wheel rube to recoil from the experience. I set off down the street behind the supermarket and gasped as the 250cc engine whooshed me along. OK, changing gear was as subtle as switching the points on a railway track, and continuing in this manner led briskly to the marque's fabled flaw: drum brakes and tyres which hissed rather than screeched like proper rubber. This hiss was a commonly heard sound from the back, as an MZ's rear brake pedal had more leverage than Jeremy Thorpe's lawyers. Meanwhile, on the front you could strangle the lever all you liked: the cable might just as well have been attached to a bell to give pedestrians a chance to jump clear.

Vic's Trophy was a decade behind the times – partially functional yet largely hideous – but its avowed lack of Ram-Air allure meant you got a lot of bike to the pound. MZs were cheap to buy and much cheaper to insure than the snazzy 250 killers from Japan.

At that time I had yet to snap out of the delusion that buying a used motorcycle from a dealer was the way to go. After all, they wouldn't knowingly buy in junk, any more than they'd sell it to a customer. And if there were problems they'd be there to help. In nearby Wallington, Hughes Motorcycles had the sparse wooden interior of a prairie schoolhouse. Down either side, half a dozen bikes were arranged like pews, mostly Triumphs, a BM or two and the odd MZ. From behind his counter at the head of the showroom glowered 'Preacher Hughes' himself, the shop's owner, burned off his Rhodesian farm by a thankless congregation (perhaps) and someone who didn't suffer fools – or even moderately bright individuals.

Customers' pathetic bleatings would invariably fall on deaf ears, but 'Hughes' was not your usual sarcastic 'Yes, mate, what can I do you for?' git you met in the bigger and busier dealers, like the hairy thugs running Aeros in Norbury, or Elite Motors (pronounced 'Ee-light's') in Tooting. At the time notions of American-style customer service were still fogbound somewhere off the Azores. At Elite's they wouldn't even look at you unless you had the original part, knew its seventeen-digit part number and didn't mind waiting two weeks or more after being smacked around a bit with a dented Dunstall silencer. Many years later I read a story in *SuperBike* magazine, in the days when bike mags still ran occasional fictional contributions. It was titled 'Triumph at Pughes' and was unmistakably a long-abused customer's revenge fantasy based on the Wallington grouch.

Oblivious to Hughes' widely acknowledged misanthropy, I managed to prise a 1974 four-speed MZ TS250 from him for £180. The TS model came out after Vic's Trophy, but before the five-speed 250/1 Supa 5 that was then going for just £410 new. While not fully in the Ugly Bike Hall of Shame, my TS was still recognisably an MZ. Front forks were long telescopes, and the tank and the headlight were separate, but all the other functional features were there, including the removable ignition key-switch that was common to all MZs. Should you be daft enough to want to nick an MZ, just buy the key-switch from an MZ shop, head out on to the streets and take your pick. Or just save up and buy a proper bike.

I never really gelled with my MZ. Had I been invited to be a stunt rider in a Bond movie, required to bounce off kerbs, jump lines of stationary cars and scurry across the Vatican's rooftops, an MZ wouldn't have been my choice of machine. Something was wrong with the MZ or me, and whatever synergy arced intermittently through the footrests, bars and bench seat, the result still felt like sitting on a plank balanced on a pair of space hoppers.

The ill-suited ergonomics weren't the only flaw. The 250 two-stroke engine accelerated smoothly enough, but when you closed the throttle it had the habit of kangarooing – lurching fore and aft – as the decelerating engine hesitated between gulps of fuel. Slowing into a bend with the 'all' (rear) and 'nothing' (front) braking, smooth progress was difficult to maintain. And with deceleration came the TS's most enduring curse: the rrrring-ding-ding-ding-ding, rrrrrrring-ding-ding-ding-ding-ding chorus from the didgeridoo silencer. It's a detestable din that can be recalled all too easily, even many years on, like the grating warblings of early, dial-up internet.

But I had a lot to learn and the TS was my first pedal-free motorcycle. It wasn't until two bikes later that I discovered what it meant to feel great on a bike. First though, I had to wade through the mz-rable purgatory of my Zschopau years, which, bafflingly, were to include more than one MZ.

At the supermarket I'd hooked up with Starfire Steve, a bright chemistry student who, like me, was into rock climbing. If Vic rode the ugliest bike on the planet, Steve had just bought himself one of the prettiest, a green and white UK-spec Triumph Tiger TR7. Here was a real motorcycle with disc brakes and a growling hunk of an engine that made the MZ sound like a fly in need of a damn good thwack.

That summer of 1977 was the Queen's Silver Jubilee, one of the last genuine flings of traditional British patriotism, spoiled only by those stud-nosed punk rockers. In June, at the peak of the celebrations, Steve and I rode to North Wales to tick off some classic routes. I was finally heading back to the Promised Land to do some real climbs, not piss about at Sobell or scrape the moss at Harrison's. Ron Fawcett and Pete Livesey were the wiry-limbed rock stars of the day, lifting British climbing to new levels with outlandish routes. Being mere mortals, Steve and I carried the classic climbers' guide to Snowdonia, the green edition of Ron James' *Rock Climbing in Wales*, and we knew what we had to do.

I remember being acutely nervous the night we left London, an insecurity based chiefly around the MZ and my lack of long-distance experience. Like most young riders running crap bikes, I was clinging to a steep learning curve, just like the bloke on the cover of Ron James' guidebook. As always, getting on the road was the tonic. I lashed on my kit bags and assorted bin liners, then kangarooed over to Steve's to find his Tiger round the back, purposefully laden with ropes and camping gear. Steve had calculated we could get to North Wales overnight, via a complex combination of traffic-free back roads which required more than simply memorising 'A' and '5'. His route took us west and south of Birmingham to meet the A5 near Shrewsbury, where we'd catch the Romans with their pants down. It was as we approached that junction, shortly after dawn, that I found I just could not keep my eyes open any longer. Unknown seconds were passing before I'd wake with a start, inches from a tweeting hedgerow. I revived myself with shouts and spasms and bashed my crotch against the MZ tank in an effort to keep awake. If only I'd known it was just a temporary surge of sleep-inducing enzymes that could have been purged with a swift nap.

As the A5 approaches the massifs of Snowdonia it briefly becomes a spectacular road, Wales' answer to the A82 through Glencoe in Scotland. After several hours on the go, our engines were fully warmed through and humming away, while we clung on like zombies. We left the A5 at Capel Curig, where Joe Brown, Britain's first rock-climbing celebrity, ran one of his climbing shops. It was some of Brown's routes from the fifties that we hoped to climb in the coming days. Around us lay peaty wastes and glittering llyns, and directly ahead the distinctive 3500-foot-high pyramid of Yr Wyddfa, or 'Snowdon' to you and me. At the Pen-y-Gwryd Hotel, where Irving and Mallory had trained for Everest, we turned again up to Pen-y-Pass at the head of the Llanberis Pass, then coasted in neutral down to our camp at the Cromlech Boulders, right below the striking right-angle crag of Dinas Cromlech.

Twenty-five years earlier in this very arena, Joe Brown and a chum had succeeded in hauling themselves up the square-cut cleft of the Cromlech to sign off Cenotaph Corner, the classic route in the Pass. Three years before our arrival, Pete Livesey had found a way across the fingertip flakes on the seemingly blank vertical wall to the right, and Fawcett himself would, a couple of years after the Jubilee, put up the even less repeatable Lord of the Flies. It was all moving so fast in the late-seventies that they had to invent new sub-categories of the 'E' for 'Extreme' grade. Lord of the Flies was an E6 6a. These days climbers are injecting themselves with neat gecko serum to knock out E11 7a routes.

None of these modern routes were remotely do-able by Steve, let alone me. We just wanted to try some old favourites from the more achievable Joe Brown catalogue, and Ron James' little green bible listed them all. If it was raining in the Pass we'd ride twenty miles down the Nant Gwynant valley to the limestone crags at Tremadoc on the coast. In early June Beddgelert village was strung out with bunting and VE-Day-style street parties. The Queen's quarter-century didn't mean much to us, we were strung out ourselves on Bwlch y Moch, battling with routes like Meshach, Shadrach (both VS) and, after a bit of a run up, The Fang (HVS: Hard Very Severe).

That was a carefree summer of peeking out of the tent for a break in the rain, coiling ropes and easing into our too-tight EB rock shoes, and blurting out, 'You got me?' – climbers' code for 'Take the strain, I'm about to fall.' We came back in August for more of the same, and at the top of our game, Steve led us up Cenotaph Corner, our hardest route so far.

One night, as we queued up in a chippy in Bangor, the news buzzed across the telly behind the counter: Elvis was dead. But that meant no more to us than June's jubilee. We were absorbed in the quest to climb all the HVSs we dared, and would end each sore-limbed day with another great ride over the dry-stone passes of Snowdonia to our roadside camp. When our time was done we loaded up and rode back down the A5 to London.

I don't recall the impact, but as they wheeled me into Kidderminster Hospital, I definitely remember coming round below a ring of pretty nurses' faces. That vision of *Charlie's Angels* heaven quickly dropped back to earth once the crotch ache from having rammed myself against a TS 250's tank took hold.

As we'd passed through Kidderminster a VW Kombi had pulled out on me from a side road. The back tyre hissed, the front didn't, and losing little speed, I bashed through the van's side window with my budget Kangol head. 'SMACK' fist into palm, just like the bloke in the 'Think Bike' TV advert. On the bright side, the MZ was now a foot shorter and ready for the scrap heap. Until that happy event came to pass, the wreckage was looked after by nearby friends of family friends and I was discharged a few days later with the first of my biking scars stitched up under my chin. Oblivious to any traumatic recall, but clearly suffering some residual brain damage, I soon got another MZ, a yellow 150 this time. Rrrring-ding-ding-ding-ding, rrrrrrring-ding-ding-ding-ding-ding.

By the end of the summer I was back in the education system, what they called a Sixth Form College just down the road from my old school. The plan here was to snatch two A-levels in a year: Geography, which I liked – mostly; and Geology, which I wanted to like but mostly didn't. I rode the 150 daily to college and, as always, easily made friends with other bikers. Among them was sullen Rod, who had an RS100 two-stroke Yamaha that he detested, along with just about everything else.

Around this time I took my motorcycle test down in Croydon. As any learner will recall, the motorcycle test circa October 1977 added up to nothing more than a bloke with a clipboard watching you ride off round the block. Once round the corner, should you wish to, you could strip off and wheelie down the street with one hand on your hip singing, 'Don't cry for me Argenteeeenarrrr!' Just as long as all was in order when you came back round the last corner, having covered the distance at a steady 29mph. Then, as he'd clearly warned you he'd do, Mr Examiner stepped out into the road, raised his hand and commanded you to brake hard. This you did. All that remained was to read a nearby car number plate and answer a few questions from the Highway Code. You might only be shaving once a week, but if you passed you were ready to let rip on the fastest road-going motorcycles on earth.

I was still living at home and putting away wages from the weekend job at Sainsbury's. When the full licence arrived I proudly snipped off the L-plates from the 150. My old schoolmate Robert was dead impressed. I could take him on the back now and ride on motorways with the big boys. We sat in his room listening to the dangerous riffs on *Rattus Norvegicus* as if they were hardcore rockporn and his mum might burst in at any minute. Rob was only emerging from his Carpenters period, but who among us has not harboured uncool musical predilections? The Stranglers sound had a malevolent, prowling, lock-up-your-daughters quality and wasn't like anything we'd heard. Founder and bass player Jean-Jacques Burnel had been recently profiled in *Bike* magazine, brooding menacingly over his T160 Trident. Rob was never going to be a biker but still fancied himself aboard Kawasaki's latest Z1000. With my vast biking knowledge I was able to authoritatively parrot magazine reports and inform him that it was a sadly softened version of the original 900cc gunships.

One day at a hole-in-the-wall MZ shop in Brixton, right over the road from the famous Pride & Clarke's bike emporium, I pinched a bundle of red and silver MZ stickers while geezer was round the back. It was a shabby act of opportunist retaliation against the hated bike shops. And what does a boy do with sixty shiny MZ stickers? Stickers cry out to be stuck, so with the forethought of a burglar tweeting a selfie off a stolen smartphone, I plastered them all over my blue Kangol and thought I looked the dog's bollocks.

My juvenile criminality wasn't limited to self-adhesive labels. When off the shop floor at the supermarket, I'd got into the habit of knocking back yoghurt pots that had got split in transit. They couldn't be sold or repackaged, so no harm done, I figured. Also, a side benefit of looking after frozen food was being able to lock myself in the walk-in freezer. Sure, as I slammed the door the fans would spin up, chilling the cell back down to minus 15°C, but it was a place where no one in their right mind would look for me. Should anyone burst in, I always had my stocktaking clipboard at hand to claim I was solicitously checking the status of Birds Eye mint peas as they were on special and selling fast. In fact I was just relaxing in my icy hideaway and occasionally snacking.

The problem with frozen food was that you couldn't eat it straight out of (or indeed inside) a freezer. Yes, you could suck on a prawn until it gradually released its succulent briny tang, or less successfully attempt to bite into one of those overrated Arctic Rolls. But most of it was uncooked and inedible and some of it, such as the nauseously named Brain's Faggots, remained inedible on humanitarian grounds. Choc ices were the sole exception, even if this was a simple era before Magnums came in eight varieties, including ones made with Fair Trade chocolate and ewe's milk, plus detailed instructions on how to recycle the packaging. In 1978 choc ices were basic: you had your milk-chocolate briquette or you had your plain.

After a while neither could fully satisfy me so I developed a taste for fresh cream fruit pies from the dairy counter. One time in a moment of weakness, I chose to work through a twin-pack of these moist blackcurrant beauties in the comfort and warmth of the gents' toilet cubicle. Here I was caught with cream on my face by Les, the creepy manager of tinned and dried goods, and presented to the store manager for a dressing down. It was well known that night managers like Les and Eddie were helping themselves to food by the car-boot-load, so again I figured my indiscretions were trivial by comparison. The warning had little effect and I continued to take swipes at damaged or just desirable delicacies until one day I fell into Eddie's trap. Gotcha!

Out of a job and feeling sorry for myself, I took consolation by ring-ding-dinging straight up to Coburn & Hughes in Hornsey to put down a deposit on a new T140V Triumph Bonneville.

3

BLUE REMEMBERED DOWNPIPES

Triumph Bonneville T140V

It was 1978 and according to the papers, Britain was continuing its steady descent. Strikes were rife, 1.5 million were out of work and the Yorkshire Ripper was midway through his grisly spree. Things were so bad even the rich were poor. However they measured it, the 'wealth gap' hit an all-time low that was never to be seen again. But biking in Britain was booming and the annual sales rush was bearing fruit. 'It's going to be a hell of a year for new bikes,' promised the January edition of *Bike* magazine. The megabikes were coming, even as a Honda spokesman claimed rather unconvincingly, 'We are hoping for an end to the escalation,' following the release of the six-cylinder, 105hp CBX. It was an evolutionary spike in bike development that produced some duds but many more brilliant machines, while at the same time bringing about legislation that would eventually reduce motorcycling to a leisure activity for middle-aged men.

Meanwhile, at the back of the cave some diehards were still blowing over the embers of the Jap Crap versus Brit Shit debate. You threw the term at one if you proudly rode the other. Kraut Crates and especially Wop Slop were exotic sub-genres, although Yank Wank didn't really come into it: Harleys back then were poorly made tractors as yet unfashionable in the UK. While this chauvinism never escalated to the previous decade's much exaggerated Mods and Rockers brawls, you were usually blindly loyal to one, but a little curious about the other.

The once dominant British bike industry was unravelling. Stuffy, complacent management who lacked vision had seen to that, though variable build quality – old designs and crude manufacturing techniques – was most users' actual experience. Through the sixties the Japanese were, like the Chinese today, on the march, making ever faster and well built, if on occasion hideously styled, small bikes. Initially they imitated and innovated, until finally they began to invent their own spectacular machines.

When I joined the scene in 1977 (rego years 'R' and 'S') the choice of motorcycles in the UK was pretty fruity and about to go apeshit. Some have suggested that the late-seventies eruption of powerful Japanese bikes was the manufacturers' desperate response to falling sales in the US, which had peaked around five million in 1975. That downturn has been attributed to free-spirited post-war Baby Boomers finally settling down, though these Boomers seem to be a conveniently elastic category trotted out to explain many social trends.

The dreary derivatives of the previous decade's technology (MZs being an emblematic example) were being junked, starting with the environmentally intolerable big two strokes. In Europe, the balls-out, straight-line performance of the famed Kawasaki H-series triples was seen as pandering to the annoyingly large but obviously unsophisticated American market.

Those with more than the fabled six brain cells of a KH250 rider also appreciated spirited bend-swinging as well as brakes that worked in the rain. That was why frame builders like Peckett & McNab, Harris, and Rickman had plenty of work. And however it was conjured, we all wanted smart looks.

In our day there was no reverence about or value in classic or, as we called them, 'old' bikes, which chiefly meant cantankerous Brit hand-me-downs. Guys were buying ratty Vincents for a hundred quid or Panthers for twenty. Your dad's old BSA or Triumph was going so cheap that blokes were shoehorning them into daft, coccyx-crushing, armpit-baring choppers.

The seventies have been called the decade that shaped modern motorcycles, not least for delivering the transverse, four-cylinder Japanese engine that soon became universal. Honda's original CB750 may have been astonishingly modern in 1969, but to us it looked about as exciting as your mum's hairdo. In the latter seventies we biking anoraks agreed that Kawasaki's Z900 was easily the most desirable big Jap bike, even if it only resembled the original kick-arse Z1A which pulled 125mph across three lanes of motorway. The later Zed Thou lost the critical '9' connection and the new, glacier-blue Z1R discarded its predecessors' voluptuous curves for the futuristic slab sides of a *Blake's 7* film set.

Sharp edged or curvy, in looks and performance the big Zeds ran rings round Honda's ploddy SOHC CB750s, while their sexy Z650 version trounced Suzuki's GS750 plank too. It was the same with Suzuki's new GS1000, which soon gained a reputation as the first big Jap with OK handling. For the moment Yamaha were steering clear of the high-performance fray with the previous year's XS750 triple. 'Supershaft' ran the print adverts featuring a crop-haired but regrettably flat-chested black chick in a half-unzipped jumpsuit. Once their XS1100 tractor came out, subsequent 750 ads dropped the supershaft pun and compensated with more appropriate 'Black

Magic' seventies cleavage. Well-engineered, high-revving, twin-cam engines made 130mph performance achievable on the big Jap bikes. But in most cases, holding on to the gibbering machine at such speeds was another matter. Crafting a frame that managed the accelerating and braking forces better than a Uri Geller spoon was considered the preserve of European manufacturers, especially the Italians.

In this Wop Slop category neither the 900SS Ducati nor even Laverda's Jota caught our eye half as much as Guzzi's fabulous 850 Le Mans. As Bill Haylock in *Bike* put it, 'how could a guy not fall for the horniest thing you've ever seen on two wheels'. In red nothing else came close, even if the other two were having greater success on the tracks. The Jota and Le Mans cost over two grand each, but the shaft-drive V-twin proved that a curve-lean profile of parallel lines could be confidently wheeled into a Louvre des Motos alongside a Z1. Chuck in a Morini, an R90S plus your favourite Triumph and you could lock up for the night.

Ducati's 500 Desmo and Laverda's Montjuic were a pair of short-lived, middleweight parallel twins that were more admired than owned. If you were going to spend that sort of money, Morini's 3½ Sport V-twin was a much better candidate, if for no other reason than their audacity in not calling it a 350. That's what Honda would have done.

And so in pubs and cafes around the country the debate ran on. The Italians made the most exciting machines with the worst electrics, finish and fittings, 'spoiling the ship for a ha'p'orth of tar', as the expression went. The Japs were reliable, something that won them many fans, and were becoming increasingly inventive at shaking off their bland 'UJM' image. 'Universal Japanese Motorcycle' was the damned-with-faint-praise label coined by the US magazine *Cycle* in a 1976 review of Kawasaki's Z650. Though Lord knows there were blander Japs out there than the spunky middleweight Zed.

The Krauts – in other words BMW – unapologetically continued to produce expensive, well-engineered flat-twins associated with smug, know-all beardies. BMWs just weren't dashing enough for a young blade, perhaps because the ads haughtily claimed, 'Ven somsing is right it should not be changed. Only Improved.' When it was revived a couple of years later, Audi's 'Vorsprung durch Technik' was a much wittier way of evoking Teutonic superiority.

Meanwhile, the fish 'n' chip Brits had a long heritage of producing love-hate machines, but everyone else seemed to be doing it a little better, without resorting to nostalgia or tradition. With the writing on the wall, in the early seventies the Conservative government had formed Norton Villiers Triumph, or 'NVT', consolidating Triumph-BSA with Norton-Villiers, the salvageable vestiges of British motorcycledom. The by-then irredeemably toxic BSA marque was buried in favour of Triumph – but Villi-who? To me Villiers conjured up some long-dead, two-stroke farmyard muck sprayer.

Not so with Triumph or Norton; they were still something to aspire to. Sure, their leaky engine casings brought about the 1973 Oil Crisis, and Lucas electrics certainly contributed to the nationwide power cuts of that era. But these two virile survivors of the Jap invasion had one thing your yen could not buy: lashings of that indefinable property – character. Even their solid, two-syllable names gave an impression of stoic Britannic fortitude cast in the soot-blackened foundries of the Industrial Revolution. In actor Eric Bana's 2009 film *Love the Beast*, Jeremy Clarkson assures Bana his recently smashed-up Ford GT Falcon Coupe isn't worth rebuilding because 'muscle cars are crap'. Then, in one of his occasional spells of profoundness, Clarkson offers to explain 'character'. 'The cars [and bikes] we love the best are the ones with human traits, warts and all. Anything else is just a machine.' Jezzer nailed it. Did my repugnant MZs have character? Do bears floss after meals? Proper Brit bikes of the era had the love-hate qualities of character. Much Wop Slop and Yank Wank too. But Jap Crap and Kraut Crates, not so sure.

By the time NVT entered my consciousness they were only months from liquidation. Just as with my Honda 'More Sense. More Style' brochure of 1976, I'd become fixated on a small, four-fold NVT leaflet from a year earlier. It was titled 'The Powerchoice', as if it announced some new TV action drama like *The Professionals* or *The Persuaders!* On the outside two bikes were tantalisingly blurred by the zoom-pulling trick to suggest speeds a modern camera simply couldn't capture. Open it up and you were invited to choose 'A Two or a Three': an 850 Norton Commando Mk3 or a Triumph T160 Trident. Points of note included electric starts (with back-up kicks), left-hand gear change for the Norton and rear disc brakes. 'Instruments and Controls'? Yes, the Mk3 came with those too. The Trident's 'For Men Who Can Handle Power' was a little off-putting for the time being, but in the black and gold livery I'd seen elsewhere, the Interstate Commando looked like a rumbling bundle of motorcycling bliss. Commando – what a great name for a British bike. What red-blooded young seventies male wouldn't want to be associated with a plucky wartime saboteur, crouched in readiness with his Sten gun and grappling iron.

It took a while to brush away that rosy haze and admit that both were dinosaurs taking their last breaths as the Japanese meteor impact changed the motorcycling climate for good. The same could easily have been said of the Bonneville. By 1978 NVT had collapsed, and following the famed sit-in, the Triumph factory at Meriden in the Midlands was now said to be run by a loyal, streamlined and motivated 700-strong workers' co-operative. According to a 1976 magazine article, shop floor or director, all earned the same £56 wage – thirty per cent below the national average. Twenty years ago during the heyday of the Triumph Engineering Company, wages had been among the highest in that sector.

But I wasn't interested in any of that. All I knew was that MZ-ing was stunting my development and I was eager for a real bike. Commando, Bonnie, or even a Silk 700S, the light, simple water-cooled two-stroke twin. It was fun to flirt with leftfield options, but I snapped out of it and picked the Bonnie. In the spring of 1978, aged nearly eighteen and expelled from Sainsbury's just hours earlier, I ordered a £900 UK-spec T140V in burgundy.

Anyone who ever dealt with one of the many franchise dealers trading under the Coburn & Hughes banner won't be surprised to learn I actually got a blue, US-spec T140V with a few bits missing – and I could take it or leave it. The US model came with a smaller teardrop tank and high bars, because Americans were like that – cruising around upright with their annoying confidence, straight teeth and indifference to the practicalities of large tanks. Brit bikers? We crouched over flat bars in grubby oilskins, our crooked Stadium goggles perched over a ketchup-rimmed grin.

High bar or low, the 750 Bonnie displayed a characteristic I'd not experienced before: torque or low-down pulling power. It took a long, long time before I became immune to the loin-stirring, smile-inducing shove persuasively unleashed between 2500 and 3000rpm. I was to find the Triumph also had another sort of potential pulling power. It's hard to be certain, but I was convinced that on occasion girls would glance at me as I torqued along in my demi-orang-utan stance. Even my mum and sister recognised that the Bonnie was a machine with charisma.

Realising I was on to a good thing, I eagerly bought into the full 'Brit biker look' with a cream silk scarf made of nylon and long woollen socks (also nylon) rolled over my Kett boot tops. They were complemented by a miraculous advance in textile innovation, a black 'greaseless' Belstaff Trialmaster jacket (you can guess the fabric). My Brit biker's costume was topped off with a pair of those metal-framed, flat-glass Stadium goggles. In the rain the heavy leather padding became saturated and the feeble knicker-elastic strap lost all tension. On a wet winter's night, unless you spat in them they'd steam up, but that made little difference once the elastic failed and the goggles slid down your face, leaving you with a dilemma: 'Can I shove these effing goggles back over my stinging eyes before I need to change down and brake for that roundabout?' But it was The Look.

After the MZs, riding the Triumph was like being led out of the castle's dungeon and into the bright sunshine on the shoulders of the town's fairest maidens. Suddenly I knew what it was all about – the surge of a powerful engine, the throb from the deeply chromed pipes and the bite of hydraulic disc brakes. Well, as long as it wasn't raining. The chaps at Meriden had got carried away with the chrome and splashed it all over the disc rotors to thwart unsightly rust. It wasn't a flaw unique to Triumphs by any means. For years many Jap bikes carried tank-top warning stickers along the lines of 'Brake performance may be delayed in wet conditions'. The Bonnie was no different. Pull on the brakes in the rain and nothing happened until the pads cut through the watery film, at which point they'd grab the rotor like a bear trap. Result: dampened underwear, but not in a good way. Smart riders unbolted the rotors and got the deadly chrome skimmed off, or took note of the 'Cast-Iron Disc Conversion' adverts in the magazines. Others like me held back in the wet and hoped for the best, or fitted a cable-operated wiper-like gadget cooked up by some garden-shed boffin who'd had one fright too many.

Starting my Triumph required an exacting ritual. Unlike those nancy-boy 'Powerchoice' bikes, the Bonnie was kick-only, which could be interpreted as 'for men only'. First you'd turn on the fuel taps and 'tickle' or flood the two carbs by pressing on tiny plungers. Once petrol was safely dripping onto the top of the gearbox, you turned the ignition key and pressed on the (chromed) kickstart until you could feel the engine compression resisting. You were now ready to enact a triumphant, manful lunge by lifting your body weight on to your right leg while swinging the other leg upward like one of Pan's People. Then, at the peak of this gymnastic arc, the right knee locked out and you came down on the kickstarter with all your weight. It was a solid, well-designed mechanism perfected over the eons. There was no risk of overdoing it. But any pussyfooting could result in a painful backfire – this beast had to be grabbed by the hair and heaved into life. 'Tickle and prod,' they called it. Until I started riding for a living, I never failed to get a thrill from kickstarting the Bonnie. Once the technique was mastered and performed with gusto, it worked every time, hot or cold, rain or shine. Electric starts were for those pansies who rode Jap Crap in full-face helmets.

One in three 750s sold in 1978 was a Triumph, but unfortunately I bought mine at a bad time: I'd been banned from riding. A few months earlier, before I'd acquired a full licence, I'd ridden the 150 MZ up to Liverpool for an interview on the slim chance I'd pass my two A-level exams and get into college there. Returning at night, I mistakenly assumed that British motorways were lit, making the two-hundred-mile ride back to London a little safer. They weren't lit, but progress was easy enough in the slow lane, slipstreaming lorries at 52mph with my learner plates rolled up in my pocket (learners weren't allowed on motorways). Smelling a rather putrid rat, a police car pulled me over using the old 'dodgy back light' pretext and I had my first experience of the good-cop, bad-cop routine. It worked. I confessed and got three months. At that time motorcycle injuries and deaths were horrendous and I was right in the most accident-prone age group. I suspect magistrates were encouraged to dissuade youngsters by banning us hard at the first infraction, however slight, in the hope we'd lose interest, get a car and free up some beds in the wards. Like many others, I carried on as normal and rode the Triumph along the back streets to college until the revived licence popped back through the letterbox.

One Sunday evening some clumsy scumbags in a van tried to steal my pride and joy, but the gumbies hadn't noticed it was chained to a tree and smashed their Transit's headlamp trying to move it. I walked out and glared menacingly, jotting down their van's number.

'You ain't seen us do nuffin'!' They scowled back with more convincing menace, the Triumph hanging off the kerb like a rowboat on the sands. They drove off, I moved the Bonnie into the front garden and a day or two later sank a section of girder into the paving as a ground anchor. I couldn't report the thieves to the police for fear of revealing my unlicensed and uninsured status.

Far greater crimes were being committed. For a start I was still riding around in my cheap Kangol splattered with the shiny MZ stickers which had become the subject of an international search warrant by the Stasi. And at college, which was soon to end, the blue-eyed babe I fancied was playing it hard. Did I give her a lift on the Bonnie to a bus stop one time, or did I dream it? The term ended without romance and a few years later the campus got levelled and rebuilt as a bus garage.

With sixth-form college over but the exam results unpublished, Steve and I took in another fabulous summer's climbing aboard our Triumphs. We chased the happy highways down to Harrison's in the evenings; up to the grippy gritstone crags of the Peak District; back over to the mountains of Snowdonia or down to the Gower. Blue Remembered Downpipes.

One time, cruising for kicks up Brixton High Street, I came across a trio of French kids on overloaded Peugeot mopeds.

Washed up by the roadside, they'd got lost while looking for a campsite. I'd never seen real Frenchies close up before so it was quite exciting, despite Opposition leader Thatcher's recent warning that many Britons were 'really rather afraid that this country might be rather swamped by people with a different culture'.

'Shingforh? Do you noe zi wey to Shingforh?' they asked.

'Shingforh? Oh, Chingford? Blimey, that's out in Essex somewhere, isn't it?'

I must have had my *A-Z* with me and looked it up. Lee Valley, on the very edge of the street atlas' coverage. It was obvious they'd never find the way there before their holiday was over, but perhaps they reminded me of my first aborted moped adventure to Wales. And anyway, we bikers looked out for each other. When a leather-clad pilgrim was stranded by the roadside, it was customary to offer assistance.

'Well, it's about twenty miles. Tell you what, follow me. I'll take you there.'

'Merci beaucoup, monsieur.'

And so, with an afternoon to kill, I led my caravan of plucky Gauls up to the Elephant, over Tower Bridge and up Mile End to Stratford, Leyton and 'Shingforh'. This part of London was new to me too, and exploring it was all part of motorcycling's grand adventure.

Back home, my exam results dropped on the mat but may as well have stayed there. For me it was time to look for a job. It would only be for a short while, just to get enough money so I could emigrate to Bristol. What was so great about Bristol? Steve and I had stopped there on the way back from Wales to climb at the Avon Gorge. Specifically, we went to bag the classic Malbogies, a route that had first been climbed by none other than Chris Bonington. He was to British mountaineering what Barry Sheene was to motorcycling; even non-interested civilians knew his name. Something must have impressed me about Bristol – probably simply that it was a manageably sized city that was close to Wales but didn't have the depressing stigma of 1970s Cardiff or Swansea.

I went for an interview at a factory in Croydon that manufactured typewriter-correcting fluid. The amenable guy measured me up, looked at my education and employment background (the cream cake episode redacted) and advised me to find a different job. I was clearly far too bright to be supervising stock levels and loading vans. My first real job interview and I'd been praised with faint damnation.

'What do you like doing, Chris? What do you enjoy?'

'Well, riding motorbikes I suppose. And rock climbing.'

'How about despatch riding? Ever heard of that? The money's good, you're your own boss and you get to ride a bike all day. I have a friend who's just opened a courier company. Hold on... here's his number. Give him a ring.'

Despatch rider. Sounded exciting. My mum's brother had been one during the war until he copped it at Monte Cassino. Croydon man's lead didn't materialise, but the idea took hold and my road for the next decade or more was set.

4

LONDON CALLING

*And [they] are stayed neither by snow nor rain nor heat nor
darkness from accomplishing their appointed course with all
speed.*

So wrote Herodotus about ancient Persia's horseback courier
service during the first millennium BC. The idea of using motorcycle riders to perform the same task must be as old as
affordable and reliable bikes. In WWI the British army used
motorcyclists, often women, as message or 'despatch' runners,
hence 'despatch riders', and in the late fifties, BSA Bantams
made scheduled runs between London's printers and advertising agencies. But as a same-day on-demand delivery service,
it was in the late sixties that the job took off, in the increasingly congested capitals of Europe and the US. In London
you could probably factor in the seven-week postal strike of
early 1971, the first time post offices and mail-delivery workers went on strike simultaneously, right across in the country.
Using motorcycles for deliveries was seen as quicker and less
expensive than taxis or minicabs.

At that time, minicabs themselves had only been operating as an alternative to licensed black taxis for about a decade. Some bright spark realised that as long as the minicab driver didn't solicit trade on the street but instead received work via a controller over the radio, he wasn't in contravention of a Victorian edict concerning carriages licensed for hire and reward. Once those bulky minicab radios were adapted for bikes, the modern urban despatch rider was born. The earliest outfits included GLH and Yellow Express, as well as Mercury Despatch, whose orange-liveried Suzuki GT250s were most people's first introduction to bike messengers in London.

Up in Kentish Town, two miles north of Oxford Circus, Capital Couriers was a new player looking for a bit of Mercury's action. Its strategy was to grab one of the other vivid options in the colour spectrum and then outdo Mercury with eye-catchingly goofy bikes. The result: Honda C50 mopeds dipped in a vat of rich, placenta-pink paint and fitted with plywood boxes the size of an oven. It was a branding exercise worthy of a child's school project.

I must have spotted Capital's advert in the back of *Motorcycle News* (*MCN*, which I read weekly). The interview process took one phone call.

'Hello, I see in *MCN* you're looking for despatch riders.'

'Yes, mate, what you got?'

'What bike? Triumph Bonneville?'

'Bourneville? Wassat, a two-fifty?'

'Seven-fifty. T140V.'

'Tea for TV? Sounds great. Come on up for a pager. You know where we are?'

I'd never heard of Royal College Street or Kentish Town. Was there a Royal College there? And anyway, why was Kentish Town north of the Thames and miles from the county of Kent? As I was soon to learn, the metropolis was not an intuitive city to navigate, especially for a kid whose knowledge of central London extended to hand-held visits to Madame Tussauds and the Tower of London. It transpired that Kentish Town was vaguely in the vicinity of my pioneering moped expedition to the Sobell Sports Centre a year or two earlier: Elephant, Blackfriars, King's Cross, north by northwest. I had made my first connection. It was to be the key in getting to know the city.

Although I was in no position to judge, Capital Couriers was your typical cowboy outfit, the latest venture from Dennis, a chubby cockney Greek entrepreneur with a thick black perm like a scorched Brillo Pad. To cover his bases he maintained close connections with the massage parlour next door and had accounts with a few others in the vicinity. That's how it was in that newly liberated but pre-politically-correct era. Just up the road, The Falcon pub laid on lunchtime strippers before it became a New Wave music venue. Evening time there'd frequently be a job delivering a takeaway to the blacked-out 'sauna' nearby, like something out of *The Sopranos*. Presumably a bloke got peckish for a lasagne while enjoying a blow job.

The tiny office was on the corner of Camden Road. Not the nearby Camden *Street*, not Camden *High Street* and obviously not Camden Square, -Terrace, -Walk, -Way, -Row, -Passage, -Mews or any of the half-dozen other Camden-somethings in the vicinity. How easy despatching must be in somewhere like Manhattan, where numbered streets go up and the dozen avenues run across town. Capital was the last in a short parade of shops below a terrace of sash-windowed flats. The last time I looked, it was occupied by a charity treating substance abusers. Back then, the office looked like it had been knocked up by a glue-sniffer who then used the off-cuts to bang out the mopeds' load-carrying oven crates. I parked my Triumph a safe distance from the pink mopeds. I'd never seen contraptions like them – nor would I until the pizza-bike trend hit town twenty years later. Dennis was standing outside, fag and coffee in hand, proudly surveying his fleet of lurid deathtraps as well as his Triumph TR7 sports car. Pink mopeds with giant boxes: 'Denny, me ol' son, you are a fa-kin geee-nius!'

The Honda C50 mopeds could be bought for fifty quid. The paint job and boxes cost another tenner, tops. With that done, Denny signed up sixteen-year-olds with a provisional licence picked up free over a post office counter. He charged the kids twenty quid a week bike rental, bleeper and fuel included. If they could ride a pushbike, they could master a clutchless step-thru in a matter of hours. Just stamp on the gear lever and turn the go handle. At that rate, in just a month the mopeds would be as good as paid for, and from there on it was money in the old bank. Den was angling to upgrade to the new Jag XJ-S like the one that Gareth drove in the *New Avengers*. It was merely a matter of time.

Dennis looked over to me, dropped his fag to the ground and scrunched it. 'You 'ere for a job? Pop in and see Mario. 'E'll sort you out.'

Then as now, central London comprised two districts that mattered to messengers: the City and the West End. The City occupies the site of the original Roman settlement, whose pottery and other relics are still regularly unearthed. London grew from there, although 'filled up' might be a better way of putting it, because by the time of the Great Fire of 1666, the capital within the old Roman walls was notoriously congested and squalid. Then, as the empire flourished and merchandise flowed through the nearby docks, the City evolved into the trading and commercial district that is today's 'Square Mile'.

By the time I got to know it, the City was run by the 'Corporation of London'. To my suburban eyes it had the air of a Vatican-like enclave, concentrated in the EC2 and EC3 postal districts. In places along its convoluted boundaries, fiery-tongued dragons braced against the shield of St George marked the City's former gates or 'bars'. It had its own mayor and police force, as well as arcane privileges, taxes and responsibilities dating back to the reign of William the Conqueror. Fewer than 5000 people actually lived in the City, the majority in the recently completed Barbican estate. Of all the English municipal districts, only the Scilly Isles had a smaller residential population, but weekdays from nine to five, the City's ancient foundations creaked as some 200,000 office workers streamed in from the suburbs.

Two miles away, the West End was more familiar to me, quartered by the grand axes of Oxford Street and Regent Street, which met at Oxford Circus. North of the 'City of Westminster' which had been established as the seat of the monarchy and parliament during the Norman era, the West End had been remodelled with Georgian elegance, a spacious neighbourhood quite different from the old City. Oxford and Regent streets informally divided the postal district of W1 into four neighbourhoods: Marylebone at the top left; Fitzrovia top right; Soho bottom right; and exclusive Mayfair to the left, alongside Hyde Park. The liberal attitudes of the late seventies permitted a red-light district of discreet services offered by 'models', as well as in-your-face sex shows to fill the lanes of southern Soho, close to Piccadilly Circus and a short walk from Carnaby Street.

The City was the home of financial institutions in tall buildings, a conservative place where old boys' networks made money from money. The West End was much more lively, the creative and entertainment quarter accommodating publishers, advertising agencies, film- and record companies, as well as cinemas, theatres, restaurants, clubs, hotels and shopping boulevards. Between the two were Covent Garden, Bloomsbury – de facto 'West End' to us – plus Fleet Street and Holborn, off which lay the ancient Inns of Court, a maze of cloistered courtyards occupied by the judiciary.

From Mayfair westwards was largely wealthy and white collar, while east of the City the East End was predominantly working class. And beyond both was the Outer Zone, a ring of suburbs where people lived in houses and children played in parks.

For us, though, the bulk of the work involved bouncing around the City and the West End like the pinball in Brian Protheroe's song. Had he teamed up with WH Auden, they could have composed a catchy tribute to despatchers, along the lines of Auden's 'Night Mail' poem but set to the rhythm of a 250 Super Dream with a dodgy camchain. Models' portfolios to Soho or Chelsea, affidavits to Lincoln's Inn Field, artwork or transparencies to Covent Garden, financial reports from City to City, press releases to all the papers, VT footage to the two TV stations, shoes from King's Road or Shoreditch studio, master tapes to pop star's pad, tissue samples from out of town lab – and any number of cheques, forgotten keys, plane tickets or wallets. If you needed it there within the hour, or just wanted to impress someone with a posthaste hand delivery, call for a leather-clad biker boy. By the mid-eighties, as commerce in London thrived, we could barely keep up.

But in the late summer of 1978 my knowledge of the streets of London was based primarily on the Monopoly board game. I knew the expensive dark blues, greens and yellows – Mayfair, Piccadilly and Bond Street – were posh areas and therefore West End. The cheapies like Pentonville, and Whitechapel? Out east somewhere. As for south London, that was all one big suburb with little activity requiring bike couriers.

Armed with my Monopoly know-how and a good sense of direction, I got my very first job – a delivery to Chiswick in west London, close to the river. That'll be easy: head south and simply follow the north bank of the Thames upstream. It was a foolproof strategy refined along the hostile banks of the Nile by the likes of Livingstone, Burton and Speke.

That might have been an efficient route had the River Thames run as straight as a Roman aqueduct, but being a real river, the Thames meanders north and south by up to two miles. So it was, some two hours after undertaking what should have been a nine-mile, twenty-five-minute ride along the as-yet undiscovered trade route known as the Westway, I got the package signed for without a word of complaint. That came to be the everlasting paradox of messengering: clients might have been paying twenty times the cost of overnight postage, and on occasion we obliged by pulling every trick in the book to get it there fast. But usually no one gave a toss on receipt, far less offered any thanks for executing a high-speed delivery that left a trail of destruction fit for an episode of Ogri.

Early on, I remember doing an urgent 'wait-and-return' to Ashford in Kent, a 110-mile round-trip for which I got paid both ways, plus waiting time. It was good money so I belted up and down the M20 to make it better, and as I rolled back into Maiden Lane, WC2, I announced to the guy with some pride, 'Ashford and back, two hours five!'

'What a wing you are,' he said dryly as he scribbled a signature and handed me back my clipboard.

'Well, fuck you, pal,' I thought. I never dared make such a boast again – not to a customer at least.

No, the real pressure to deliver promptly was not so much to please clients but to get more work and the buzz that going for it generated. It was a form of gambling: how fast and hard could I go before blowing it with an accident, an altercation or a pull from the rozzers (police). We were paid by the job and £1.50 (about a fiver today) was the minimum fee for a W1 to W1. As long as there was the work, the quicker you rode the more you earned, and that could be multiplied by getting two or more jobs in the same direction. Just like a truck haulier, running across town 'empty' set your earnings back three spaces. Every mile had to pay, even the ride to and from work.

The best way to achieve all this was to keep in touch with base; never let them forget about you. Handheld two-way VHF radios had been around for years but required expensive hardware and licensing. Being a fly-by-night outfit, Capital Couriers supplied us with the cutting-edge alternative: pagers or 'bleepers', the mobile phones of the day. By some electronic miracle devised by Motorola, Mario could ring my pager's unique number and seconds later it would bleep on my shoulder – a signal to call base now. With luck I would hear it and respond. I soon learned to hoard 2p coins and memorise the locations of payphones around town.

The first few days continued in a litany of agonised blunderings with regular reference to the soon-to-be-despised *A-Z.* But gradually the key traffic arteries began to take form and join up. Even if it did follow the meandering river, the Embankment was still a quick way from Westminster to the City; Park Lane was rated at 40mph so pushed to 50 was a fast way of skirting Mayfair. You could also snatch a quick burn-up in the underpass linking Piccadilly to Knightsbridge. Nailing that underpass eastbound was a bit of a gamble though. At any time of day a tailback could stretch from Piccadilly into the chicaned tunnel. Come round the exit lefthander too fast and you'd ram the back of some limo and find yourself sailing over car roofs, as happened to one over-exuberant guy at Capital. Meanwhile, in the congested City with its medieval street plan, there were no top-gear runways, except the brief thrill of London Wall.

If you had any distance to cover you wanted to get onto one of the axes, and chief among them was the Euston Road. Ask any London despatcher and they'll confess to a love-hate relationship with the Euston Road and its western extension, the Marylebone Road. In a city centre where most of the flow was east to west, this thoroughfare was practically an urban freeway. Not only that but the underpass below Euston Tower had no unsporting bends, so when the rare chance presented itself you could belt through it at a fair lick.

A canny or sufficiently hyped-up rider rarely got stuck on the Euston Road. Three lanes and the median railing also discouraged jaywalking pedestrians, which made speeding safer, and those lanes also offered the harried courier a choice of two channels between the slow-moving traffic. With a slim bike and a confident attitude you could slip by up to 20mph faster than the cars either side without it getting too risky. But it was still nerve-wracking. Whether they did it for just one summer or for an entire decade, this practice of 'lane splitting' through moving traffic will have been burned deep into a despatch rider's psyche. It was a live version of the yet-to-be-invented video game in *Tron*, a 1982 sci-fi movie, but with nurse-meeting consequences.

Best of all, the usually reliable Euston Road was a quick way west out of town, and what a relief it was to do that once in a while. At Marylebone it rose up over the Edgware Road on to a flyover that whisked you over Paddington and Notting Hill's Portobello Market, with nifty exits down to Shepherd's Bush for Hammersmith and the M4 to Heathrow, and then Wood Lane for the BBC TV Centre. Soon after that the elevated racetrack came back down at East Acton where the still brisk A40 Western Avenue ran on to Oxford and beyond.

This flyover was the Westway. Completed in 1970, it was actually less than three miles long, but if necessary could be covered safely in as many minutes. It was the only motorway in town and after hours of stop-start pushing and shoving through the West End's gridlock, it gave you a chance to purge the cylinders. And it wasn't only despatchers who thought so. A year before I became aware of this westbound runway, The Clash had sung about tearing along the flyover after dark on their original *The Clash* album. And a year later Chris Petit's road movie *Radio On* featured the Westway flyover too. If only London's planners had kept at it and cleared a Northway, Eastway and Southway, the capital could have been a contender for courier's City of the Year.

At Capital I bonded with the only other rider running a big bike. Nick had a CB750K6, a too-close descendant of the revolutionary 1969 superbike that led to the current megabike frenzy. Nick and I soon engaged in amiable 'Brit Shit/ Jap Crap' banter.

'Bland.'

'Unreliable.'

'Over-complicated.'

'Crude.'

'Sewing machine.'

'Pneumatic drill.'

This sparring ran for days at a time, but always with a twinkle of affability. Of course I was only partly joking. His gargantuan, four-pipe CB was far from what I aspired to in a big bike. In that category even Suzuki's cackling GT750 triple had more going for it. No, at that time I was fully enamoured with my Bonneville, and I wasn't the only one. With my inaugural Chiswick debacle still only days old, one morning I bounded up the stairs of a redbrick Edwardian block off Oxford Circus. A pretty receptionist was just tidying up some photocopies rolling off the machine behind her.

'Ooh, are you the bike? Won't be a minute,' she said with a smile, glancing over her shoulder at the skinny bloke manning the Xerox. 'Are you new? I haven't seen you before.'

She had an optimal blend of nice hair, posh accent and comely figure all of which combined to produce a pleasing, knee-weakening effect.

'Yes, last week. I just started,' I spluttered.

'Ooh. What sort of motorbike do you ride?'

'Triumph Bonneville. Seven-fifty.'

'Oh,' she replied with a light gasp, which I unhesitatingly interpreted as dazzled admiration.

I reached out for something on which to steady myself, but then Xerox bloke chucked some documents in front of her in a huff and broke the spell.

'Ah, here we are. Thank you, *Jeffrey.*' She pronounced his name with a bite. With a final shuffle, the documents were slipped into an addressed envelope which she handed to me with another smile.

'There. Don't ride too fast now. See you soon!'

I relived that early encounter for hours if not days. Had I just had a near-miss in the rain and she been an equally attractive but stuck-up bag asking me patronisingly not to drip on their carpet, I'd have probably lost interest in despatching and been dishwashing in Bristol by Christmas. Sadly, I was never to collect from John Princes Street again, but my faith in the Triumph's magical charisma was enshrined.

Another time, as I was leafing through my *A-Z* in Westbourne Grove, an Australian tourist asked to take a picture of the bike.

'What, with me on it?'

'You bet. My son back in Melbourne will love it. He's always wanted a real motorbike.'

And in Victoria Street another time I came trotting back to the bike to see a pinstripey old gent stooped over the Bonnie.

'Oh, do excuse me. I was just admiring your superb motor cycle. It's a beauty. Does it really do a hundred-and-sixty-miles-per-hour?' The way he asked conjured up a chap who was getting on and beginning to see signs all around of the things he could have done if only he'd dared.

'I don't think so. That's just the speedo.' Though there was a good chance that at full-chat the jumpy Smiths instrument might well flicker wildly anywhere between one-sixty and zero while actually doing eighty.

Non-biking civilians who didn't know a pushrod from Rod Stewart responded to the Bonnie in a way no other bike of mine ever inspired, whether flash or trash. I put it down to a warm nostalgia for British engineering at its gentlemanly apogee ten or twenty years earlier: sporty, but never aggressive or ostentatious. British sports cars from the same era probably evoke similarly fond reactions. And it wasn't just a patriotic thing. In the sixties, three-quarters of new Triumphs were sold in North America, where they loved Brit Iron too. The Bonneville was of course named after the salt flats in Utah where from the mid-fifties onwards, land-speed records were set by American daredevils on Triumphs.

Nick at Capital was of that fifties generation, a white African born in Kenya, which I suspected he'd left under murky circumstances. Or maybe he was just a public school casualty and general-purpose misfit – there would be plenty of those in the despatching game. Though professing to have been well brought up, Nick had a dark edge that was at times a little scary. My mum spotted it straight away the one time he came round. Occasionally he'd expel misogynistic or racist rants, or pull off episodes of crazy riding. But he was also supportive when my Brit shit-heap needed some TLC.

With more experience and a decade my senior, he was my guide into the world of motorcycle despatching. We'd hang out after work and talk bikes. He had a lockup nearby where a mate kept a gorgeous burgundy T160 Trident that was 'resting'. I'd never really fancied the triples. It seemed the Brits were overreaching themselves with that extra pot, at least without a few more decades of development.

Nick also introduced me to the exotic Levantine delicacy known as the doner kebab, the fast-food fad that had recently followed croissants from the Continent. The hideous rotating stump of raw, compressed animal matter appeared oddly appetising when you'd subsisted on crisps and Nutty Bars all day. One chilly night on Chalk Farm Road Nick instructed an oil-splattered vendor to wipe himself down and shave me a freshly grilled morsel with his huge knife.

'Try that,' he said. 'It's delicious.'

At that age and that time of night, my taste buds weren't as fussy as my eyes, and once some crispy salad, a spoonful of hummus and 'chilli sos?' had been ladled on, it went down well enough. Despite containing enough salt and grease to tan a herd's-worth of buffalo hides, it took a few years for me to come to my senses and revert to my original misgivings.

Like a lot of young riders getting to grips with despatching, or perhaps just adulthood, I became enamoured with my new-found self-importance and the perceived urgency of my errands. Soon I was riding around like an arrogant twat, slashing across lanes, kicking back at cars that cut me up and scaring pedestrians unnecessarily. Necessary intimidation was entirely legitimate, as I had to vehemently explain to a traumatised plainclothes cop I'd nearly run over. But it didn't take long before I got a taste of my own medicine.

One day I turned north off Shaftesbury into Great Windmill Street, former site of a fifteenth-century windmill but at that time the hub of Paul Raymond's porn empire. The narrow lane was clogged with stationary traffic that showed no signs of moving, so with little hesitation I rode up on to the equally narrow pavement. Just as I passed a doorway a bloke strode out, zipping up his flies with the satisfied mien of one who'd just had a twenty-quid bunk-up. I grazed matey's girth, chirped an 'Oops, sorry mate' and dropped back on to the road behind a van. Striding up behind me unseen, bunk-up man belted the back of my helmet with a thwack. 'Yew FAKIN' CANT!' he yelled and stormed off up the road, justice served and, most annoyingly of all, getting to Brewer Street quicker than me. I was suitably shamed and made a vow to in future always give way to pedestrians when riding on the pavement.

Sometimes though, the rules just had to be broken. One evening at the Colindale Blood Bank I was handed a padded vinyl case with 'Urgent – Human Tissue' emblazoned in red across the top.

'How long will it take to get there?' asked the receptionist.

'Er… Children's Hospital, Great Ormond Street? About twenty or twenty-five minutes?' I replied, quickly juggling what might be possible with what she wanted to hear.

'Oh,' she said with a frown. 'Well, please be as quick as you can.'

Crikey, this was urgent. I'd never picked up blood before. Was some poor child actually haemorrhaging on the slab, nine miles away, with their life in the balance? As I kicked the Bonnie over I wondered – should I? Dare I? Is it allowed? I decided tonight, yes it would be. The time was 7.22pm and the Highway Code was being temporarily suspended.

I flicked the headlight on high and roared off down the Edgware Road for Staples Corner, then hit sixty-five along the short stretch of the North Circular before swinging through the traffic for the roundabout under the A41 Brent Cross flyover. From here the broad Hendon Way was always a reliably fast run with only two sets of lights on the way to Finchley Road. I braked hard towards them, squeezed between the queued cars and pushed out past the white line. Cross traffic swept from left and right, but once a space opened up, and contrary to all my licence-preserving instincts, I launched myself across the red light and belted on towards Finchley Road.

The next stage was going to be dicey: slow traffic, buses and at least half a dozen lights to negotiate before Swiss Cottage. Where necessary I skipped round the outside of traffic islands, and on the reds pulled up out front, watched for a chance, then launched again.

Amazingly no one seemed to be hooting at me and no sirens wailed. At Swiss Cottage I slipped into the flow coming from the left and managed to cross Adelaide Road on green. Swift, smooth progress with minimal right turns: that seemed to be the secret to racing efficiently across town, all fed by the colossal rush brought on by concentration.

Like a rally racer I was visualising the next 'bend', or in my case a junction or traffic light, so as to calculate how best to clear it. Opposite Regent's Park I slipped left on to Prince Albert Road. Some countries allow this manoeuvre at traffic light junctions on red, but not the UK. Once through though, I kept it down to 55: we all knew that along residential '30mph' streets, 40-ish was the working limit. Stray beyond that for too long and things could happen too fast, with fines probably involving a ban.

At Camden Parkway the evening traffic made it too difficult to shoot across the junction, but six weeks in the game and I'd already learned the trick of watching the other lights change to red in anticipation. The middle lamp flicked to amber and as soon as the road cleared I was off again with a squeal from the K181 and a good four seconds before my light turned green.

Running alongside the railway tracks, Park Village East, NW1 was a nifty back road linking Regent's Park with Euston. Nick had put me on to it. Braking at the end, I crunched the side stand into Granby for Hampstead Road, where I knew the lights took ages to change. So I dashed across to the central strip, and then sped off south once it was clear left.

ETA just a couple of minutes now. Scrape left into Cardington and down the side of Euston Station – watch out for taxis! – then slip on to the busy Euston Road and heave over to the right lane quick to line up for the lights into Woburn Place. There was no chance of pushing across three lanes here, but once barrelling down Woburn I ran all the reds as before.

Just after Russell Square I was looking out for a pedestrian passage I'd spotted one time. It led directly into Queen Square, so avoiding the two-minute schlep via Theobald's Road. There it was, Cosmo Place. I rode onto the kerb; some tourists stopped in their tracks, startled by the revving Triumph's full beam and my determined glare. I passed them, weaved briskly among Cosmo's early-evening revellers heading for a pre-show meal, and dropped into Queen Square without so much as a 'bloody bike messengers'.

By now I was buzzing like a midsummer hive and with the engine baking my shins I sprinted down to the hospital, grabbed the blood, leapt the steps in a single stride and landed at reception.

'Hi. Got some blood here from Colindale.'

I checked my watch. Just coming up to 7.37. Fifteen minutes and as many red lights. Not bad.

In the UK the practice of using 'blood bikes' dates back to the 'Emergency Volunteer Service' of the early sixties. A couple of years after my dash the 'Bloodrunners' service was established and still thrives today. The volunteers' machines get hi-viz stickers like those used on police bikes, except with 'BLOOD' stencilled across the windscreen. And although some are also fitted with blue lights and sirens, that's just to make the riders even more noticeable in traffic. Bloodrunners aren't instructed or permitted to run red lights, ignore speed limits or pass round the wrong sides of traffic islands as I'd done that evening, although on the job we despatchers flaunted those latter two rules daily.

What would have happened had I got stopped by the cops? I like to think they'd at least have escorted me to my destination on a blue light before throwing the book at me. As it was, even though we all clocked up our share of actual rather than metaphorical ambulance chasing, it was amazing that no one reported me.

That memorable blast across town was typical of the immunity we despatchers felt from the Law and the laws of physics, engendered on that occasion by a well-meaning if mistaken sense of entitlement. It was how we treated every job when under pressure or in the mood – 'You want urgent, I'll give you urgent!' – and why we were to become notorious in the years to come.

5

Security Despatch

Honda CB400T, MZ TS250/1

Just before I started at Capital I'd gone for a job at Security Despatch in Covent Garden but was advised by a nice, well-spoken chap to first get a few months' experience. And so I did. But in Kentish Town, Mario and Dennis were forever arguing. It's hard to think what about, but one day Mario finally had enough of the Greek and stormed out. Or perhaps he left before the undertow pulled him down. Clients were going elsewhere and Capital couldn't even lure in enough unemployed teenagers to ride their mopeds. That these were the colour of an eight-year-old girl's bedroom might have had something to do with it. Capital was wobbling like one of its top-heavy C50s, and it looked as if Dennis might have to revert to what he knew best: serving faintly disguised knocking shops with lasagnes on the side. Having paid my dues and with Mario gone, I went back to Security and signed on as rider 106, their hundred and sixth operative.

Security Despatch had been established in late 1974 by a trio of ambitious riders then working for Yellow Express, itself formed following the 1971 Post Office strike. The three went into business with an entrepreneur, whose Belgravia basement served as their original office. They took on all available work at first, but their long-term plan was to secure upmarket accounts from PR-, model- and press agencies. Within a few years Security relocated to a proper office in Russell Street, Covent Garden, ideally situated between the City and West End.

When I arrived in Russell Street, Covent Garden's nearby seventeenth-century piazza – London's first square – was undergoing a makeover. The famous wholesale fruit and vegetable market had been relocated across the river in Battersea a couple of years earlier and Covent Garden was in the process of being turned into today's successful tourist precinct. Outside Inigo Jones' St Paul's Church, where aspiring flower girl Eliza Doolittle had stood in the opening scenes of *Pygmalion*, today licensed buskers pursue similar recognition.

The trendies were homing in on Covent Garden, and the old Georgian coffee houses had become wine bars with names like Brahms & Liszt (Cockney rhyming slang for 'pissed'). SD's office was located above Brahms and here I received my clipboard, some reflective stickers depicting SD's subtle 'leaping panther' logo, plus my Motorola handheld radio. I also got a laminated photo ID card which instructed anyone who found me lying unconscious by the roadside to call in immediately – the client would be wondering where their stuff was. Walking back to my Bonnie with that lot in my arms, Russell Street felt a lot more than two and a half miles from Capital Couriers at the scuzzy end of Royal College Street.

Soon after I started at SD an article appeared in *Bike* magazine titled, 'Toff Security, Posher Than Yer Average Despatch Company'. Written by a former rider, it described how the management and many of the riders at Security Despatch had public school or university educations. The *Bike* feature portrayed Security as an exclusive club of louche, articulate dropouts, and the antics and attitudes of this maverick band of riders made the place I now worked for sound exciting and glamorous. The article also highlighted tensions between the management and the workforce, some of whom had been with the company since the early days but had passed the peak of their motivation. There was a high turnover of staff and actual profits were still nebulous. The company relied on a few indefatigable hands, many from the lower orders and not mentioned in the article, but who turned up come what may.

Despite my equally common background, my Bonneville fitted in well with the other unconventional machines, and as bike messengers became fashionable, we liked to think we added to the buzz that typified Covent Garden back then. One of the attractions was that, unlike other major players such as Pony Express and Mercury, Security didn't employ riders on fixed wages and nor did it have us riding liveried company bikes with matching company bibs. Instead, SD drew on a pool of free-styling, hard-charging dissenters committed to expressing their individuality and belief in personal freedom. For the management, that became part of the problem.

At the office I kept a low profile until I found my feet. They came in handy one evening when Shaun, a lanky Ozzie, gave me a lift home for some reason. A side benefit of his Z900's high, wide bars was demonstrated when, somewhere near Sidcup, Shaun unexpectedly opened her up and I pivoted backwards around the grab rail I was clutching. Luckily my feet caught under his outspread arms, so saving me from a broken neck.

Other characters at SD included swaggering Tim, who rode an R80 with a Windjammer fairing, Krausers and spots, between them bearing the implied message: 'Comin' Through.

Outta My Effing Way!' If you passed him out on the streets he'd hastily turn up the wick, exaggeratedly flipping the BM through the traffic to verify his alpha-rider status. One warm day he was told off for walking into an office bare-chested, prompting the unwarranted company directive: 'All riders must remain fully clothed'.

Northern Kevin was another hard-charging show-off. Seeing me opposite him at a rainy Ludgate Circus one time, he threw his XL250S hard left up Fleet Street. The back wheel stepped out but he kept his nerve and his feet on the pegs.

'Ya see me back there? Back end came rah toot,' he bragged back in the office.

'Yes, mate. Nice save.'

'It weren't no save.'

There was also the eccentric, Maurice Seddon. Probably in his late forties, he sounded like a toff but may have merely been posh. His rode a bonkers 1950s BSA B33 clad in self-promotional banners and which powered an array of his hand-made electrically heated silk underclothing about whose virtues he prattled on if you strayed too close.

Dressed in full-race leathers that matched his CB750 Phil Read Replica, ageing actor Richard Wyler may have been a dashing Clint or Connery clone in the sixties. But like Maurice, he only seemed to rock up when he was free and in town. Looking back, few of us appreciated the colourful lives both Wyler and Seddon had led. Most dismissed them as a batty inventor and an aloof flash harry.

If it was attention you craved, there were other ways of doing it, such as riding a stripped-down, high-compression R90 proddie racer with pipes fit to raise the dead from Inigo Jones' nearby churchyard. Strung out like dirty washing between the clip-ons and rear-sets was balding, long-haired Christian. He'd fled East Germany, just like that MZ racer back in the sixties, but rode as if they might come and snatch him back any time. His tape-bound leathers were fifty shades grubbier than Wyler's HRC get-up, and his racing plates were for real. For Christian, despatching was a means of funding his British racing campaign as well as an effective way to terrify tourists.

Fit for nothing taller than a 400/4, Pat was 'dat fonny lidl Oirishman', but the controllers depended on solid riders like him. Rarely sick, crashed, flat-tyred or otherwise indisposed, Pat would come into work early and keep going all day. He introduced me to my first rude Irish word – something like 'soktopper', as in, 'use yer indicators, ye feckin' soktopper!' – though he never told me what it actually meant.

The Essex Boys may also not have known the difference between a serviette and a napkin, but were good workers: Cliff on his RD400, Boris on a Guzzi Spada and older Dave on a high-mileage XS500 eight-valve. Dave advised me on the best way to prolong the life of the era's predominant air-cooled engines: let them warm up fully before tearing off each morning, and change the oil frequently – it was cheaper and less hassle than a new top end. Dave still lived with his mum despite being at least twice my age, and at the Friday evening spin-down, when wages were paid, spliffs were rolled and beers cracked open, Dave would dispense a selection of mysterious capsules and pills. Suitably resuscitated, the throng would offload their week's burdens, query payments or head for the pub, where the grubby despatchers, eyelids lined with a day's worth of sooty kohl, looked out of place among the smartly dressed trendies we'd soon be calling yuppies.

As far as I could tell, the 'toff' angle described in *Bike* was a red herring, or perhaps a shrewd form of spin on SD's part. Despatching attracted artful roger-dodgers from all backgrounds, footloose young guns who weren't yet fixed on a career and were reluctant to clock on to a steady job. Bike messengering was an occasionally exciting but ultimately dead-end job. With no ranks to rise up, once you knew the streets and a few associated tricks as well as the next guy, you were top of the crowded heap. Beyond that lay van driving, office-bound controlling or starting your own despatch company. And soon there would be scores of those looking for good riders immune to the job's less glamorous aggravations. Most despatchers didn't stay for more than a few months or didn't stick at it full time. The son of the actor who played Cowley, the grumpy chief in *The Professionals*, turned up for a bit, but like many, he didn't last.

Early on at SD I discovered two things that greatly improved my day-to-day despatching. Firstly, the little-known *Nicholson Greater London Street Atlas* was miles better than my crumby *Geographers' A-Z*, even if 'A-to-Z' had become shorthand for an urban streetfinder. In my few months of using an *A-Z*, I'd already uncovered several errors and omissions, and even with an eighteen-year-old's eyesight, the density of detail on the critical central London pages was a strain to read. On top of that, the grubby brown newsprint pulped like toilet paper when exposed to rain, and after sustained use the whole lot would start to disintegrate. I binned the distended remains of my *A-Z*, bought a *Nicholson's* and never looked back, right until the very, very end. Cloth bound and stitched with thicker and brighter paper, it mapped well beyond the boundaries of Greater London and brought up very few errors. Best of all, the congested mass of streets in the centre of town were depicted at an enlarged scale. Anyone who used a *Nicholson's* back then will fondly remember the much-thumbed pages around 140 to 145 covering the City and West End.

The other gem I uncovered was that, as of 1665, all of London's street numbers radiated from Charing Cross. Perhaps the practice of painting red crosses on the doors of houses affected by the deadly bubonic plague of that year had something to do with it. The Great Fire the following year may have reduced the first numbered buildings to ash, but wherever you were in London, with your back to Charing Cross, odd numbers started on the left side of a street, even numbers on the right. Once I'd assimilated this, homing in on a building in a street became a whole lot easier.

Charing Cross is London's geodetic datum; all distances from the capital are measured from this point. However, 'London – Mile Zero' is not indicated by the ornate Gothic 'cross' you see today outside Charing Cross Station, but by the bronze equestrian statue of Charles I that stands on its own traffic island some 200 yards to the southwest, by Trafalgar Square. This was where the original Eleanor Cross stood, the last of a dozen such monuments commissioned in 1290 by Edward I to commemorate the funeral procession of his late queen's body from Lincoln to London. It was destroyed by anti-royalists during the Civil War in 1647; the cross outside the station is an embellished nineteenth-century replica. A couple of original Eleanor Crosses do survive today, including one at Waltham Cross, a suburb on the north edge of London.

There may have been little obvious logic to the ordering of London's postal zones – for example not one of the zones between SE1 and SE5 are adjacent, and ten miles separates SE2 from SE1 – but London's street numbering finally made sense. Of course some streets broke the rules. Take Tottenham Court Road ('TCR'): the numbers ran consecutively all the way up the east side to the Euston Road and back down to Centrepoint. But on adjacent Gower Street it was odd left, even right. Was that because TCR was a *road?* If only it were that simple. A little further east, Grays Inn Road and Farringdon Road also followed the odd/even pattern. For some reason TCR, on the border of WC1 and W1 postal districts, used the older 'circular' or consecutive system. So too did cul-de-sacs (understandably), roads along the Embankment, which had buildings on one side only, and places like Bedford Square between Gower Street and TCR. Although in Bedford's case, Number 1 was not at the corner closest to Charing Cross and the numbers ran anticlockwise. It was the same story in other West End squares, but in the City squares numbers ran clockwise. As with railway gauges in some countries, because of separate jurisdictions or authorities a consistent standard was never adopted, and the resulting anomalies now survive as one of London's navigational eccentricities.

As for the difference between 'streets' and 'roads', that was marginally less complicated. A road was a transportation route connecting one locality to another, sometimes with the place in its name, although it may not be located in that place. A street was once defined as a paved or improved road, usually within a settlement, and one street might be named after the settlement. So, to return to the Camden example, Camden Road linked Camden with nearby Holloway but Camden Street was in Camden, as was Camden High Street. Tottenham Court Road, however, didn't lead to some forgotten Tudor 'court' way out in Tottenham, although TCR's continuation, Hampstead Road, did lead to Hampstead. And at nearby King's Cross, Caledonian Road soon joined the Great North Road. And that road, the A1, did lead four hundred miles to Edinburgh in Scotland, or 'Caledonia' to the Romans.

Paving main streets within a busy settlement would have been a worthwhile investment, preventing them from turning into quagmires, but the much longer link roads outside a municipality – king's highways under the crown's authority – remained largely unpaved. That explains why the A5 to North Wales was called Watling Street. It was part paved in the Roman era but then, like all roads in Britain, it fell into disrepair for well over a thousand years until the art of road building was revived by the likes of Telford and McAdam.

As I continued to feel my way around the roads and streets, avenues and lanes of the two-thousand-year-old city, I tuned into the secrets of its arcane layout. But there were many occasions when I'd ride up and down and up a road (or street), utterly unable to unearth any sign of the building that must exist and was urgently awaiting my delivery. I'd radio base, they'd call the client, the client would call their client and they'd walk out into the street (or road), wave a lantern and guide me in.

Considering the use it was getting, my young Bonnie was doing a lot better than I had a right to expect. A year earlier *Bike* magazine (along with *MCN*, the fount of all my biking lore at the time) had run a reader's report of his T140V, titled 'The Love-Hate Machine'. It described a litany of maddening minor faults, leaks and all-out seizures which were common to many British products at the time. And yet the loyal owner kept coming back for more. When his Bonnie was in a state, he admitted no one would buy it. But when it was fixed up, love was back in the air and who'd want to be riding anything else? All I can deduce from this experience was that his might have been a slapdash example from the NVT era, while mine, built maybe two years later, was a product of the Meriden co-op, lovingly assembled by underpaid enthusiasts until that iteration of Triumph also foundered in the early eighties.

I didn't run my Bonnie hard, rarely over 60mph, as beyond that speed all was wind, noise and vibration. With the Bonnie the grin-factor was all about exploiting that low-rpm torque. Living in south London had its benefits, among them the grippy lefthander at the bottom of Brixton Hill just past St Matthew's Church. Even after a long day in the saddle, I'd always do my best to line myself up at the lights beforehand so as to hit that bend ahead of the pack and grind the side stand in a long shower of sparks. Banked over far less than I imagined, the wheels unloaded a little and the Triumph crabbed to the right, but remained planted like a chubby genie on his magic carpet. Shifting into fourth to charge up to the lights by the prison, it was a great way to sign off the day. But it wasn't always like that. Another time turning hard into Charing Cross Road opposite Leicester Square, the right pipe dug in and I flipped like a tossed coin, scattering alarmed tourists. Not so cool.

An important item in the professional despatcher's armoury was the handheld Motorola. It separated you from the sad-arsed bleeper boys frequently seen beating the crap out of another faulty public phone box that had swallowed their last bit of change. I knew the feeling. In the dark period just before British Telecom was privatised, my all-time record was traipsing to no less than eight phone boxes before I found one that worked.

At SD I was instructed in radio protocol: charge it up nightly and always start transmissions with your call sign, location and maybe status, which was either 'POB' (package on board) or 'empty' (package delivered). No chitchat. When asked, provide signal strength and clarity on a scale of five. 'Five by five' was good; 'two by four' meant you could hardly hear then and might want to twiddle the mysterious squelch button. 'Roger roge' for 'OK' or 'message received and understood' was in the approved lexicon, as was 'say again' for 'please repeat'. But 'over' or worse still 'over and out' was from bad movies only, and not even funny as a joke. With the strap looped under your left arm and behind your neck, the radio lay flat on your right shoulder in its holster, the handset close to your ear. On the move the transmit button was easily engaged with your left hand as you brought the radio to your chin to speak – the right hand took care of the steering, acceleration and the front brake. There was no need to slow down to talk and the radio was always with you, even when waiting in an office (though they rarely worked indoors). As you rode around the speaker blared away, boosting your self-importance. But for the radio to be of any use, you needed to listen out for your call sign.

'Wanasx, Wanasx.' Pause.

'Wanasx, Wanasx, Wanasx.' Longer pause.

'Wanasx-Wanasx, Wanasx-Wanasx.'

'One Oh Six. Marylebone Road.' No need to say where I was going, the controller ought to know.

'Wanasx, I been calling you and calling you and calling you.'

'Just come off the Westway. Decca in five minutes.'

'Roge, One Oh Six.' Sigh. 'Call me when you're empty.'

If this was delivered in a resigned tone with no further instructions, you'd failed in some way. Perhaps there'd been an urgent pick-up in Notting Hill also for the West End, but you'd been hammering overhead along the Westway with one eye on your mirrors, oblivious to the controller's pleas. That was why you'd purposefully mentioned 'Westway' – it proved you'd not merely forgotten to turn the radio volume back up after dozing for twenty minutes in the over-warm reception of a Ladbroke Grove studio.

I joined SD in early winter when the students and fair-weather dilettantes had scarpered like rats from a shipwreck. There was lots of work and soon I was earning £250 or more for a fifty-hour week. True, running costs might reduce that by a third, but it was still way more than I could spend while still living at home. Just two years earlier at Sainsbury's I'd been on twenty quid a week, but despatching came with a range of stresses greater than being caught red-handed in the freezer with a half-bitten choc ice. Traffic, police, unpredict-able pedestrians, taxi drivers, maddening delays with other pressing deliveries on board, rude receptionists or a bladder about to blow. All that took some time to diffuse and some-times one night's rest wasn't enough. I remember falling sleep after a particularly hectic day, the Euston Road playing in my mind's eye. I was out – then suddenly jumped upright with a fright, wide awake.

'FUCK! I've still got that SE21 in the frigging topbox!'

It took me a few seconds to realise it had been an unusually vivid dream, the brain mulling over the day's unresolved anxieties. I sat for a minute thinking. I did deliver it, didn't I? Yes, I definitely dropped a letter off at the fancy house in Dulwich. I had a signature and the time. It was safe to lie back down.

Earning all this money while learning the craft, it seemed a waste to throw it all away and move to Bristol – to do what, exactly? There wouldn't be any despatching there worth the bother, and unemployment was climbing month on month. Instead, I began to entertain thoughts of knuckling down at Security on a more suitable machine. The Bonneville was too good for all this rushing about, and the hefty kickstarting ritual was losing its shine when done forty-four times a day.

If I'd followed convention, that bike would have been a CX500, Honda's innovative shaft-drive V-twin that had come out that year. By the early eighties, the CX was supposedly the definitive despatcher's ride, but from the start I took against the top-heavy 'plastic maggot' and its string of cam chain failures, something that bedevilled many Hondas at that time. Actually it was more than that. You couldn't accuse the CX of being another UJM, but typical of the Japs, they hadn't gone far enough to make it a brilliant bike. My choice of work bike was to be much blander.

Read the following and try and guess which bike was being described. The road tester was commending this bike to 'poets, romantics and all people who have soul' because 'it possesses virtues true to the ideals of biking … in allowing its rider to develop an empathy with [the bike's] inanimate character'. Furthermore, 'it can be flicked through corners almost like it's a Ducati' at which point '85–90mph country lane scratching is within reach'.

Some sort of gutsy Morini? Perhaps an RD350LC, a bike built especially for us 'Yur-peens' now that the US had killed off road-going two-strokes? Couldn't be, could it? LCs weren't out for another year or more. Oh no, our man was getting worked up over the new Honda CB400T Dream. I can't actually recall reading that road test when it was published a few months earlier, but if I had, it's unlikely I'd have taken it in. I've no doubt it was written from the heart, but after barely two years on two wheels, I knew it all and could see what this bike really was. My motivation for getting a Dream was bleakly pragmatic – to paraphrase Honda's slogan of '76: 'All Sense, No Style'.

The 400 Dream replaced Honda's CB400/4, a bestseller in Europe but apparently a flop in the States. Couldn't be having that, so the new twin featured three-valve heads, riveted Comstar wheels and... and... nice ergonomics. Everyone likes those. As the adverts had it, 'It's more than a sports bike, it's a mid-range super bike,' and as demonstrated above, most road testers conceded that the new twin was a better machine than the charismatic Four. For me though, it was a command from the head not a plea from the heart, a terse instruction to secure sensible and economical transportation. With such a practical machine the controllers at SD would recognise my commitment to the job. I'd work like a drone and earn more money.

Some time before Christmas I picked up my burgundy turkey for around £850 from the then fashionable Mocheck dealership in Clapham. For Prime Minister Callaghan, a nice chap who nevertheless seemed out of his depth, the epidemic of crippling strikes dubbed the 'Winter of Discontent' was about to do him in. For me, not in anywhere near deep enough, it was to be a winter of dissatisfaction.

The 400 Dream was indeed a boringly perfect bike, and as I soon found, perfectly boring. Sure, with a press release out of Shoe Lane to deliver to thirty different drops before close of business, the 400 started on the button, ran, turned and stopped like a... No, I refuse to use the D-word.

I suppose if I'd come to the Dream directly from my MZs I might have been more impressed, but what a dreary progression that would have been. Above all, it was the engine characteristics that killed the spirit of enjoyment. When Brit aficionados accused the Japs of turning out bland sewing machines, it was bikes like the 400T they had in mind. Perhaps it was down to torque, the often misunderstood turning force of an engine: Honda claimed twenty-four torques at 8000rpm – my Triumph probably had nearer forty, but at half the engine speed. It seemed I'd stumbled upon one of Motorcycling's Incontrovertible Truths: tractor-like torque at low rpm feels good.

I stuck with the 400T while the Shah fled Iran, strikers left the dead unburied in the morgues, Sid Vicious joined them, and one Monday morning in San Diego a teenage girl flipped to overload, giving the Boomtown Rats an idea for their second number one. In town even Leicester Square became a huge rubbish tip and Elton John's solemn 'Song for Guy', about the death of his record company's young bike messenger, got to number four in the charts. But long before all that had come to pass, I was certain the 400T wasn't going to grow on me. I just could not bear that thing any longer. I was having to get my kicks pondering over the meaning of 'Crane Fruehauf' and other back-of-lorry curiosities. Going to work held fewer thrills, so some days I chose the Triumph, especially when London got caught in an icy spell for a few days in February. The low-slung, high-barred Bonneville was so much easier to control on compacted snow and ice.

I offloaded the Dream on some snivelling pedant who insisted on having Mocheck perform a forensic evaluation before agreeing to the sale. This went on for a couple of weeks, and when he finally required that I deliver it to his place, I in turn decided to see just what 8500rpm felt like through the gears down the Epsom bypass. The guy probably still owns it now.

Back at SD, one Friday evening semi-posh Dave let me try his Commando. This was the barrel-tanked Interstate Mk3 version I'd lusted over in the NVT 'Powerchoice' brochure eighteen months earlier. A short sprint round Covent Garden couldn't qualify as a detailed evaluation, but it was enough to assure me the Bonneville had been the right choice. The Norton's engine wobbled about on its isolastic rubber mounts, not unlike an MZ on tickover. That may have helped isolate vibration, but produced a disconcerting inertia that flung the mighty 850's motor up and down like a buxom sprinter. Or maybe the rubbers were shot. In a hurry to catch the Japs, the boffins at Wolverhampton hadn't only isolated the quivering engine from the frame with rubber, but the swingarm too. As the isolastic rubbers wore, predictably unpleasant handling anomalies appeared.

So the 400T made me want to jab out my eyes out with a red-hot poker, and a ten-minute ride wrote off the hitherto glorious Commando. Was it any wonder that in my confusion I thought MZ's TS250/1 Supa 5 would be a remedy? I found a lovely low-mileage example in the *MCN* classifieds with front and rear crash bars and a neat topbox with a top rack: a well-equipped working machine with not a mark on it. Riding it back the twenty miles from Surrey one chilly Saturday morning, I came round the last bend before home and, just as I passed my old school's playing fields, down I went on some black ice. Not even an hour old and my lovely five-speed MZ was already disfigured. There was no real damage bar my faith in the universe, but as I was picking it up a police car stopped to see if I was OK.

'You wanna watch out, son. It's an icy morning.'

I thanked the officer for his sage assessment of the riding conditions, but was careful not to prolong the encounter – the MZ was as yet uninsured.

The Supa 5 didn't make work any more enjoyable than the Dream, but then it came pre-tuned with low expectations: it was an MZ. I plastered the box with SD stickers, put my head down and carried on messengering. Why? Because after a winter of hard yakka the savings were piling up and 106 had a cunning plan that was going to put a smile back on his face.

6

STREET RACING FOR REAL

Ducati 900SS

It's difficult to write about motorcycling in Britain at this time without acknowledging *Bike* magazine's assistance along my road to nerdition and its influence on my late-teenage world view. *Bike* was the first UK motorcycling magazine with attitude. It gave an irreverent kick up the arse to dreary, cork-lined monthlies such as *Motorcycle Sport* and *Motorcycle Mechanics*, which must have been cracking reads before television was invented. When I started reading *Bike*, and for many years after, it was the bestselling bike mag in the UK, and at the time you could see why.

The magazine had been conceived in the early seventies by Mark Williams, a restless media entrepreneur and contributor to what was then known as the underground press. The early issues went down well but, too soon, Williams was forced to sell the magazine on to another company – something he apparently still regrets. *Bike* magazine *was* Mark Williams, and few bike mag readers celebrate him for coming up with *Which Bike?* a couple of years later, even if he's called it a superior publication.

When I started reading *Bike*, Williams was still writing occasional features as well as his opinionated 'Running out of Road' column about his 'fast' lifestyle. Month in, month out he was either lauded or pilloried on the Letters page, but then so was much of the magazine's content – no different to today's opinionated online bike forums. Readers would also take the time to remind the editor that British bikes still ruled, that a road test's conclusion didn't correlate with their own view, that the 75p cover price was too high, or that the mag was sexist. But for all its failings, *Bike* had come at just the right time to capitalise on the biking boom. Mark Williams was also one of the few Brit bike journalists who was genuinely into off-road riding as much as hurtling along the Embankment on a Jota (at 3am while high on drugs with a Puerto Rican art dealer he'd picked up at a swanky Mayfair party).

Perhaps some of his implausibly tall yarns in *Bike* weren't so far removed from the truth after all. A mid-1979 issue featured a rambling two-parter by Williams titled 'Freeway Madness', a hedonistic fable set in California about shagging, tripping, drug running and then laundering the profits. It read like *Easy Riders* meets *Fear and Loathing* and felt a little dated, even then. Shortly after that Williams wrote his final column for *Bike*, admitted he was still stuck in '71 and had run out of road for real. Fifteen years later, having edited a provincial Welsh newspaper, Mark Williams flew a little too close to the sun and did a couple of years for the very activities he'd fictionalised in 'Freeway Madness'. Some former *Bike* readers were unsure which was the greater tragedy: being busted for coke and currency smuggling, or ending up as editor at the *Brecon & Radnor Express*.

For a couple of years at least, *Bike* was my sort of magazine, reporting on its subject with an enthusiasm and objectivity that comfortably distanced it from its pudding-basin rivals. In the early days I gobbled it up cover to cover, although it had its share of dull content. The greasy northern custom bike scene, trikes, customised Gold Wings with alien bimbo paint jobs – *Bike* covered it all. And when they went to the Isle of Man TT or the Bol d'Or 24-hour endurance race, they didn't get anal about pole positions or lap times, they just got down with the other revellers celebrating the two-wheel carnival. They even put their name and presumably money behind a production bike race series with Avon Tyres.

Motorcycling was heading towards the end of its most successful and outrageous decade. Cocking two-fingers at the Oil Crisis and the general collapse of British industry, dirt biking had boomed and street scramblers (road bikes with wide bars) had evolved into trail bikes (civilised motocrossers with lights). The Japanese and the Italians in particular were coming out with machines not based on a pair of Sheffield-cast pistons going up and down like two arthritic sauropods at the lakeside, reminiscing about the good old days before those mammals came along and ruined it for everyone.

It was a great time to be riding and once in a while a *Bike* feature resonated like a double bass twanged right by your ear-hole. The gang gunning across France to the Bol on big Italian V-twins; Bill Haylock's ride through the Western Isles recalled like some hazy, childhood fairy tale; a giant test of four big trail bikes up in the Lake District. And then there was 'Street Racing for Real', a review of Ducati's 900SS Desmo written by the latest editor, Dave Calderwood.

It was already fairly clear that *Bike* had a soft spot for Ducatis. One or two staffers actually owned them, and despite the Italian marque's well-documented flaws, they were admired for their uncompromising engineering, sharp handling, great looks and brakes that worked in the rain. Ducatis were the extreme antithesis of UJMs.

Bike's contributors often expressed a rebellious attitude that today comes across as a little juvenile, and some of the readers' letters using wilfully misspelled 'biker talk' were just plain embarrassing. There was much mention of 'straights' with their mortgages, Cortinas and, horror of horrors, V-neck jumpers. Dave Calderwood's 'Street Racing for Real' kicked off with a rant in this heroic vein, mocking society's fixation with money and even supermarket hygiene, a subject I'd once been close to. 'Buy a disinfected, cling-film-covered pack of apples and get a lemon free – yourself!' he spat, in the best tradition of upcoming alternative comedians like Alexei Sayle and Ben Elton, but without the jokes. The citrus reference may have triggered a spasm in my subconscious. At SD there was a light-hearted 'Lemon of the Week' award for doing something daft like racing off to Ashford Middlesex when it should have been Ashford in Kent.

Daringly, Calderwood even picked on 'safety anxiety', including the surely sacrosanct 'Think Bike' campaign; foreseeing the eighties consumerist boom, he also attacked 'gotta-have-one-like-the-rest' neuroses, deriding 'this pseudo-life where cringing blockheads worry themselves sick at every turn'. I liked that one. But hold on a minute. This was the same guy who'd commended my disastrous Honda 400 Dream to 'all people who have soul' because it allowed 'its rider to develop an empathy with its inanimate character'. This Calderwood cat was clearly a complex chap. Was he secretly more like the characters in *Abigail's Party*, Mike Leigh's seminal 1977 play, than he'd have us believe? You didn't have to be a social anthropologist to chuckle knowingly at the scene in the play where they argue over the artistic merits of the popular seventies painting *Wings of Love*. A steady seller in Woolies, this faintly Dali-esque picture depicted a naked couple gazing out unperturbed as an oceanic tide floods their infinity patio and a giant Sky Swan cradles the man in its wing, apparently lining up to take a jab at his pecker.

Bike was squeezing out the last drops of Williamsian rebelliousness, best expressed by riding a fast, noisy motorbike, and Ducatis inspired *Bike*'s contributors more than other marques. The last line of Mike Nicks' review of Ducati's Darmah roadster stuck with me too:

> *'In Italy, Darmah is the name given to a tiger in a famous children's story. In Zen Buddhist lore dharma means the one true way. Ducati could really have spelt it either way.'*

Writing like that was why we lapped up *Bike* as if it were the very tablets brought down from the mount.

By 1979 the 900SS was one of the most desirable bikes around. Like cousin Daisy in the *Dukes of Hazzard*, it met with universal approval, one of the few production bikes to personify the drama of raw super biking, where braking, handling and power were in harmony.

Based on the 750 Desmo racer immortalised by Paul Smart's win at Imola in 1972, the 900SS was Ducati's second step on their march to glory. At the 1978 Isle of Man TT, Mike Hailwood, Britain's greatest road racer from the sixties, came out of retirement on a tweaked NCR '900TT' based on the round-case 750. Then aged thirty-eight, and twenty years after he'd first raced on the Island, a pot-bellied Hailwood won the Formula One race, lapping at nearly 110 and passing former rival Phil Read on a 750 Honda. It paralleled Hailwood's last TT race eleven years earlier, when he'd trounced then rival Giacomo Agostini on an MV Augusta. On that occasion Hailwood's four-cylinder Honda set a lap record that lasted till the mid-seventies. Though I wasn't into road racing, it was hard to remain indifferent to Hailwood's astonishing and almost casual comeback on the Island.

Calderwood's 900SS 'Street Racing for Real' test came to me as my bike preferences were solidifying. Although it's unlikely they were ever pitched against each other, to me the SS and the Triumph were cut from the same mould: a similar low-revving engine, the same charismatic profile and the same 'just enough to get the job done' restraint. On the face of it the Desmo (a cool-sounding abbreviation for the desmodromic valve operation that was unique to Ducati bikes) was everything I thought I wanted in my ultimate machine. Weighing around 440lb (201kg), just 60hp got you to 130mph – one of the fastest bikes on the streets. Over the winter I read Calderwood's road test over and over, scrutinising every word and, you'd hope, picking it apart. Unfortunately, even if the warnings were right there, like a slack-jawed, doe-eyed disciple, I read only what I wanted to hear:

> *'… whether you're zamming along a twisty lane or pootling around looking for chicks, you've got control that's… finely tuned and uninhibited by dead weight'.*

Nice.

> *'Time and again I'd slink into the office slyly grinning yet reluctant to tell the tale of that morning's excitements. No-one ever really believes such stories.'*

Like it!

> *'That's the problem with the 900SS. You keep forgetting you're part of the outside world and that you're supposed to obey mundane things like speed limits… staying on the left side of the road and so on.'*

Get me on a drip, I'm delirious!

The Triumph had gone. One weekend an 'Ogri and Malcolm' twosome straight out of *Bike*'s back-page cartoon came round

– big Ogri there to make sure little Malc didn't get reamed. Adios WHX 791S, the only one of my forty-odd bikes from that time whose number plate I can reel off without hesitation. The MZ stayed on for a couple more months – maybe it was longer, who cares. By then the Supa 5 was like a former chum I no longer had time for now I'd hit the big time.

Meanwhile, my mum had mistakenly conflated Ducati with Bugatti's sporty heritage so had therefore theoretically approved. But as I paddled the long black shark up the garden path, her wise words rang across the tiles.

'I think you've gone a bit too far this time, son.'

This was of course music to my ears. At nearly nineteen, the ultimate motorcycle experience had come early.

Those early weeks on the SS were a mixture of breathtaking thrills and nagging disappointment. Certainly the motor's delivery was effortless and smooth for something that looked so crude. But ergonomically – a word only starting to be associated with bikes back then – the SS didn't work for me. Perhaps I'd spent too much time sitting in the wind on my US-spec Bonneville, but the SS's pegs were too high and too far forward, the thin seat also felt too high, plus the clip-ons and controls felt all wrong. Even in the last days of twin shocks, the rear suspension was unnecessarily harsh – or maybe that's why they were the last days. Over-sprung and under-damped, the bike juddered on fast bumpy sweepers and didn't induce the bend-swinging confidence that Dave C had promised. Only the magnificent motor delivered the goods reliably and on time. Maybe even ahead of time. A week out of the showroom it propelled me into a £70 speeding fine.

Above all, it was the hypnotic din punched out by the 900's Conti silencers that captivated me. All V-twins have a rich, distinctive, offbeat timbre, even CX500s muffled by water-cooling, actual silencers and anti-charisma wadding (to be on the safe side). But the sound ejected from the Conti's

was timber-shivering and addictive, whether it was the un-
steady tickover that sounded like an HT lead was loose, hard
accelerating or, best of all, decelerating hard when the note
rose in pitch like the Doppler effect of a passing racer. Some
have speculated that a V-twin's beat sparks a primal reso-
nance deep in the human brain or bone marrow. One time
when I was sure no one was looking, I decided to see if there
was anything actually in the slender Conti megaphones. Like
a Houdini-swallowed sword, my broom handle disappeared
clean up the pipe to the bend under the engine. There was
nothing in there bar cheese-grater-like perforations on the
inner wall of the pipe, and even those scoops pointed 'down-
wind' so as not to impede the escaping gases.

As with the Bonnie, there was a starting procedure
which you followed with respect. The SS ran massive 40mm
Dell'Orto 'pumper' carbs with ticklers and a coarse grill over
the bell-mouthed intakes to stop passing birds getting sucked
in. Chokes were for those other bikes; with the 'Cat you just
tickled the carbs, yanked the throttle so the accelerator pumps
squirted neat juice into the intakes, and then stomped on the
lever. Even though this was akin to starting a pair of hi-comp
XT500s, it was about as easy as it got for a bike this size. The
big V soon settled into its idiosyncratic tempo.

I kept the SS in a lockup in Thornton Heath, from where
I resumed my after-work prowling of south London's streets,
hurling my right-angled desmodromic throb at the cowering,
pebble-dashed semis where fretful Abigails were doubtless
serving up dips while privately fantasising about an axe-frenzy
at the Whitgift Centre. One night some fellow bikers even
waved and cheered as I passed them on the SS, or at least
that's how it looked. Maybe something was on fire behind me.

Though indifferent to the social side of biking, I figured I ought to see what this fabled TT was all about. In
1979 I rode the SS up to the Island to see if 'Mike the Bike'

could do it again. As it was, he only managed a fifth on his 900TT, but that was a lot better than me. TT week brought me close to breaking point with my street racer. Like thousands of others, I was up early on my first day, putting in a forty-five-minute lap on the unfamiliar, damp and bumpy circuit. I remember trying to hold on down the supposedly flat-out Cronk-y-Voddy straight, tank banging around and both wheels seldom in touch with the road. The worse moment came the following day. Pootling around, still learning the circuit, I approached the right-hand turn at Ballacraine. 'Take it easy now, don't show off in front of all the blokes sitting outside the... CRASH... pub.'

Helpful spectators helped me restart the Desmo while my red face was mistaken for a temporary traffic light. It turned out the kickstarter had grounded going into the bend at a very reasonable 40mph. That was it! I was selling the Desmo as soon as I got home. First though, I jacked up the unyielding Marzocchis and forced myself to live with it. Though I didn't know it then, my chum Dave Calderwood was on the Island too, having a similarly difficult time getting to grips with a MkII Guzzi Le Mans.

Back home, I decided to give the slim black duke one last chance before consigning it to the rest of the low-mileage superbikes adorning the back of *MCN*. I fitted some Girling shocks and tested them along the A22 Caterham bypass. The chassis remained as rigid as new PM Thatcher's Caligula smile, but the bike still jumped off line when cornering over expansion joints.

I removed the fairing – I couldn't see through the blotchy Plexiglas anyway. And suddenly everything was different, as if a hitherto unnoticed receptionist had removed her glasses, shaken her hair free and – why not, we're all on holiday here – undone a couple of buttons on her blouse. Whether it was ditching the crudely moulded fibreglass or being able to see the front wheel, confidence in the twisty bits improved greatly, even if the ride remained the same. And the Desmo – never such a sow's ear to start with – looked even meaner and leaner with the indicators removed and the Bosch headlamp poking out like a Soyuz probe.

One summer's evening I got a delivery to Worthing on the south coast. I scooted over to the lockup, swapped the SP for the SS and forty-five minutes later dropped off the package at some edge-of-town business park. Remembering to collect a stick of rock, as office tradition required of seaside jobs, I rode back up the A24. Holding a steady ton, I spotted a couple also enjoying an evening blast in their open-top MG. I wound in another 1000 revs and we exchanged waves as I hurtled past in the gathering dusk, checking the mirrors for the police while singing: 'Ride the streets for money, I don't care what's to the left or to the right'.

Despite the usual office frictions there was a good vibe at Security at that time. One of the usually diffident bosses invited me to his Knightsbridge pad one time, and even lent me his Guzzi 850 T3 for the weekend. With a mate we set off with the SS for a ride into the West Country. The high-barred, fat-saddled Guzzi was clad in a Pantera fairing, a half-priced Brit copy of Craig Vetter's famous Windjammer that parted the air like the *Cutty Sark*. The linked cast-iron discs originally developed for the automatic Convert model were a great idea, but alongside the crisp SS, the Guzzi's engine made a floppy-lipped warble that delivered a flat, woolly response. 'Long-legged and easy to live with' ran the saucy adverts at the time, but a Le Mans would surely need some spiked trainers too if it was to reach the same top speed as the SS.

One of the controllers rode a red Le Mans and whatever form it came in, you couldn't deny that a Guzzi V-twin motor was just so well suited to a motorcycle: a big, air-cooled, flying

V that was easy to get to and set just right for a shaft drive. In a suitably arid climate they were said to be reliable too, but the lumbering T3 cruiser put me off ever owning a Guzzi.

Occasionally I'd run the SS in town, purely for the attention, you understand. As we rumbled through the narrow streets of Soho, heads would compliantly pivot while small plumes of mortar loosened and spiralled down from centuries-old brickwork. The limited steering lock put paid to any cutting and thrusting through the traffic, and even simply turning into side streets had to be carefully anticipated, but it gave a buzz to the day. Once in a while a lot of riders at SD enjoyed the same relief with their inappropriate 'weekend' bikes.

I sent off to Sports Motorcycles in Manchester for the curvaceous fibreglass tank-seat unit they'd fitted to Hailwood's 900TT, which they'd prepared and sponsored. A trendy Pirelli Phantom was waiting for the Metzeler to wear out, and I considered properly rear-setting the pegs. While waiting for the tank-seat unit to arrive, one evening I rode over to Croydon to see *The Texas Chain Saw Massacre*. As with many of these slashers, it didn't take long before you were gagging for the annoyingly preppy teenagers to get the chop, but karma was at play that night and it was I who was about to get minced. Coming back, I had another golden moment overtaking a fast-moving Rolls on the Croydon flyover before heading down to Five-ways junction at the bottom of Purley Way. Approaching the lights fast, I assumed the guy ahead had seen me, but at the last second the VW Kombi (another Kombi!) pulled across my path. And stopped.

Three Brembos and my new Achilles Stadium helmet prevented any serious injuries, but the bike was less fortunate. The massive forks were only slightly bent – instead the frame's downtubes transferred the force to the alloy crankcase's mounting lugs. At the time a pair of crankcases cost the same as a new bike.

In the eighteen months it took to get the Desmo back on the road a lot of establishments put themselves on my arson list. They included the well-known Ducati dealer in Caterham who offered to undertake the repairs: they tried to buy the bike off the insurers behind my back, probably to support their own SS racer. After much aggravation, I reclaimed the Ducati, strapped the damaged engine on the back of my Honda work bike and rode it to some place in Watford that had promised to do a faultless alloy welding job on the crankcase. 'Leave it with us, mate. You won't even see the join.' Then the Sports Motorcycles tank-seat unit arrived but leaked from the seams and the filler cap.

Back on the road at long last, I was getting a feel for the rebuilt bike on a mid-winter ride from Dover to Brighton. Near Hastings I was pulled again; only sixty in a forty this time, but I couldn't afford much more of this or I'd lose my licence again and need to get a proper job. Just as I was getting back into the Desmo, I accepted that southern England was just too small, too crowded with police and too bumpy for my uncompromising street racer. It was all there at the end of Calderwood's *Bike* magazine test, back in 1979.

The Ducati 900SS is possibly the purest form of motorcycling there is, a kind of nirvana of all the thrills and sensations that makes it all worthwhile. But it wouldn't suit everyone, or even most bikers, so be careful before committing yourself. Street racing for real? Well, maybe.'

Can't say he didn't warn me, but the bottom line failed to connect with the lustful teenage hindbrain. The Ducati didn't turn me into a street racer, but then street racing was the day job. With only 3600 miles on the clock the half-finished SS went to another seeker of the ultimate experience. Not long after, Ducati's 900SS got gelded, just as Calderwood had predicted. Flashy cosmetics, silencers branded 'Silentiums', for pity's sake, and even air filters, all helped kill any spark in the S2 Desmo. Just as with the Z1s, the spell had been broken, and only the huge success of the showy Hailwood TT replica postponed the Italian marque's demise. But just as Triumph would do, Ducati returned and today neither they nor Triumph appear to have looked back since.

Every few years I have the same dream: my only recurring dream. In my dream it suddenly dawns on me with glee that I've somehow overlooked the fact that I still own the 900SS. There's no doubt about it, it's still there in that lockup in Thornton Heath, waiting to be kicked back into life like some forgotten Norse god glowering in his cave. I like having that dream.

7

DISCOVERING THE DIRT

Suzuki SP370 and TS185

Before the 900SS even had its first service, I spent another
750 quid on a new Suzuki SP370 trail bike from Gus Kuhn's
in Stockwell. Three grand on two bikes in seven days. How
keen was I? In parallel with my street-racing programme I was
curious to give trail riding a go. Exploring the countryside on
a bike looked like fun, but with far fewer risks than snatching
the same thrill on the highway.

Just up the road from Mocheck's, Gus Kuhn Motors had
been in Stockwell since Fred Flintstone chiselled out his first
rockbike while courting Wilma. Kuhn's had a similarly solid reputation, which, by the time I came along, was something of a unique selling point. Grubby, hole-in-the-wall bike
shops were commonplace across London back then, some
with workshops that looked like a sick bike's equivalent of
a Crimean hospital ward. Kuhn's service area was not like
that. The place was as tidy as my mum's bathroom and the

mechanics wore clean overalls and addressed you politely, inviting you to appraise their work. Today such attitudes are widespread; in the late seventies it was all a little unnerving, at least at the places I patronised.

Discount dealers like Coburn & Hughes may have grabbed initial sales, but it was becoming common knowledge that saving a penny might cost you a pound later. Or in my case, with C&H and my new Triumph, the pound was paid promptly on collection of the machine. Otherwise, you had places like Pride & Clarke's (or 'Snide & Sharks', as we knew them), who'd been round the corner on the nearby Stockwell Road even longer than Kuhn's. Or Hughes Motorcycles with his unsympathetic 'futue te ipsum emptor' attitude. At least with Elite's and Aeros in Norbury you got as far as the counter before some sneering ruffian with a roll-up drooping from his lower lip mumbled his 'Yesmate…' without breaking eye contact with his microfiche reader.

Bad service wasn't just limited to bikes. As better technology produced better and cheaper stuff, vendors and services were remorselessly fleecing the slobbering shopper. TV shows like Esther Rantzen's popular *That's Life!* stepped up to champion the put-upon consumer by exposing miscreants and a growing awareness of this abuse helped establish the imminent Sale of Goods Act. Marches on Alabama were all very well, but it was time for civil rights to move over and make way for consumer rights.

Gus Kuhn himself had good form. Back in 1926 he'd lapped the Island at 60mph on a Velocette, and by the sixties, Kuhn Motors were famed for their Norton racers. In 1970 a young Barry Sheene rode a Seeley-framed GK Commando at Brands and Montjuic Park in Barcelona. When racing got too costly, Kuhn's moved upmarket to become one of the most successful BMW dealers in the land, just as Stockwell was becoming yuppiefied and rebranding itself as 'St. Ockwell'.

By the time I was looking for an SP370, Kuhn's were briefly dabbling in Suzukis. As buying a Suzuki from Aeros probably involved an unspeakable initiation, I decided to see if getting one from a well-regarded dealer made any difference. In an effort to make the most of the good times, Kuhn's had also taken on Laverdas, and the day I picked up my silver dream thumper, a snarling orange Montjuic twin was parked out front on a heavy chain, gnawing at a loose Comstar wheel. With its granite-cast engine and Laverda pedigree, a 'Monty' had been a contender alongside the Ducati, but cost just £150 less. Jota, SS, Le Mans: those Italians had all the answers when it came to road bikes that looked as good as they went.

But the Japs had clearly got to grips with trail bikes and Suzuki's slick SP370 trailie compared well with the much ad- mired XT500. It had a lighter, wet-sump motor and claimed to have suspension technology derived from Suzuki's RM mo- tocrossers. With persuasive marketing like that, I was easily won over.

Several other guys at SD ran four-stroke trailies, and in town they were a winning combination. When sitting upright, vital visibility was excellent and the slim engines made slicing and dicing effortless, even with the wide bars. At the speeds we rode in town, drum brakes did the job in all weathers, and up to a point trail bikes were designed to be dropped with- out drastic damage. Add the light weight, and a punchy en- gine with low gearing, and you had a nippy work bike plus something for the weekend. The only drawback was that trail bike handlebars shared mirror heights with Transit vans, something which got awkward when splitting lanes down the Euston Road. After smashing a few, I, like other trail-biking despatchers, perfected a trials-style, off-centre hip-pivot ma- noeuvre to avoid white van man rage.

At work I gravitated towards others with an interest in trail biking. Chriscol was one, a part-time fireman who rode

Honda's new XL250S with those amazingly grippy Bridge-stones and a 'bigger-must-be-better' twenty-three-inch front wheel (a short-lived fad). He lived over a parade of shops on the Isle of Dogs in the East End with an older woman and her kid, something he was a little embarrassed by. To me, only just planning to move out of my mum's house in Norbury, it seemed like the ragged edge of modern living.

That summer of 1979, as Thatcher's new administration announced how things were going to be run around here from now on, Chriscol and I hunted down tracts of wasteland for goofing about on trail bikes. Jumping, sliding and tearing up a steep learning curve, we'd ride until something broke or the sun went down. At these places we'd meet fellow dirt hounds who tipped us off about other dirtsome venues, and so the network of play areas spread: Roundshaw Fields off the Purley Way, or 'Croydon Airport' as we called it. Aveley gravel pits out in Essex. An overgrown patch of scrub opposite Brent Cross, mined with broken concrete and rebar – we only went there once. And Frylands Wood off Featherbed Lane in New Addington, on the southern perimeter of London's urban sprawl.

Forty years earlier, Luftwaffe bombing intended for nearby Biggin Hill Aerodrome had quite possibly adjusted the topography of Frylands Wood. A huge bomb crater surrounded by mature trees offered any number of ways to tip in and spring out, with a spot of wall-of-deathing in between. With helmets ditched at the earliest opportunity, the primary calling at all these locations was to jump. To jump far, jump high and jump long, over and over and over again. There was no end to the thrill of jumping: the surge of a good launch, the momentary buzz of weightlessness and the satisfying impact softened by groaning springs, thick-soled boots and bent knees. In this pre-full-suspension era, such larking about had never been realistic on pushbikes. I could vouch for that because one childhood summer on Mitcham Common I tried jumping my Moulton. Back at the store, my mum had some difficulty insisting that the seat-post bent flat against the back wheel was a legitimate warranty claim.

While I was learning what the SP370 could do, Eddie Kidd, a dashing daredevil with matinee idol looks, was making a name for himself as the new English Evel Knievel. He was soon stunt doubling for Hollywood stars and a year later starred in his own film, *Riding High*. In it, Kidd played a small-town bike messenger who pitted himself in a contest against the world's top stunt jumper, a boozy slob by the name of Judas S Chariot whose haircut, twilight-Elvis outfit and nationality were uncannily similar to those of the real Knievel. As far as I know, it was the only film to feature a motorcycle messenger until Mike (*Abigail's Party*) Leigh came out with *High Hopes* in 1988. Setting aside the latter film's crude caricatures of grasping Thatcherite yuppies and put-upon ordinary folk, Cyril the courier used the word 'over' on the radio – an unforgivably monumental gaffe.

Not that *Riding High* was exactly *Chariots of Fire*. But watching Eddie Kidd gunning around the godforsaken wastelands of estuarine Kent on a YZ400 and then jumping the gaping viaduct at the film's climax was certainly better than *CHiPS*, the soggy California highway-cop drama series which started airing in the UK that year. In it, Ponch and corn-fed Jon threw their big Zeds around as best they could, but the storylines were as wooden as chipboard. And the synching of a four-stroke's deep growl over what was clearly an RM250 tearing down the freeway with the money for the orphans' fund yard sale was utterly maddening to us moto-nerds. This was supposed to be a show all about motorbikes!

Bizarrely, inapt motorcycle dubbing continues to this day – and never worse than when a two-stroke's grating racket is slapped over a meaty V-twin. Nine years later the Comic Strip team released *The Strike*, a Hollywoodised parody of the 1984 miners' strike and one of their best films. In it, the village idiot lends the Scargill figure (played by 'Al Pacino') his black Harley to race after the militant coal miners who are determined to blow up the nuclear plant in defence of their jobs. With what I like to think is a knowing nod to this persistent continuity gaffe, the Harley starts up sounding like a DT100. Then once underway, it morphs into an actual YZ250 motocrosser with leather saddlebags as a number of respectable stunts pay homage to *The Great Escape* and *Riding High*. And all the while the noise it makes flips between DT, YZ and XLCR.

My SP soon acquired its own soundtrack. Perhaps a little later than most teenagers, I discovered the superb racket a big single was capable of once the silencer was removed. Some sort of cylindrical pre-silencer was integrated into the header system and helped lessen the din, but as with the Ducati's noise-trumpets, I was now one of south London's peak-level noise polluters. And the SP never barked a finer bark than when decelerating hard down London Wall towards Moorgate. The skyscrapers lining that short urban drag strip obligingly amplified the racket. 'Excuse me,' would come a yell from the eleventh floor, 'some people are trying to manipulate share prices up here. *If* you don't mind!'

One day on the Suzuki I discovered a trick of award-winning idiocy. If, when decelerating, I briefly flipped the kill switch off and on, a first-rate backfire detonated somewhere down below. Pedestrians jumped, pensioners soiled themselves and crows fell stunned from the sky. Again, be it London Wall or coming off the Westway into White City – hard off the throttle with some Doppler deceleration, then kill, flick, BANG! Terrific! Imagine it, nineteen, a card-carrying motorcycle professional and still an abject pillock. It was a way of brightening up the day, but after a while I gave up the kill-switch game. Whatever it did to the engine, it felt potentially as damaging as hyperventilating over a tinful of pan-warmed Evo-stik.

Resigned to doing my civic duty, I slipped on a cheap reverse-cone megaphone and instead perfected my road-cornering skills, just as I refined my aerobatics on weekends. One must have helped the other, because a Sunday morning spent pounding the earth until the sump plug caved in seemed to have softened the suspension. What other explanation could there be for me getting the SP's footrests to graze the bitumen while cornering hard into Newgate Street below St Paul's approving dome?

I'd found another new game to help juice up the adrenaline glands desensitised by day-long messengering: filing the Suzuki's footrests on any bend that would have them. One sunny day up in Wanstead I left a satisfying scrape on some back-street switchback, so I swung round the block to do it again and blew it with a harmless lowside. A passer-by who'd noted my pointless circumnavigation quipped, 'Y'oright, mate?' without breaking step.

'Yep,' I groaned, getting up with a limp, righting the bike and bending the brake lever straight.

Darn. Why did that happen? Why did we fall off bikes when we didn't want to? What immeasurable variant of traction caused the tyre to give way? I decided to leave that to another time and proceeded, sore hipped, to my drop.

'One Oh Six, empty, Wanstead.'

'Rrrroger, Wanasx. Call me Aldgate.'

Taking on road and trail seven days a week, the plucky 370 got beaten to a pulp over that summer. Protective clothing comprised my leather work trousers, which went well with my new shin-plated Alpine Stars, and a pair of rib-backed MX gloves. There was a whole new world of off-road gear to explore. Problem was, from a couture point of view, motocross gear seemed patterned to suit some sort of heavy-metal acid-disco fusion. There were no tasteful touring outfits in dirtworld. Oh no. Instead, thoughtlessly lurid designs were thrown at textiles like rotten tomatoes at a sheep thief clamped in the village stocks. Where possible, I'd go for much cheaper, army surplus clobber.

'Anti-mustard-gas overtrousers. Woodpulp and lycra. Includes integrated braces. Unissued. £2.50.'

'Field gunner's overmitts with otter cub fur lining. Size XXXXL only. £1.50 each.'

Yes, we'd discovered Laurence Corner in Euston, by the underpass and opposite Capital Radio. It was a repository of largely useless, often overpriced but theatrically tempting 'work wear' as well as obsolete scientific instrumentation deemed too good for *Blake's 7*. In the coming years it was to become to us despatchers what Sex – Vivienne Westwood's King's Road rubber-and-vinyl boutique – had become to the early punks.

Laurence Corner's wasn't the only mud-plugger's outlet in town. Giro, one of the trail bikers at SD, put me on to a little shop jammed between the theatres and literary emporia of St Martin's Lane, a minute from the office. Out front, Ralph and his wife sold model cars to middle-aged collectors. But Ralph was also an enduro racer in the expert class, and with the right nod, an initiate got led up to the mezzanine floor where a creditable array of off-road clothing, oils, tools, levers, duct tape and other accessories was on display. To find a place like this within sight of Eleanor's Cross was nothing short of an all-terrain miracle. Most weeks I'd pop in to Ralph's to replace the casualties of the weekend's antics.

Unfortunately, I hadn't discovered trail biking at a very propitious time. Barely had Thatcher cleared out Callaghan's collection of novelty Toby Jugs, then her government set about sponsoring a Wildlife and Countryside Bill which, among other things, aimed to restrict off-road access by motor vehicles. At that time I didn't appreciate that a barely used track winding through the Peak District had the same ancient right-of-way status as the busy road I'd take to get there. Whether road or dirt, a road could still be a legal right of way, even if a Ford Fiesta wouldn't get twenty yards along it. Conflicts with other users had escalated following the boom in recreational use of off-highway vehicles. Under pressure from organisations like the Ramblers Association, many of these 'green lanes' were being downgraded to plain footpaths or bridleways limited to walkers, horse riders and bicycles. And once mountain biking became too popular, they got banned from some places too.

Founded in 1970, the Trail Riders Fellowship fought closures while promoting responsible riding – riding that didn't involve creeping up behind a rambler and playing the kill-switch game. Certainly, in the crowded confines of southeast England, finding a green lane that was more than a few miles long was as likely as running over Gloria Gaynor on her met-alflake 390 Husqvarna in the ISDT. But I knew no different and just made do. And if I'm honest, I could appreciate that riding north Kent's Pilgrim's Way on some notionally road-legal PE175 was incompatible with hikers who, just like me, sought the countryside as a place in which to commune with the birds and the bees.

And so, as disgraced politicians came and went, inflation soared and brilliant films like *Life of Brian*, *Apocalypse Now*, *Nosferatu* and even *Derek and Clive Get the Horn* hit the screens, Chriscol and I were happy to fool around on those isolated patches of wasteland which still had a few years in them before being turned into wildfowl refuges or hypermarkets.

By the time the leaves of 1979 began to curl, my SP370 was also ready to drop. The engine puffed blue smoke on chilly autumn mornings and the drivetrain, always annoyingly slack, now had more play than an a VHS tape of *Pot Black* highlights. I could fix it; I could run it into the ground until it sank; or I could just flog it and move on. Option three it was then. Someone came round, handed me a hundred quid and left me their 1975 Suzuki TS185.

The basic TS was a few rungs down the trail bike evolutionary scale but lapped up the same seven-day-a-week beating as the SP. Only, being cheaper and lighter, it got launched off bigger jumps and down steeper drop-offs. One Monday morning near Blackfriars Bridge, I came back to see a traffic warden hovering around my TS with a frown. She was actually considering writing me a ticket for riding a muddy bike!

By now I was devouring American *Dirt Bike* magazine the way I used to read *Bike*. Until *TBM* came along in 1995, there were no dirt-biking magazines in the UK that I found worth reading. Doubtless thanks to colossal sales in the US, *Dirt Bike* could tell it like it was, and tested dirt bikes with a zeal and candour the Brit mags never matched. New KX125 handling funny in the whoops? Take to the steering head with a grinder and blowtorch until it's sorted. Carb not picking up crisply in the mid-range? Rip it out and drill the jets, then meddle with airbox vents and inlet tract until the engine sings like Lene Lovich being lowered into an ice-cold vat of Liebfraumilch. A Brit mag would have just written the bike off as a turkey.

Even though back then it still mostly covered competition two-strokes, *Dirt Bike* was an education. Rick Sieman (the magazine's founder), Paul Clipper, Tom Webb and the helpful but mercilessly sarcastic Mr Know-It-All expanded my dirt-jargon and 'sano' techniques. Things like moving forward and weighting the outside peg when cornering hard, or setting up suspension sag, chain slack and forks. A staunch supporter of off-road access to the western deserts that he loved, the forthright Sieman eventually paid a heavy price for standing by his belief in the freedom to ride, as his forthright, funny and sometimes angry 1995 memoir, *Monkey Butt!*, recalls.

In the UK the best we had was the weekly *Trials and Mo-tocross News*: a combination of a horse-racing gazette and *Motorcycle Sport*. But it had a used bikes section and regulations or 'Regs' – announcements about upcoming races and events, which were beginning to interest me. With my fine-tuned jumping talents needing an outlet, a growing collection of mismatched gear and a new ACU racing licence, I was ready to take up enduros. These day-long events required you to ride at a pace rather than against the clock or other riders; that this 'pace' still meant riding your arse off for hours on end was beside the point. The only alternatives were trials, which looked a bit finessy, and motocross: forty minutes of balls-to-the-wall hysteria on highly-strung competition machines. Enduros were different; besides pacing yourself (fat chance), you needed the skill to repair the bike, and obviously the 'enduro-ance' to keep at it for several hours. Sounded a lot like despatch riding but without U-turning taxis. And best of all, enduros were do-able on trail bikes because they actually required a road-legal machine.

The best events were in Wales or up north but, prudent as always, I signed up for my first race in some woods near Orpington in Kent. I then set about preparing my machine, using the know-how I'd gleaned from Mr Know-It-All's ruthless lacerations of his craven prey. If I waggled the bars the TS's steel wheel would flap between the skinny forks like a sack of wet laundry. On *DB*'s advice I cut, bent and bolted an eighth-inch U-plate of steel between the fork legs and cured that. I then fitted a Michelin Trials tyre as this was designated an eco-conscious 'no knobblies' event. Best of all came the big moment: sticking racing numbers onto the yellow racing plates I'd bought from Ralph's in Covent Garden. I wouldn't be unbolting those any time soon. My TS185 – the very same model ridiculed in *Riding High* when contestants failed to leap a bath of 'foaming acid' – never looked more purposeful.

I rung-dung-dunged my way down to Petts Wood, hoping I wouldn't DNF ('Did Not Finish') so I could at least get back home. When my time came, I lowered my new lightweight Scott goggles and bimbled off between the tapes and into the woods. Bikes shot past me all morning but I plodded valiantly around the tiny, convoluted circuit. It didn't take long to realise this wasn't exactly like coursing across the boundless Welsh moorlands, far less fighting for survival in West Virginia's gladiatorial Blackwater 100 enduro, but with its crisp new tyre at half pressure and no unruly powerband, my little TS did rather well. I may even have won some under-250cc, novice, two-stroke, open-face, trail bike class.

All fired up by my promising debut (and with the smashed-up Ducati still in its year-long stasis), I took a day off work and rode forty miles down to Slab Common near Bordon in east Hampshire. It was army training land, too sandy for agriculture, but I'd heard they held enduros there once in a while, proper enduros with laps measured in miles, not yards.

Going there when there wasn't an event on, I was taking a big risk, because the warnings were clear: if caught riding on army land they'd confiscate your bike and probably shout at you too. Unperturbed, I rode down the A325, made sure I had the right place, then slipped up a lane that led into the woods. Checking no one was around, I scaled a ditch and rode into the pines, then leant the TS against a tree to let the tyres down.

This was going to be a great day out. It was time to move on from childish jumping and pathetic attempts at wheelies. Then, just as I screwed a valve cap back on, fifty yards away I saw a troop of kitted-out commandos creeping through the undergrowth, faces blackened and machine guns in hand. Shite! I crouched down and froze. 'Evade and escape', wasn't that what they called it? My instincts proved true and the column of squaddies moved into the deadly heart of Slab Common, oblivious to the enemy saboteur in their sector. I felt chuffed my leopard-like stealth had outwitted an elite squad of black beret killers, but clearly my big day out on the sopping sands of Slab Common was over. I pumped the tyres back up, polished off my chunk of survival fruitcake and crept back out of the woods. He Who Dares, Rides Home.

Those two Suzukis were my entry into the thrilling world of dirt biking that went on to provide all the attainable thrills and adventures that the Ducati would never deliver, even if I'd had the skill and opportunity to ride it well. In the words of Kenny Roberts, who the previous year had successfully adapted his flat-track power-sliding skills to come from nowhere and pluck the GP crown from Sheene,

> *'Dirt racing is more enjoyable… you can make a mistake and fool around a bit, which you can't do with road racing unless you wanna get hurt.'*

Perched at the other extreme of the speed and talent galaxy, that was my conclusion too. Dirt bashing was good honest fun with a wide margin between sustainable thrills and mortal dangers to both rider and licence.

8

ON THE BEACH

Yamaha XT500, Mobylette

Blue Hills on the north coast of Cornwall. A stream cuts down to the sea, passing the slag heaps and ruins of a former tin mine. Me and Colin, a mate from SD, took turns riding around on my latest acquisition, an XT500. We dribbled down progressively steeper slopes on the overrun, then blasted back up with a jaunty hop of the front wheel. Hell, we even progressed to actual jumps just to show how at ease we were on Yamaha's big trailie.

Brought up not far away, Colin had come to London via Barrow-in-Furness, looking for work on his functional MZ 250 'Toucan' Trophy. In the dire industrial climate of late-seventies Britain, it's hard to imagine a more dismal setting than Barrow, a stagnating iron-smelting and ship-building port suspended from a Cumbrian peninsula, like a soiled nappy held at arm's reach. Even the very name conjured up some carcinogenic foundry worker, old Jack Barrow, heaving carts of molten slag twelve hours a day before shuffling back to his soot-caked hovel and his consumptive brood. Of course, I'd never actually been to Barrow; it might have been like Paris in the spring. For Colin, who'd eloped from Cornwall but hadn't made it as far as Gretna Green, the smoke stacks and tenements of Barrow made a temporarily arresting contrast to the Beatrix Potter idyll of his ivy-clad Cornish village.

The day before, he and I had watched the Land's End Trial pass through Blue Hills. Run most years since 1908, the Trial was a rally of eccentrically inappropriate cars and bikes that set off overnight to cross the width of southern England and finish up at Land's End. On the way, various short, observed sections required contestants to tackle loose or slippery climbs and other obstacles without either stalling the car or taking a steadying dab on the bike. The tricky climb out of Blue Hills was a popular stage with spectators. Some contestants tried finesse, others used momentum, but tackling the Trial on a knobbly-tyred enduro bike or a supercharged 4WD hill climber was not in the spirit of the event. Old BSA steam mangles mixed it up with Jap trailies, rear-engined Hillman Imps and MGs.

Yamaha's XT500 was the original do-it-all Jap thumper. The Brits had been producing 500cc street scramblers for decades, but engineering-wise the most recent example – BSA's B50 Victor (badged as a Triumph in the brief NVT era) – didn't look much different from the bike your dad had ridden off the Normandy beaches on D-Day. Most manufacturers produced street scramblers – Ducati's 450 Desmo Scrambler was a mango-coloured beauty – but they were mostly road bikes fitted with wide bars, longer springs and maybe a bigger back sprocket. Nobody was fooled.

In a bid to take on the dominant Huskies (and with Kaaden's secrets now widely known), since the early seventies the Japs had been producing light and powerful two-stroke off-road racers such as Yamaha YZs and Honda's CR Elsinores. Desert racing was becoming hugely popular in the western US: the 1971 Barstow to Vegas race across the Mohave Desert had a start-line a mile wide, crammed with 3000 bikes. With YZs catching on, Yamaha US proposed that Yamaha in Hamamatsu design them a big 500cc dual sport as well as a similar, dirt-oriented version. When the XT500 and TT500 scrambler came out in 1976, the Brits were typically slow to catch on, but in France and Germany they got it right away. The first two bikes to finish 1979's original Paris–Dakar Rally were big-tanked XTs. And the following year XTs took the top four places. That led to the Rally replica XT600Z Ténéré, which created a whole new genre of bikes.

Unfortunately, in the UK, the XT was condemned as a bit of a trolley in the dirt, even if it did make a great road bike. Unlike the SR500 all-road version which followed, the XT quickly became a Jap classic. Part of the XT's mystique lay in its all-terrain potential and allegedly difficult starting. Later models came with a cam position marker behind a little window on the cylinder head which you were supposed to line up before taking a swing. But having come from a kick-only Bonnie, a 900SS and a summer on the SP370, all without the benefit of a decompression lever to lift an exhaust valve, for me the XT never put up much of a fight.

My XT500 was a first-generation '76-er and I soon replaced the convoluted under-and-up exhaust system with a rasping American J&R pipe. The J&R came with two silencers: a hefty, domesticated reverse-cone mega, which was handy for visiting your gran and for MoTs. And the Other Pipe. For a sawn-off bazooka, it was a conventional looking can, but like a Conti, it was essentially a straight-through howitzer with all the restriction of an LA storm sewer. A perforated liner was supposed to hold a wad of fibreglass against the outer can and while it did so, the J&R boomed out a thud that made your hair stand on end. You rode around trailing a bone-powdering clamour akin to a swarm of zombies let loose on Japanese taiko drums. Then, within a few miles the fibreglass got blasted out of the end and the spell was broken – it just sounded horribly loud.

Unlike the SP, the XT's dry-sump engine used the frame's backbone as an oil tank and Gambier Reeks bike shop down the King's Road advised me to add an extra oil line to the cylinder head to keep the rockers lubed. Brakes were 'dependable' drums, and although electrics were six volt, that chiefly translated to a crumby headlight. Plenty of twelve-volt bikes also came with crap lights in those days.

Not far from Blue Hills was Perranporth, where, on weekdays outside of the summer season, at low tide you could discreetly ride across the tourist beach to reach an empty, mile-and-a-half runway called Perran Beach. It got cut off at high tide, but if you timed it right, there was no stopping you carving arcs across a huge strand of wave-smoothed sand. Unfortunately my XT was running Avon Speedmaster road tyres at the time. They came with a signed guarantee from the Marquis of Avon himself that they'd outlast the owner, especially if that owner risked riding around in the rain. The Avons also limited the foot-skimming fun to be had banking the XT on the sands, so I turned my attention to Colin's even less agile Toucan. Dismissing the corrosive potential of fresh Atlantic brine on hot East German alloy, I aimed an ill-timed sweep into the surf, just as the surf rushed up towards me. The long pipe's noisome drone became a plangent gurgle, the motor died and, stranded up to my knees, another wave rolled in and washed over the MZ's motor. For this MZ, the day's fun was over. We found some rope and towed the drowned bike home.

Colin and I returned to Perran Beach another time on a borrowed XT shod with bristling Metzeler knobblies. It turned into one of the best day's beach riding ever. We slipped off Perranporth seafront on to the sands, cantered briskly beyond the headland, ditched our lids and let rip. A good bike is a slider or feels like it could be, and with its tyres, controllable grunt and low saddle, the XT had all these credentials, even if we were just muppets in oilskins. The game was to crank it over until the rear Metz started breaking away, then progressively feed the power on to maintain the drift.

Sliding a bike controllably is where motorcycling gets transcendental. In my early moto days, down on Sainsbury's shop floor after hours, or up in the warehouse, I'd spend much of my time astride an imaginary flat tracker, bars wrenched at full lock while sliding immaculately from corner to corner. I'd hurtle past the dried fruit and preserves, snicking through the gears, then swing the back round in a perfect feet-up one-eighty, grab the fork tube and blast down the soft drinks aisle towards the '8 Items or Less' checkout. Yes, in those benighted days they still used 'less' instead of 'fewer'. If it felt good in the head, on a Cornish beach it was spellbinding. The same intoxicating sensation as surfing or skiing: a magical combination of precarious, motion-dependent balance. Lose control of one and the other soon followed.

That day our crossed-up, beach-carving antics got the better of us and next time we looked up, the tide had cut off access back to Perranporth. Unless we fancied hanging around till 11.17pm, the only way out was over the dunes behind the shore. Colin reckoned it passed through a restricted military area associated with the nearby army camp at Penhale. What if we set off an unexploded shell, or stumbled over some secret experimental facility, got drugged and woke up spliced to a pig's head, like that bloke in the Lindsay Anderson film?

'Ow, dey bin doin' dat fur years down 'ere. Caan' ee tell?' said Colin, in his finest Kernow burr. In fact he wasn't joking. Just eight miles down the coast at Nancekuke, the MoD were busy decommissioning an old nerve-gas production base, though that information wasn't released for another twenty years. Anyway, I was confident my escape and evasion skills honed a few weeks earlier at Slab Common would pay off here. Two-up, we rode up and down the beach, looking for the least steep gully climbing up into the grassy dunes.

'Canee get up there?'

'I suppose so. It's the easiest one so far.' And, taking as good a run-up as the incoming tide allowed, the XT churned its way on to the scrubby heathland, aided by a shove from Colin, who picked up a faceful of sand for his trouble.

On top we followed the coastal footpath to an overgrown road that led inland to a locked gate. The question was, were we where we shouldn't be, trying to get out – or about to break into some ghastly, bio-genetic gulag? The five-bar gate was locked solid and the fence either side was no less resilient. Lifting the XT over was out, so like Steve McQueen on the run from the Jerries, we knew there was only one thing for it. *Vorsprung durch Springen* – the gate had to be jumped.

We needed a ramp that could support the accelerating 450lb mass of me and the XT as we made our bid for freedom. Miraculously, a bit of kicking around in the undergrowth unearthed the very components we needed: three pallet-sized sections of sturdy iron railing. Wider and more rigid than a plank, by overlapping the three sections we could construct a vaguely concave ramp, like those on the pointy end of aircraft carriers. The ramp's irrefutable geometry would catapult the XT high over the gate. Even Eddie Kidd or the cast of *Colditz* would've been impressed.

The heavy railings rested like fallen dominoes against the gate and Colin was ready with his Leica. I felt confident our launch ramp's profile would provide more than enough lift, but I didn't want to fly on the borrowed XT any more than necessary. Too much speed might flip the bike backwards; not enough would see it drop front first and break something.

With very little hesitation and my helmet at Colin's feet, I took a run at the gate. Colin's one shot caught me at the peak of my arc, suspended a foot over the gate with the front wheel way high and canted to the left, me off the seat, ready to take the impact. A second later the back wheel thudded on to the road, launching me forward over the fully compressed forks.

'D'you get that?'

'I think so. You went a lot higher than I expected. Is the bike all right?'

I bounced up and down on the springs and looked down at the back wheel.

'Looks OK.'

'What about the ramp. Shall we leave it?

'Let's leave it.'

We rode on down the private road. The heath to either side was pockmarked with shell craters, but we remained undetected by armed patrols in nerve-gas suits. Within a few minutes we reached a regular road, strapped on our lids and were home for dinner.

It turned out we'd unwittingly starred in our own version of *On Any Sunday*, the 1971 movie that dazzlingly documented dirt biking's free-spirited thrills in and around California. In the closing scenes Steve McQueen, desert racer Malcolm Smith and flat tracker Mert Lawwill goofed about in the surf, just as we'd done. Director Bruce Brown had shot the no-less-inspirational *The Endless Summer* surf movie a few years earlier, and for a short while *On Any Sunday* lifted motorcycling's image from the cycle-psycho exploitation trash that filled US cinemas at that time.

Back in the capital, a form of that exploitation genre had hit the mainstream. Set in a fuel-starved, post-apocalyptic dystopia, *Mad Max* burst on to UK screens in a cloud of smoking rubber, cordite and leather. It was a post-punk resetting of *Vanishing Point*'s loner-in-a-V8 battling not the cops and his

111

own demons, but a bunch of marauding brutes on scrapheap-challenged Zed Ones. Filmed on the cheap, *Max Max*'s cost-to-profit ratio is still right up there with *The Blair Witch Project*, *Deep Throat* and *Night of the Living Dead*.

Meanwhile, in pre-apocalypse London, leather trousers and steel-plated Alpine Stars Hi-Points became à la mode. One day in Wardour Street, a young media-type in dreadlocks ran up to me and asked, breathlessly, 'Where d'ya get those boots, mate?' In a few enlightened Soho receptions an overdue appreciation of the Mad Max chic got us despatchers noticed in a way that was hard to pull off in a dripping one-piece Rukka smeared with diesel soot. But for me it all came too late for the dishy blonde at Decca Records in Great Marlborough Street. There seemed to be a rapport but my not coincidental pleas over the radio, 'One Oh Six, empty – ahem – Great Marlborough Street…', were no longer producing the desired collection point. Decca must have got an account with someone else.

And the XT? It never really ran that well. That J&R was probably to blame because I'd yet to learn that more noise doesn't always equal more power. In an attempt to improve things, I probably made them worse by ditching the whole airbox assembly and clamping a K&N filter to the carb. At that time my understanding of 'jetting' was only slowly losing its juvenile connotations with romping BOAC air stewardesses.

Still, the space freed by the airbox became a handy stash for a tool roll. That was until the day I was dashing back along the Commercial Road to the City in a bigger hurry than usual. It was a warm spring afternoon and as I pulled up outside the Bank of England to call in, I learned the first rule of bike fires: stopping makes them worse, much worse. Beneath the seat the canvas tool bag had lodged itself against the J&R, now running hotter than ever on the over-lean fuelling brought on by the K&N. As long as I'd been moving, it had smouldered harmlessly, but trickling through the City's congestion had raised the temperature and produced flames.

'Wanasx, Wanasx?'

'Yeah, One Oh… Hang on a minute I'm having a fire.'

Just a stone's throw from Pudding Lane where the Great Fire had kicked off, office workers trotting into the tube paused in alarm while I yanked out bits of burning canvas and blackened spanners fell to the ground with a clang. Luckily I'd caught it early and there was no significant damage. Not all my bike fires would end so well.

There was no real harm done when the XT got stolen out of my mum's front garden either. It was recovered within a couple of weeks, not smashed up, stripped or burned to a crisp, but fully intact and flooded. When I collected it from the back of Sutton police station, even the headlamp was half full of water and bright green slime hung from the footrests. Perhaps the scumbags who'd nicked the XT hadn't known how to start it so had dumped it in nearby Carshalton Ponds. With the crankcases similarly contaminated, I pushed it home before giving the mysteriously drowned thumper an oil transfusion. First charred, now drowned, what next – crushed in a landslide? A few weeks later I sold it to one of Colin's Cornish mates. One day he accidentally jumped it down a mineshaft, but like the legendary *Top Gear* Hilux, it survived that too. I knew I'd be getting another XT one day.

The TS185 was also off sick so I downsized all the way to a mate's mum's Mobylette before being persuaded to rent a works' Honda 400/4. I didn't mind as I was keen to see what all the clamour had been about over the 400/4, the super mini superbike. Or so I thought until the day I actually rode one. Even accepting that SD's Four-Fours were part of an abused fleet passed from rider to rider, I still recall running up the A1 near Mill Hill thinking, 'What is *wrong* with this bike? Are all the cylinders firing?' Everything – power delivery, braking, steering, suspension, the very sound it made – seemed dead, flat or wooden. The 400/4 may have been a hit in Britain and the cover star of Honda's 1976 brochure, but the magazines had been right after all: the insipid three-valve Dream was indeed a less awful machine. What a chilling thought.

Looking at a 400/4 was a pleasure, but riding one was another of motorcycling's big let-downs. I got the TS running again, but little did I know another two-wheeled lemon was rolling towards me like something out of *The Goodies*. Goody-goody, yum-yum.

9

DIRT AND DESPATCH

Yamaha IT250G, Honda XL250S, Yamaha DT175MX, MZ TS250

The year 1980 saw a never-to-be-repeated peak in motorcycle sales in Britain. Perhaps some imminent law hastened a buying frenzy, but whatever the reason, a staggering 315,000 new bikes were registered for the road. Thirty-five-years on, that figure is less than a third. On top of several thousand unplated competition machines, in 1980 nearly a fifth of all bikes on the road were new. I played my part in this sales fever by racking up another eight bikes in just twelve months, and that included a long spell on crutches.

My dirt-riding talent may have been some distance behind my enthusiasm for it, but I was already tiring of turning turkeys into do-it-all greyhounds with only duct tape and old inner tubes (cable ties hadn't registered yet). Either way, I must have been taking US *Dirt Bike* seriously, because I decided I was now ready for the real thing. *DB* had been raving with typical Californian fervour about Yamaha's new IT-G series of enduro bikes. Suzuki's 'pure enduro' PEs has been around in the UK for a couple of years as a 175, 250 and 400, but the blue and white IT-Gs were said to have less fierce motors and more refined monoshocks with clever progressive linkages. The 'IT' prefix referenced the Yamaha's success in the gruelling ISDT six-day enduro, and as anything new had to be better, riders were lapping them up on both sides of the Atlantic.

Manufacturers were only just beginning to discover ways of spreading the power of a two-stroke across a wider rev band. Perhaps recruiting factory riders to sign up for voluntary lobotomies was taking its toll at the races. As the trade maxim went: 'Win on Sunday, Sell on Monday'. What had taken them so long? Tuned-to-kill might have worked on Kenny Roberts' GP TZ750 until they tried flat tracking with it, but off road the irregular speeds and terrain were tricky enough without trying to keep an engine spinning between 6150 and 6450rpm, lest it choke up. Whatever *Dirt Bike* may have actually said, I was convinced that with the G, Yamaha had made great advances in the porting, induction and the expansion chamber. This baby would trickle through the woods like a TS185 on a lead – and then when the call came down the throttle cable, it would explode like a champagne cork off the podium.

An article in *Bike* titled 'The 100mph Dirt Bike' suggested that an IT425 might be a bad idea. With the IT175 doubtlessly too peaky, the 250 was the sensible middle way. Sure, it consumed twice the fuel of a bad-running XT500 with tadpoles in the lights, but as with the Ducati, the only way to know for sure was to pay up and find out.

Down at Meeten & Ward in Surbiton the stiff-necked sales chappy busied himself tidying up the counter while I eagerly talked myself into another misguided purchase, that year's third bike. Accepting my faultless reasoning – lighter, faster, bouncier – with a 'Right you are, sir', he rung up twelve hundred quid and a few days later I picked up my new, blue

IT250G. It made over 32hp, had nearly a foot of suspension travel and weighed twenty per cent less than the XT. Altogether it looked a little intimidating, and that was before I started it.

I'd never owned or even tried a real competition bike. All I knew was it came with the all-important number plate so I could run it on the road, once I fitted the alloy tank that came as a spare – plastic tanks were still illegal then. On the road the IT would largely be wasted, but surely my dirt riding would advance just as briskly as my street racing had on the SS.

The IT was a proper dirt racer. Everything was purposed to make operation and maintenance efficient: the gear *and* the foot brake levers had swivelling tips; a single fastener removed the airbox cover with one twist; there was a tool bag on the back and the rear wheel had those foolproof snail-cam adjusters. What ever happened to them? Things that didn't matter that much, like batteries, key-lock ignition, lights, indicators and silencing were either tiny or non-existent. I followed the running-in procedure carefully, using the best oils, hoping to dodge the required engine rebuild for at least a few months, even though that was all part of owning a high-performance competition two-stroke.

While running-in, the power felt fine, nothing special apart from the din. Far from the jungle pounding of an XT500 spitting fibreglass from its J&R cannon, the IT produced a manifestly obnoxious cackle that could have served in some CIA interrogation cell, once *Gourd of Satan* at volume eleven had failed to soften up a recalcitrant Sandinista detainee. The description 'a chainsaw on crack' hit the mark, but such was the price of highly tuned two-stroke performance.

With fresh oil in the gearbox and the rings quite possibly bedded in, one day I rode the IT to work. All was going well until, while casually overtaking a string of cars up South Lambeth Road, I was unexpectedly snatched into the gnat-wide maelstrom of the powerband. My blue and white apparition hurtled forward on one-and-a-bit wheels, its hideous racket amplifying exponentially alongside a simultaneous expulsion of thick, oily smoke, like 007's Aston Martin fending off some baddies. Any passing armed policeman with a sense of social justice would have shot the bike out from under me and clipped me round the ear. All I remember from that brief experiment of despatching on a motocrosser with lights was the deep, deep shame I felt at noting the ear-shielding grimaces of hunched-up passers-by mouthing, 'What the fuck IS that?!'

As luck would have it, the powerband was sufficiently high up the rev scale to be avoidable with care, but as I'd foreseen, it complicated off-road riding. One weekend Giro, a New Zealander from SD, and I rode out to Aveley gravel pit in Essex, just past Dagenham. Merely getting there and back swallowed two gallons of fuel and half a bottle of pre-mix, the thirstiest bike I ever owned. Today Aveley is a nature reserve and bird sanctuary, but in 1980 the gravel pit was one of our best dirt-biking finds. With treeless acres of ramps, banked pits and walls, it may well have featured briefly in that Eddie Kidd movie. Was riding there legal or just tolerated? We never knew, but other bikers would rock up on anything from stripped-out C90s to full-bore motocross exterminators. I was pretty sure the IT was going to be too demanding for me to ride well, but that day at Aveley would decide whether I invested in it or threw it out into the classifieds.

No surprise the highly strung IT indeed proved to be a one-trick pony: yank it open, hold on and hope the turbo-like rush came and went before you needed to stop or steer round something. Even the most elementary manoeuvre like a bend, a climb or a down change required anticipating which way the engine's switch might get flicked and how you'd deal with it.

Giro ran a nimble, twin-shock XR200, which was infinitely more useable. That added up to greater confidence and therefore more fun. Providing you weren't too tall, the 200 was by far the best of the XRs at the time, and what the masterful Giro couldn't do on it didn't need doing outside of an Eddie Kidd stadium event.

One of the gravel pits was backed by a twelve-foot-high wall of dirt where a digger had once clawed. If I'm generous I'd say it was ten degrees from vertical, but that didn't stop a couple of fearless local kids launching themselves up it on their denuded, step-thru Hondas. Like a sprinter at the tape, when hovering at the crest they had to launch their weight forward to avoid falling back down and getting staked by a C90 footrest. To me the stunt contravened the much respected laws of physics. How did you even practise something like that? If I were to run at the wall, surely I'd simply ram it like something out of a *Road Runner* cartoon, snap my neck and wonder, 'Well, what did I expect?'

Giro had never watched *Road Runner*. He inspected the curved base of the wall and I got in position with the camera. As he made his pass I captured the XR pressed vertically against the wall on crushed suspension: Giro hung over the bars, nose to the fender. A split-second later some latent horizontal momentum pitched him forward over the brim and he landed safely.

The best I could manage on the IT was railing a few berms and pointless, blue-smoke power wheelies. Compared to the user-friendly XR, or even a Yamaha DT400MX one guy there let me try, the IT was far too manic. Back in town, an enduro mate of Ralph's had just ditched his unreliable KTM and gave me his XL250S plus cash for the IT. Within a fortnight the wicked IT had snapped his leg; meanwhile I broke an indicator lens on the XL, failing to show schoolmate Rob how to drift like Mert the Dirt.

The trouble with that XL250S was it lacked the torque of a 500 or the weight of a 185. The middle way was not always better. Chriscol and a couple of others at SD swore by their 250-Ss, but though it sounded right on paper, it wasn't for me and helped set my opinion at that time that Honda made bland motorcycles: XS650 vs CB500T; Z900 vs CB750; Derriboot vs CX500. The comparisons were plain for all to see.

For me the XRs were Honda's only outstanding bikes of the era and miles ahead of the four-stroke competition. Instead, I recalled that DT400's super-smooth power delivery. It managed it at the cost of catastrophic fuel consumption of course, but it did suggest that even though the days of noxious two-strokes were numbered on the road, they could produce masses of *useable* power. So the XL-S was replaced with one of the most popular trail bikes of its day, Yamaha's brilliant DT175MX.

Mine came with performance-enhancing 'Moto-X Fox' tank stickers and an oversized 4.50 rear tyre to snatch back that advantage. Far superior to the KEs and TSs, everyone and his dog was running 175 MXs for green-laning and easy enduros. With the same dopey thinking that supposed a bigger tyre was better, I figured screwing in an expensive NGK racing spark plug would be one of the simplest performance enhancements going. The only tangible difference it made was the shorter time it took to burn a hole in the piston while coming down the M2 towards the Medway Bridge after a weekend's jumping and sliding. Off to the mender's and into the classifieds. My strategy for dealing with my mistakes was to flog them and move on. There were plenty more mistakes to be made out there, and that summer my bike sampling hit its frenzied peak.

This restiveness was apparent at work too. I was getting sick of not being fed. A year and a half at Security put me among a minority of long-established employees, but in that time I'd failed to break into the Golden Circle, a mythical band of favourites who were fed the best work. There was some doubt whether 'feeding' really existed, at least on the scale and for the reasons that we non-beneficiaries perceived. It was true that, except in the midsummer doldrums, you barely saw some riders in the office from week to week and yet they seemed to be earning up to twice as much. How was that possible if we all put in the same hours and our radios broadcast all the controllers' transmissions (but not other riders' replies)? Was there some code used to get the cream jobs? 'Three Zero, err, you're breaking up. Call me on the phone when you get there.'

Maybe I didn't suck up to the controllers enough, or was ignored because I didn't join the gang in the Marquis of Anglesey on a Friday night. Or could it be that turning up to work on crack-snorting IT250s and Mobylettes didn't send the right message. What happened to that sensible young lad on his new CB400T with a windscreen, topbox and matching handlebar muffs?

One quiet day I got a job to Cleckheaton near Leeds, which I interpreted as a bit of a break. I was on another MZ TS250 by then – a yellow one, that's all you need to know. My drop was opposite a baker's, and although I rarely followed the informal office etiquette of returning with gifts from distant lands, I bought a big pie for the controller.

'Here, Barry, a present from t'north.'

Actually I liked old Whispering Baz. He looked like Tom Waits with smallpox, never got worked up, and came across as neither snarky nor a cross-eyed toff.

'Wassat then?'

'Cleckheaton pasty, speciality of West Yorkshire.' (I made that up. It was probably just the usual mishmash of boiled hooves and offal.)

'Ta.'

Security wasn't so special any more. Eccentrics like Christian and Richard Wyler on their racers, and Maurice on his heat-generating contraption had moved on or been persuaded to do so. The shallow pleasures from delivering to famous people and hanging around in model agencies, and the thrill of cracking out a multi-drop press release without missing a beat were getting mundane. I'd met my share of pop divas, actors and lords, but despatching had become just another job with as many aggravations as kicks.

The management were set on sanitising our image, replacing grubby stoners with smartly trimmed pros who didn't just roll in when they needed some extra cash to placate the landlord or score an eighth. As the Institute of Couriers described the late 1970s in its self-styled history of despatching, 'It was the lifestyle issues of the job that were to bring many failings to the service'. That wouldn't do at all. Our job had become so mainstream, Avon featured a scruffy Mercury despatcher alongside his GS425 in a double-page advert for their Roadrunner tyres. The tried and tested implication being, 'if the pros use 'em, they gotta be good'.

Nearly two years earlier I'd planned to ride for a few months, bag up some cash and head west, but I'd become one of these lifestylers. Learning to beat the odds and perfect the dodges in the World of Despatchcraft was a game we all enjoyed, but I'd largely got over the unsustainable thrill of the chase. The money was now just a means of gorging myself on biking's steaming banquet. 'Just one more winter and I'll jack it in.' Who among us didn't make that vow from time to time.

Nowadays online talk from old hands can tend to brag about the encounters, the earnings and the dangers: 'I jumped Tower Bridge while delivering cocaine to [supermodel's name redacted].' Hang out backstage long enough and eventually you'll get to meet the band, but keeping up enthusiasm for the weekly combat when the bike was playing up, the weather crap, the work lean, the receptionists disdainful and the near-misses unnerving took fortitude not all could maintain. Over a couple of years you might get to the peak of your skills, but you were a ball balancing on a jet of water surrounded by hundreds of others, deftly bobbing up and down. I knew only one rider who slipped off that jet. He took the bend on the Chiswick flyover at some crazy speed on his CB1000 and that was the end of him.

By mid-1980 the UK economy was in deep recession. Inflation hit twenty-two per cent and unemployment soared to the highest level since before the war, and was set to climb far higher. With an XS250, a *Nicholson*'s and a family to support, motorcycle couriering was becoming a viable solution. Petrol was still substantially cheaper than milk and you could earn the average UK weekly wage of £125 in two or three days. Even if a week's earnings per month accounted for running and living costs, if you set your mind to it, you could buy a new bike every two months. All you needed was eight weeks of uninterrupted work, and some luck.

The CB1000 guy rode up each week from the West Country where he had a young family, and spent the weekdays in a hotel or on friends' floors. He was among those who were starting to treat despatching as a regular job, a job that wasn't just for cowboys, artful dodgers and adventurers akin to the 'young, skinny, wiry fellows... orphans preferred' sought by the original Pony Express back in 1860. Modern messengering was proving to be much more lucrative, and in 1981 the well-known Pony Express bike courier outfit was bought out by Securicor. And everyone knew Securicor: their armoured cash-delivery vans were as much a part of the London street scene as Routemaster buses and a regular focus of armed raids.

Like others, SD sent out reps to poach competitors' accounts. Even we riders were handed fliers and offered incentives to bring in new accounts, something I scoffed at. All established despatch companies now sought loyal, devoted salarymen, saddled with their company bibs but content to accept the gamble of piecework. The managers had to maintain a fleet large enough to deal with the work efficiently but small enough so each rider earned a wage safely above any guaranteed minimum. The fact that the work, the workers and the workplace were all unpredictable and irregular made keeping everyone happy a tricky task.

If it was quiet, you might grab a day off and get that ailing bike sorted once and for all. It was good form to call in, but you didn't have to ask, you just did it – it was part of your unwritten lifestyler's contract. After all, your workchums would benefit from the reduced pool and you'd make up the hours another day. But when several riders acted like this simultaneously, the controller would be left high and dry as irate clients called in, demanding, 'Where's my bike? My crippled grandmother could have walked it over by now!' Wedged in the middle, grovelling over the phone to clients, then covering the mouthpiece to bark down the radio at us, the controller surely had a long memory for who could be relied on.

To help shake up their image the bosses at Security ditched SD's original and elegantly enigmatic logo of a bounding panther, and commissioned a design consultancy to come up with something more crushingly obvious. The result was a graphic of a knight's armoured gauntlet clasping a rolled-up scroll.

'What do you think, Chris?' said Anthony, one of the managers. 'I think it's really rather super. It symbolises "security" and "despatch"!' Or a rather painful hand job. What next, a bike with wings? Oh, someone had that one already. With a gob like that, little wonder the Golden Circle eluded me.

Around this time I ran across Nick, formerly of Capital Couriers in Hanover Square, still astride his big K6. We exchanged the usual grumbles: low rates, favouritism, the occasional police purges. (Cop: 'What is the registration number of this vehicle, sir?' Rider: 'Dunno. Ends with a "P", I think. It's on the yellow plate on the back.')

'I'm working with Mario again. Grosvenor Cars, up behind St Pancras. Seems pretty good, actually. They're always looking for riders.'

'Oh yeah? Might see you up there.'

In my last weeks at SD I'd got to know another rider. Richard wasn't into dirt biking or a dedicated despatcher, just a lifestyler cashing in between theological studies. He inhabited a late-hippy nirvana in a lovely wisteria-clad mews cottage off the King's Road, owned by his posh girlfriend's well-off parents. As his studies suggested, Richard was engaged in examining the noble and not so noble motivations of mankind. The idea that such things mattered or were indeed worthy of study had never passed through my still unset mind, easily excited as it was by generating backfires down London Wall, or bouncing off the scenery on weekends. His kindness and Zen-like calm made an impression on me.

By this time my mum had sold the house I'd grown up in and moved to the Outer Zone. I'd taken my cue and, like so many wretched souls before and since, moved into a bedsit in Streatham Hill, a subject that not even Mike Leigh dared dramatise. My sole memories of that place were the landlady's steely warning forbidding visitors after 8pm, and lying on my bed one evening, spellbound as my Walkman played 'Sympathy for the Devil' from a cassette Richard had lent me.

Tiptoeing around my attic-dungeon wasn't such fun, so I welcomed invitations to Richard's Chelsea bolthole where the threadbare furniture reeked of pot and eclectic curiosities spoke of new worlds and different ideas. An upturned piston was a flowerpot. An oriental engraved brass grinder dispensed pepper and a woman's voice croaked hoarsely from the cassette.

'Who's that playing?'

'Marianne Faithful. *Broken English*. Good, isn't it.'

'Marianne Faithful? I thought she was dead. Can I copy it?'

(Music piracy was not born in the digital age; from the very start we copied cassettes. Sony even made twin-deck cassette players for that very purpose.)

The walls sagged under the weight of Richard's books, which included the prevailing canon of the era: RD Laing, Kahlil Gibran, Erica Jong, Baudelaire, Hunter S Thompson and Richard Bach. I had read Bach's *Jonathan Livingston Seagull* as a curious fifteen-year-old, picking it up in Norbury library and reading it right there in one go.

Under one of Richard's bookshelves was a black and white print of a grimy brick wall in some depressed northern mill town. On it someone had carefully painted in big white letters, 'This Is A Fucking Humdinger'.

'What is "hum dinger", Mister Richard?'

'Humdinger? It's an American word for "a good thing, a very good thing",' he said as he skinned up.

Hum dinger. It had a nice rhythm to it. It was to be a few years before I realised that whoever had painted that was most probably smashed off their face.

One evening Richard hung some L-plates off his Morris Traveller and accompanied me on my first drive, down along the Embankment to the Elephant and back. Another time we swapped bikes for a weekend. He wanted to see what an XT500 was good for, while I took his long-legged SR500 down to Cornwall. After I dropped the SR back, Richard handed me a book.

'You might like this, Chris. It's about a chap who rode a Triumph round the world. Took him four years.'

The front cover of *Jupiter's Travels* was a low shot across some gravel to a saturated desert sky. A guy resembling a scruffy version of the dandy TV detective *Jason King* slouched in a WWII flying jacket astride a Triumph which looked like it had been punched in the face a couple of times. The uncoordinated collection of bags carried by this two-wheeled vagabond jarred with the trim BMW touring image from the magazine ads. It all spoke of adventure and romance in far-flung lands.

Inside was a map. Down through Europe and on down through Africa, up the Americas and across to Japan and the Far East. Australia, then India and back to Europe. Imagine that. I'd barely got to grips with riding bikes in the UK and here was a guy who dropkicked *Whicker's World* into a cocked hat. I'd read Ted Simon's interview in *Bike*. The interviewer had been uncharacteristically respectful, if not downright enraptured by his 60,000-mile odyssey. 'Curiosity is greater than fear,' Simon had declared.

'Take it,' said Richard. 'It's a good read.'

10

AUF WIEDERSEHEN, PETCOCK

Honda CB350

Following Nick's tip, I was now working for Grosvenor on
Phoenix Street, NW1, a step down from Security in terms of
cachet and location, but not as bad as Capital Couriers, who
were probably moving into the pole-dancing business by
now. Actually it might just have been the weather that summer which drove me to look for a change. The June of 1980
is fixed in my memory as a month in which I had to wear my
detested waterproofs every single day. At some point each
day I had to haul myself into my human bin bag, an innovative compressed-polystyrene onesie produced by Perfec-
tos Rain & Leisurewear and about as elegant as a tablecloth
poncho. And looking like a gumby created its own kind of
road-safety hazard that was only exacerbated by riding a yellow MZ. In my sweaty, over-sized get-up I was sure drivers
intimidated or otherwise went for me just because I looked
and sounded so annoying. They had a point, but I refused to

follow convention and buy myself a costly and widely used PVC Rukka – well, not for another thirty-five years, when I finally cottoned on to what brilliant bits of kit they are.

Lawrence, the boss at Grosvenor, ran an upmarket mini-cab outfit, but like many others in the game, he saw the value in employing a few bikes plus a van or two to keep his smartly dressed chauffeurs free to do the quality work. Like many non-riders in the industry, he was suspicious of biking's combination of daredevil allure and patent vulnerability. Our agility and unpredictably in heavy traffic often took cosseted drivers by surprise, raising maddeningly contradictory feelings of 'Christ, if I'd hit him he'd have been killed. Bastard!' You see the same kind of resentment these days towards London's mushrooming hordes of commuter cyclists: annoyingly hard to spot, largely immune to traffic penalties and yet all too easy to squash inadvertently. Cycle couriers in London were a few years down the line, but in 1980 it made good business sense for Grosvenor Cars to capitalise on the motorbike messenger trend.

Because of the separation from the chin-jutting drivers who saw themselves as a cut above to the minicabbing rabble, we bikes were secondary and so any office camaraderie was rather muted. But by then I'd got over all that. You picked your mates of course, but in my experience there was no tight-knit solidarity among despatchers. You were your own boss on your own bike: that was the point. Work had become just work, but it was fun to be back with Mario and Nick. Soon XR-riding Giro joined us from SD too.

Grosvenor were too mean to provide us with Motorola handsets. Instead, we were given bulky minicab rigs which clogged up space in the topbox and, along with a loudspeaker and three-foot aerial fixed through the lid, needed wiring to the bike's battery. It wasn't all bad news though: the fixed radio had the side benefit of making my six-volt MZ redundant.

I tried running it with a second battery, but it was too much of a faff, so it was 'Auf Wiedersehen, petcock,' and thanks for all the fishtailing. It may have only been midsummer but it was time to buy my seventh bike of 1980.

Tuesday afternoons at the designated hour, a newsagent on Theobald's Road managed to acquire early copies of the next day's *Motorcycle News*. Suspiciously close to *MCN*'s London office on nearby Herbal Hill, it was the only place you could buy the paper early so as to get first stab at the classifieds. Many a seller would get caught short with a call for their bike on a Tuesday evening.

I needed a twelve-volt bike, but as usual I wanted a charismatic cheapie. No more MZs, ear drum-splitting ITs or licence-harming SSs, but certainly not the new 'Eurostyled' Honda Super Dream. I'd be eating with a spoon before I ever got one of those. As ever, I seemed compelled to go against the grain – with scores of interesting and able bikes to sample, why not? I headed out to north Kent one evening to check out a GT500. To me that Suzuki possessed some of MZ's better attributes: an unpretentious, functional machine that ought to make a good work bike, even though I'd never seen a despatcher using one. With a disc on the front and a drum on the back, one of them was bound to work come rain or shine, and at a couple of hundred quid, it was cheap.

I took a run up and down the road. For a stroker it felt torquey and smooth. Electronic ignition straight off the early Apollo programme came as standard. But something held me back. They'd stopped making GTs a couple of years earlier, but even then the bike was from that crude, pressed-steel period, and it was a ropey Suzuki at that. Suzukis were known to be the least well made of the Big Four from Japan, though their prices reflected this. Unusually, I turned away from that one. Perhaps seeing it and briefly riding it was enough to douse the appeal. I should have adopted that strategy more often.

I turned to the next edition of *MCN* and scanned the classifieds for something that was as practical as the dreary 400T but which also lit the fuse like the Bonnie, Ducati and SP. Up in the old brain some dozing synapse shifted in its deckchair and in doing so rang up a teenage memory of that enchanted Honda brochure. Or more likely, the bike was for sale, in south London and going cheap. As unemployment hit two million and Bowie confessed that Major Tom had been a junkie after all, a bronze-green M-reg Honda CB350K4 rolled onto my expanding moto-résumé.

Manufactured from the late sixties, at one time the K4 had been the bestselling bike in America. Like a dalek invasion, in the five or six years of production over a quarter of a million of them spread out across the US, exterminating Triumph Trophy and BSA sales without so much as a sink plunger stuck to their foreheads. Even I could sense the K4 possessed an intangible quality that the subsequent 360G5 of 1974 had lost. It had certainly been clinically erased from the awful CJ360T, a last-ditch, yellow-analgesic makeover shoved into the showrooms just ahead of the three-valve Dreams.

Unlike the Dream, the K4 had power characteristics which I realised were attributable to its two-valve head, or maybe it was its 180° crank. If nothing else, a basic two-valve engine couldn't rev so high and therefore gave the impression – however unfounded – of more low-down grunt. This I liked and my only real memory of the K4 is that it was a bike I felt right at home on. With the low seat, and low everything in fact, the 350 had the planted feel of an old Brit hack, but with a rare dash of Jap Crap class. Yes, it was as pressed together as a GT500 and had a swingarm like a beanstalk, but for its time it had an aura of build quality that Suzuki were only just achieving with their GSs. Best of all, the K4 signified the end of my prolonged Zschopau ballet. Maybe that's why I was so fond of it.

The solid K4 toiled its way through the city with the mute devotion of a loyal mule, filing its centre stand here and silencer there. Up front the K4 ran something new to me: a twin-leading shoe (TLS) brake. How cool was that! Before hydraulic disc brakes became the norm in the mid-seventies, smaller bikes made do with regular single-leading shoe (SLS) drums, certainly on the back wheel. But on the front, SLS performance was mediocre and the actuation grabby. Part of the problem was that with an SLS brake – invented by André Renault, no less – only one of the two shoes exerted any worthwhile braking effort onto the rotating drum to produce a useful, force-multiplying 'servo' effect as it went. The other shoe trailed, and retarded much less efficiently, rather like a bike's back brake in fact. A TLS's clever arrangement of parallel linkages had two cams instead of one, so that *both* brake shoes pressed their leading edge into the drum with equal force. Result (when adjusted correctly): much improved breaking. The drawback: precious little braking force when rolling backwards; but, unlike a car, a bike can't go backwards that fast, so an SLS on the rear covered that.

Sadly, all this superb, forward-biased braking efficiency didn't help me avoid an overdue appointment with a London casualty ward one Monday morning. Parked up on Tottenham Court Road, my speaker blared out a collection in Covent Garden. Now as then, TCR is one-way northbound. I was parked on the west side but knew that if I could zip swiftly south across the three lanes during a lull in the traffic, I could nip into Capper Street for Gower southbound, dodging at least two sets of lights and saving at least two minutes and fifteen seconds.

Naturally the three and a half minutes I waited for a gap in the traffic didn't count; it was just part of the game of snatching a quick advantage – one we'd played since before Raquel Welch stitched up a bikini from racoon pelts. Perhaps with that image occupying rather too much of my mind, I saw my chance and dashed over for Capper Street – and was promptly rammed by a car coming out of Capper on to TCR. The driver of course was looking south and was not expecting anything from my direction. It was really only a harmless tap, but I happened to be wearing my Italian elk-skin loafers, it being a warm and dry summer's day at last. Lovely shoes they were, comfy as slippers and light as a feather. But they offered little protection against the weight of a CB350 bearing down on my foot via the sharp edge of a pressed-steel brake pedal.

On the corner was a pub called the Mortimer Arms. I remember that because, once dragged inside, I bled all over their nice carpet, though as the pub was popular with nurses, they probably took that in their stride. In fact, I could have hopped my way down the block to University College Hospital, which is where I spent the next couple of weeks once they'd stitched an eight-inch gash from toe to ankle and set the broken foot in a plaster cast.

Just as I'd done in Kidderminster Hospital, I settled into the UCH regime comfortably, while calibrating the schedules of the nurses I fancied. Doctors visited periodically, accompanied by small retinues of trainees, to assess and pronounce on the newest exhibit. In the meantime the barely damaged Honda had been collected and my stuff moved out of my indifferent landlady's Streatham bedsit. The blood-soaked loafers? They were a write-off.

Giro was a real help at this time, and when the day came to leave hospital and convalesce at my mum's, he even lent me his XR200. I limped out on to Gower Street, managed to kickstart the Honda with my left leg, shoved the crutches under my bum and rode off. Of all the four limbs you use when riding a bike, the right leg is the least essential, though not everyone sees it so rationally. Arriving at my mum's on a bike caused a flurry of exasperation.

I spent another couple of weeks in the box room watching the summer pass and my foot heal, wondering what bike to try next. Even though I was only twenty and had been riding less than four years, for some reason the machines of my not that distant youth held a magical allure, while the current crop of megabikes like the CBXs, GS Thous and XS Elevens all went over my head. I did limp up to Barnet one time to check out a Z1B Kawasaki: four pipes, 125mph and one front disc brake. The Zed was still a god among bikes and the wary owner only let me ride it pillion for fear of me scarpering. It safely remained an untouched god, because I never bought that one either.

It was time to get back to work and find somewhere to live. I was too far gone to be living at home, but the thought of another dismal Streatham bedsit was disheartening. Again, the thoughtful Giro came up with a solution. He knew a bunch of fellow Kiwis who'd squatted a block of flats in Muswell Hill, right below the historic entertainment venue of Alexandra Palace (which, coincidentally, had burned down just a few weeks earlier). There were still plenty of empties.

Until that time what I knew about squatting in London was gleaned from glances at tabloid headlines about holidaymakers returning from the Costa Brava to find their home invaded by pot-smoking anarchists. That particular angle – or at least the non-Costa Brava bit – was to come later. But for now I was simply the latest in a very long line of Londoners searching for somewhere affordable to live.

In Britain squatting – the practice of occupying an uninhabited building or plot of land – had a history reaching back to before the fourteenth century. In the Middle Ages it was deemed a civil rather than a criminal offence which didn't result in being hung, drawn and quartered. Much more recently, it became a pressing issue after WWII, when thousands of servicemen returned to find that they and their families had been made homeless as a consequence of air raids and other upheavals. By 1946 over a thousand newly vacated military bases across England and Wales were occupied by squatters. The government tried to turn public opinion against them and (unsuccessfully) instructed local authorities to cut off services. Some of those families weren't relocated to approved housing for over a decade.

As the post-war economy improved, decrepit tenements as well as perfectly habitable Victorian terraces were cleared. In their place rose the notorious thirty-storey tower blocks, but still housing waiting lists ran to years while properties stood empty. By the late 1960s the community-based Family Squatting Movement in England was promoting squatting as a solution to the chronic housing shortage that continues to blight London to this day. They sought to negotiate short-occupancy agreements with councils and many of the capital's long-established housing associations have their origins in the FSM. Things turned sour when squatting attracted revolutionary groups and dropouts looking for free accommodation.

But by the time I got into squatting, the tabloid-enraging radical element had dwindled and, with some 30,000 squatters in London, the practice was returning to its pragmatic origins: somewhere affordable to live. All you needed was an appropriate target, the nerve to occupy it and an acceptance of the drawbacks, which included not having too much clobber. Being young and immortal, none of that seemed too much of a problem.

The key – quite literally – was to quickly establish sole access to the property. Breaking and entering *was* illegal, but if you could get in and change the lock before the cops showed up you could say the door was wide open and you'd claimed squatter's rights. They couldn't touch you. If you played by the book – *The Squatters Handbook*, that is, not to be confused with the bombmaker's *Anarchist Cookbook* – you posted a carefully worded statement on the door staking your claim and reminding the aggrieved that eviction was illegal.

As long as someone didn't send the boys round, it took a court order to be legitimately evicted, and that usually took months to materialise. The secret was to pick an empty council property in a Labour-run borough and not a temporarily empty house belonging to a cousin of the gangland Kray twins, or indeed any privately owned dwelling – they were strictly off limits. Labour usually ran the poorer, inner-city districts where housing waiting lists stretched out beyond the rings of Saturn. They also possessed enough habitable empties to house probably half that list overnight. Why this situation persisted we never understood and in that way squatting could be seen as a political statement. One generous explanation to the empties was that perhaps an edict had been passed that all wiring and fittings in residential council properties had to meet a certain new safety standard, but with all those cutbacks by the nasty Tory government, the cost of renovating old places to meet these regulations was too great.

Our place in Muswell Hill was a three-storey block of about twenty flats arranged in a flattened U-shape and had a reasonably good excuse for being empty. It couldn't have been more than ten years old but had been vacated when one wing subsided a couple of inches following the drought of 1976. Many properties built on north London clay suffered similar subsidence at the time. Nothing had been done to the block since, other than a half-hearted cladding of the windows with corrugated iron. No one had even bothered vandalising or ransacking the place.

So, without the need to dress up like an IRA man on parade, I hobbled into my ground floor flat in broad daylight one September morning. Once the iron was prised off the windows, I could see that the place was bare but in good order.

Some councils sabotaged empties by smashing up or blocking toilets to discourage squatters, but not here. The taps flowed, the electricity worked, the toilet flushed and only the copper immersion tank was missing a heating element. As we were to learn in future years, the utility companies rarely completely disconnected a property, and even dirtbag squatters had the legal right to these essential services.

With more rooms than I knew what to do with, I adjusted uncertainly to my new lodgings, initially camping rather than settling in. I still wasn't quite sure about the whole business. Was it really so easy or right to move into an empty flat without permission or payment? It didn't take long to decide it was. Without a tenancy agreement – however short term – a notice of impending eviction could come any time, and until it did, no one would otherwise be occupying the block. We were keeping out the vandals, thieves and rats until the place was done up – a benefit often cited by squatters. For me it was the beginning of a realisation that breaking the rules could be an option and even at times, legitimate.

Living off Pot Noodles and kebabs soon lost its sparkle so I set about scavenging the essentials to make the place habitable: kitchenware from charity shops or whatever my mum had going spare. An uncannily comfortable double mattress was dragged home from an alleyway in nearby Crouch End. I carried that bed from squat to squat for years, before indestructible Algerian bedbugs squatted it themselves.

Had Muswell Hill been some pre-war terrace in Hackney, occupied by itch-scratching junkies, militant vegans and liberally pierced dole scroungers, I'd have probably hurried back to mummy's, or slumped back into the latent perversion of the Streatham Hill bedsit scene. But the Kiwis upstairs weren't stashing petrol bombs, arguing over an inclusive manifesto or jabbing needles into their arms while signing on for their mates (that too would all come later). They were a few years older than me and most were busy with office jobs while enjoying the thrill of being young and alive and in London rather than Kaukapakapa.

There was plenty of space for my bikes too, but in my new-found spirit of transgression, I realised I could do one better and wheel them indoors. Written off the previous summer, the convalescing 900SS was now back on the scene, retrieved from the repair shop that had tried to snatch it from under my nose. It looked sexier than ever in its one-piece tank-seat unit. All it needed was the engine. That was still held hostage by the alloy welders up in Watford, who would do the job in their own effing sweet time.

11

TRIALS, ENDUROS AND THE DREAM THAT WOULDN'T DIE

Honda CB400AT and TL150, Kawasaki KLX250

I can't recall what actually happened to the K4, but moto-archaeological evidence confirms its disappearance from the fossil record around this time. In its place came my answer to the plastic maggot and now popular Super Dream.

At work Mario the controller had bought himself a Honda CB400AT as a weekend run-around. That was until he realised that, while he might work with bikers all day, he wasn't into biking himself. One weekend Nick gave me a lift up to Mario's place out near Bedford. In his garage a 500-gallon domestic fuel-oil tank kept his Peugeot diesel running on heating oil, the sort of canny dodge I admired.

'You know what, Chris, I ain't been to a petrol station since we moved in. Apart from for cigs, that is. They'll never catch me – it's the farmers and lorry drivers they're after. Costs me a tenner a week to do 500 miles. Anyway, here's the 'onda. Only 3300 miles. Whadja think?'

Honda were well known for their clutchless step-thru scooters, commonly cited as the world's most successful production motorcycle. But with full-sized machines such transmission was rare. *Dirt Bike* informed me that other contenders included Husqvarna's 390 clutchless four-speed stroker which helped Dick Burleson dominate the US enduro series for years. And there was Moto Guzzi's V1000 Convert, though that used a regular clutch to pull away. Like a step-thru, my two-speed automatic AT had no clutch: stomp into first, wind it out and off you go, or just leave it in second. When in gear and pulling against 2000rpm with the brakes on, few bikes on the metro race circuits launched from the lights as briskly as the AT.

In America, Honda had originally applied their Hondamatic transmission to a CB750A. On a bike even more than in a car, engine braking and the useful driveline tension a manual gearbox brings to the handling are vital. That's why fully automatic transmission and sporty riding usually don't mix, at least not with the technology available then. Brakes become critical – the Convert's linked foot-pedal system being a good example – though whatever the CB750A had by the way of anchors, it wasn't enough to win riders over, even in the US.

Today, scooters with middleweight bike engines run similarly effortless but much more sophisticated do-it-all transmissions. But, sorry to say, despite its clear advantages, your 100mph maxi scooter will forever be deemed an effete interloper on Planet Proper Bike.

My sort of riding was some way from gunning around the pine-scented switchbacks of Monte Carlo. But for stopping and starting and stopping again, hundreds of times a day, the 400cc Hondamatic twin was a winner. Yes, I was aware it was near identical to the dreary CB400 Dream I'd bought in haste and sold in a hurry, but the torque converter created another kind of machine entirely. With a practised flick of the hips I could hoick myself off the sidestand, kick it up and pull away in one smooth movement, all while chowing down on a succulent Spanish omelette on granary from Bruno's in Wardour Street. Having a free hand for the radio was also convenient: I could roll into a changing set of traffic lights and pull away ahead of the scrum while acknowledging the details of my next pick-up.

For a month or two, this novelty and the new workplace and bike revived my interest in the job, and that winter I re-entered the world of long hours as the Honda clocked up a thousand miles a week. Grosvenor had an account with Thames Television, which had offices opposite Laurence Corner's in Euston Tower as well as studios down in Teddington, southwest London. We'd frequently collect tapes from TV crews shooting local reports about mysterious dustbin abductions for the early evening bulletin. Other jobs included taking the 'Big Red Book' to Eamonn Andrews' place in Chiswick. He was the host of the popular ITV show *This is Your Life*, a cosy biographical tribute planted on an unsuspecting celebrity which Andrews had been presenting since before I was born. With the BBC in nearby Shepherd's Bush, a lot of TV people seemed to live in west London, and so the Westway again became a central artery in my despatching.

After a few months I became a little irritated by the way the Honda seemed to shrug off its sustained workload. One of the satisfactions of running a bike hard was keeping it in good shape in the face of gradual but inevitable deterioration. But I'd saddled myself with a Honda built during the marque's apogee, and no matter how much I thrashed it, the valiant hack would not die. Clinging on in first gear to 50mph, I craved a monumental detonation of the engine, an eruption of scalding conrods and whirring gears, preferably followed by a harmless slide into some pre-cushioned West-way Armco. But I was never to savour that lambent pleasure. The worst it could do was never exceed 55mpg and once in a while shear the sprocket holder off the cush-drive in the back hub. Probably a consequence of harsh clutchless gear changes – in the end I welded up the whole assembly and addressed the need for sprocket replacement with a grinder.

The indefatigable 400 endured partly because there were other bikes to share the load. Around that time a TV show called *Kick Start* showcased the sport of trials riding. Just two reordered letters in 'trail bike' added up to a whole new skill in finely judged balance and raw nerve. Contestants rode against the clock along narrow beams strung between stacked pallets, over old cars and huge bits of concrete pipe, as well as natural obstacles. All the action happened at harmless speeds and the only drawback seemed to be that the skinny machines would be rather hopeless road bikes.

In competitive trials the point was to 'clean' sections: ride through without putting your foot down or 'dabbing'. It was a practice we emulated in our own trials in the woods. It all helped you master balance and control, and my old TS185 had been pretty good at that. The trials bikes du jour were Spanish Bultaco two-strokes as ridden by current champ, Martin Lampkin. Yamaha were making moves with their TY250 stroker and in 1972 Honda had introduced the TL125, as svelte as any two-stroke, but with a tractable and user-friendly four-stroke motor. The legendary Sammy Miller made a name for himself both developing and winning championships on Honda trials bikes. In 1975 he helped design the Hi-Boy frame from Reynolds 531 tubing. The steel of choice on the earliest mountain bikes, it saved a massive 24lb over the original Honda TL frame. Less than five hundred Hi-Boy 125/150s were made, and I happened to buy one towards the end of the year. I took an evening train up north and made my way to a farm in West Yorkshire, where the sport flourished. Here the owner claimed the alloy Renthal bars were cast-offs from his mate Martin Lampkin's Bultaco. Martin Lampkin's handlebars! I was *that* close to feet-up royalty.

My TL150's engine was a chip off the same SOHC two-valve block used in XL125s, 185s and Giro's XR200. One of the greatest motors Honda ever made, it survives today in licensed form in China, Brazil and elsewhere. A huge back sprocket, gear ratios packed close as sardines, tiny four-inch brakes and the gorgeous chrome-plated Sammy Miller frame all helped the TL potentially chase squirrels up the trees.

I wheeled the bike on to the milk train back to London, and from Euston started pushing it home until it became light enough to ride the unlamped bike. As I'd recently learned, an Edwardian decree deemed a motorcycle road legal even without lights, speedos and other gubbins, as long as it had originally been registered in that form and was only ridden in daylight. I'm not even sure now if my £300 TL was actually registered. The yellow stick-on number plate was blank so I wouldn't have fancied my chances riding it around the West End before I scored a 'five' from the rozzers.

Knowing this, I followed a back route home through Camden, Holloway and Highgate. Crouched on the seat pad like a frog, with my knees close to my ears, it soon became clear a trials bike wouldn't make a conventional commuting machine, let alone a work bike. You could pull away in second or third gear, but by the time you were in top the poor little piston was about to pass out and you were doing just 40mph.

Come the weekend, the grounds surrounding our Muswell Hill squat made an excellent testing ground, and sadly all the testing the TL ever saw in my hands. Unless I was prepared to go through the chore of registering it, without a car, let alone a car licence, I was trapped. And even then, I would need to commit myself to riding what hadn't been possible on my previous trail bikes, otherwise the full marvel of my Miller-framed, Lampkin-barred, 200lb trials bike would never be revealed. Just like the recently departed Ducati and IT250G never reached their full potential, the specialised TL didn't turn me into a Pirelli-shod Spiderman.

Nevertheless, Giro on his XR200 and I happily contented ourselves with building ramps and leaping off the parapets around the squat. Giro astounded me with his ability to ride the TL up the walled-in bank that backed the property, just as he'd done that time at Aveley. All I could do was futile wheelies and little jumps, although the body English and clutch control required to turn at a snail's pace were useful skills for any off-roader.

One day I came home to find several tons of rubble and earth blocking our driveway. I assumed it was the London Borough of Haringey's version of leaving a severed horse's head in my bed. For Giro and me the rubble merely created a challenging new obstacle for our mini *Kick Start* course. A few weeks later the excavated waste was mysteriously removed.

Though it had been fun searching for my inner Sammy Miller, the slinky TL had to go. Through trial and error I was beginning to learn what I liked in a bike and what sort of riding I enjoyed. With my class-win in the Orpington International Six-Mile Enduro earlier in the year, I knew where my destiny lay: out on the quivering peaty mires and rubble-strewn fire roads of Mid Wales, which hosted the UK's only proper, long-lap enduro events.

At that point the Hondamatic was a dutiful work bike so was allowed to stay. That meant I had the luxury of getting a more dirtworthy machine again. Not as specialised as the IT or TL, but surely better than the TS and lighter than an SP370 or XT. Kawasaki KDXs were sweeping across the enduro results boards on both sides of the Atlantic, and again the dirt-biking press had us convinced that by owning one we would achieve the same outcome. The previous year it had been ITs, this year it was KDXs, next year we'd all paint our hair yellow and start raising hens. The reviews promised nice torquey motors, especially from the 250 KDX, and an assuredly better Uni-Trak back end. Where had I heard all that before?

I had to admit the KDXs looked great, with their long extruded alloy swingarms, white-on-green graphics, squidgy black fork gaiters and a solicitous tool pouch. But I was determined to learn from my mistakes: the TL was one of the best-looking trials bikes of the time too. I needed to shake off this 'form suggests functionality' delusion – some operator skill had to be thrown in the mix too.

Then Kawasaki snared me with a brilliantly pitched lariat: behold the KLX250. It convincingly levered the cooking engine from their inoffensive KL250 trail donkey into a KX motocross chassis, then lit it all up with those snazzy green plastics. The implication was clear: it was a 'four-stroke KDX', a cunning ploy worthy of Saatchi & Saatchi. I bought myself a year-old example for about six hundred quid.

Talking of Saatchi's, their 'Labour Isn't Working' poster had been apocryphally credited with securing the Tories' victory in 1979, though that should have been as easy as starting a warm TL150. In fact, by the spring of 1981 the Conservative government, and Thatcher in particular, were deeply unpopular. Maggie's determined attempts to reduce inflation had put one-in-ten of the workforce on the dole, with the north of England hit especially hard. Not coincidentally, skinheads and National Front mobs baited ethnic minorities and there was even talk of 'racial civil war', though that was just Enoch Powell popping up to remind us he wasn't dead yet. Winning the Eurovision Song Contest and the marriage of Charles and Diana had done little to lift the national mood. Eras were supposed to pass neatly in decades, but this felt like the grim seventies had clocked back in for some unauthorised overtime.

The only riot my KLX might cause would be surprising everyone by turning up at a finish line. With that intention in mind, I set about transforming it from playbike to highly strung enduro crossbow, deploying all the 'sano' tricks I'd read in *Dirt Bike*. The pipe breathed about as well as an anti-fascist rioter choking under a police truncheon, but the tiny UK market had nothing to offer my KLX. In the US White Brothers did list a big bore header with a tiny SuperTrapp spark arrestor that became less of a silencer the more discs you added (or was it the more you took away?). That was right up until the rusting nut became as one with the stud and you were left with what you had. On went higher bars in lustrous chromed steel, new grips (*Dirt Bike* seemed obsessed with grips), shorty levers and a quick-action throttle. Tyre levers and a wheel wrench were fixed to the H-section swingarm with strips of inner tube, razor-edged Metzeler enduro tyres shod the rims and a longer white front fender helped distinguish my KLX from the other KLX thought to be in the UK at that time.

I scanned the regs and read reports in TMX to locate a suitable event for a novice, and decided the Cwm Owen Enduro near the Welsh enduro mecca of Builth Wells was for me. Without a car licence or mates with a van, I trained the bike to Swansea the night before, rode up to the start point in the hills and crashed out in a barn with a few other earlybirds. We woke Sunday morning to a few inches of snow. The event was cancelled and I had a slippery ride back to Swansea.

The itch of Welsh mud remained unscratched, so next I signed up for the Plynlimon Enduro near Aberystwyth in West Wales. This time I trained to Hereford, rode across Wales (not as epic as it sounds, adventure riders), camped out in a forest and next morning stashed my kit in the trees and walked over to the starting area. All around me were purposeful, jacked-up dirt bikes leaning against vans clad in giant 'Renthal' or 'Girling' banners. Riders dressed like American footballers queued up at a catering van, chatting with each other. A pall of blue-grey smoke hung in the air, emitted by hideous, blood-red Maicos as well as Huskies, CRs and, yes, a couple of KDXs. Four-strokes were rare: several XRs and a DR400 or two. I was the only four-stroke KLX.

I was way out of my depth on this one and I knew it, but the great thing about the Plyn were the meaty, twenty-five-mile laps across wide-open moorland which at any other time would have seen me at the sharp end of a farmer's shotgun. It was a sorry approximation of the huge desert races that streamed across southern California's arid playas, but it was the best we had.

Apart from my prized Bell Moto 3, I was wearing a mixture of cheap or inappropriate crap from either Ralph's model shop or Laurence Corner's. The bloke at the scrutineering cast an eye over me and my machine and shouted to a mate.

'Look 'ere, Hugh, it's one of those Kawasaki Kay El Exes you were going to buy Sheila to help with the lambing.' He turned to me. 'All right? Not seen one of these before. First event is it, then?'

'Yes.'

'Oh the Plyn, she's a beauty. You'll have a great ride, I tell you. Just watch for the bomb holes on the tops and keep out of the way of the Maico boys: they don't like to brake, see. Gets 'em all cranky, like. Next!'

Butterflies roller-discoed around my stomach: it was 9.46, time for #123 to line up. I set off alongside another guy, who roosted me before the first bend, never to be seen again. My strategy was straight out of the despatcher's handbook: pace yourself; maintain a smooth momentum; be ready for anything. I was one of the last to leave and within a few miles the only bike around. My forearms soon pumped up like bricks and I panted like a spaniel in a sauna as I tried to keep the KLX on the boil. The problem was, the 17hp engine had barely enough poke to skid across an oily sheet of glass. Pulling back on the bars and turning the throttle merely resulted in a droning sound. I'd naively hoped that the 'quick-action' throttle would have a similar effect on the entire machine, rather like twelve-volt bulbs might glow twice as bright on a six-volt XT. It was not to be.

Up on a saturated plateau I was flying along at 25mph in third when a do-or-die ditch jumped out across my path. Nothing for it but to stand up, haul on the bars and yank on the QA throttle… Twenty minutes later the creature from the peat lagoon had managed to get one wheel out of the ditch when a passing pro took pity on me and helped haul out the rest of the bike.

'Better to keep on the course, mate. Stray out here and the place is full of these holes.' And off he stormed, trailing his blue veil of smoke like a Silkolene sheikh. I hadn't even been aware I was off the course, but got the bike running and went the way he went.

This sorry procession continued for hours. My class was due to do two or three laps – up to seventy-five miles – but I didn't manage that. Towards the end of one lap, I pottered gingerly down the hill's drop-offs while deranged Maico chainsaws screamed overhead in low orbit, their rear tyres snatching at the ravaged turf long enough to relaunch into the next flight. This would be the last year of Maico's dominance. Back in Germany a family feud over control of the company led to a calculated sabotage, a deluge of warranty claims, and the catastrophic collapse of the famed marque. Maico never recovered.

Neither would I – or so it felt. After hours of clinging to the bike like a wet sheet, I came in off my second lap, a limp jelly barely able to pull in the too-short clutch lever. Whose dumb idea was that? I approached the parking area that six hours earlier had been teeming with activity. Now, the last of the vans were pulling out, banners were being rolled up and a nice lady with a clipboard came over and said, 'Ah, there you are, One Twenty-Three. Well done you. We thought you'd been abducted by the aliens. Oh, is that one of those Kay El Exes? My hubby was promising me one of those.' A few weeks later a heavy letter thumped onto the doormat. Inside was a bronze-coloured finisher's medallion. I didn't really deserve it, but it was a nice thought.

I did rather better at my next enduro on the army land back at Slab Common where I'd dodged the commandos that day on my TS185. Now I was there legitimately and the moist sandy ruts of the common agreed with the KLX. As usual, most riders passed me as if I was a moped on a motorway, but who cared, I was having fun. Then the gritty Hampshire sand got to work on the chain and sprockets, grinding them all enough to allow the flapping chain to slap against the crankcase. Fully in the zone, the first I knew of it was when the oil-starved cam seized in the head. Another job for Jock Kerr Engineering, scourge of the *MCN* small ads.

It began to dawn on me that, without a van, these competitive events took their toll on the bikes in terms of work and expense and extra miles, and anyway I wasn't really cut out for racing. What I really liked was getting out of the city and into the wilds, to just enjoy being there rather than rushing to the next checkpoint. Once the KLX came back with new cam bearings, it was cleaned up for the classifieds.

12

NUCLEAR DREAD AND THE SUMMER OF RIOTS

Suzuki GS750, Honda XR500, Yamaha XT500

Whether through boredom, impulse or need, I bought myself a four-year-old Suzuki GS750DB. Most likely the Honda was off the road, probably getting its forks straightened or waiting the customary six weeks for an oil filter.

'400AT? Oooh, that's gonna be a special order, mate,' says the bloke behind the counter, sucking hard on his teeth.

'But aren't they the same as for Dreams and Super Dreams and all that?'

'Different part number, mate.' He glares. 'You wannit or what? £4.58 plus the VAT. Give us a call in March. Better still, make it April.'

Or perhaps I'd got a GS because I'd forgotten how awful the 400/4 works bike had been and was curious to challenge my dislike of transverse fours one more time. After all, a bigger engine and 60hp ought to have something going for it, even if it did all weigh over 500lb.

Along with a 550 version, the GS750 of 1976 was Suzuki's first modern four-stroke motorcycle engine. Up to that point Suzuki seem to have had a deep suspicion of camchains and valves. They even went through the costly exercise of producing the disastrous rotary-engined RE5. Even back at Sainsbury's, Steve, Vic and I had agreed that, with an engine like the back of a washing machine, the Wankel was on the short ride to the white elephant enclosure.

A rotary engine is clever: let's call it a triangular mill wheel spinning eccentrically inside a figure-of-eight chamber. The ingenious geometry of those interacting shapes sucked then compressed, ignited and expelled the mixture as smoothly as a hamster spinning merrily in its cage. Vibration may have been eliminated, but the RE5's fuel and oil consumption was on a par with the smelliest strokers and it weighed nearly as much as a Gold Wing. Following the RE5's failure, the GS750 project was as conservative as the Wankel had been radical, with performance close to a Z1000, supposedly better brakes and handling. The Japs were finally getting the hang of it.

A mate from SD had once let me loose down the A3 near Guildford on his GS1000. My recollection of my fifteen minutes aflame was of being steadily strangled by my open-face lid, which was aerodynamically unsuited to cutting through a 120mph hurricane. By Jap standards the one-litre GS was regarded as the dog's bollocks and the fastest I'd ever been on a bike apart from a momentary WFO spell on the 900SS. Hurtling past the traffic at two miles a minute on either bike sharpened the mind all right, but on a busy carriageway in Surrey it was just an unsustainable stunt to brag about later.

As for the GS750, it took less than a couple of weeks to get over that one. Only one picture survives, and you can tell from the tankbag, lashed-on radio speaker and a pannier strapped where the topbox should be, this GS was never going to be a keeper. Around town the thing was of course a tank with fuel consumption to match. One sunny spring day though, I got a job to Sussex and, unlike Basil Fawlty and his obstinate Austin 1100, elected not to give the GS a damn good thrashing. But even then it couldn't ever improve on 40mpg.

For all that, it ran reliably, propelled itself smoothly and leant as well as you'd expect with an Avon Speedmaster on the back. But there was no sensation of grunt or thrill from this most universal of Japanese motorbikes. What was it with these fours? I suspect that for me even the biggest four-cylinder motorcycle engine tuned to produce cubic amounts of torque at less than 2000rpm will still never achieve the raw appeal of a motor with fewer cylinders.

The GS750 just didn't turn me on and to underline that fact, I recall an evening blast on Giro's amazing Guzzi V50. It had barely more horsepower than some 250s but was probably lighter than most of them and over 100lb lighter than the plastic maggot. Add the brilliant linked brakes from the bigger Guzzis, and I can declare that hurtling through Crouch End that night, using bollards as slalom posts, the V50 was the best handling bike I ever did ride. That thing ran like it unrolled its own rollercoaster track before it, a rosy view helped by the fact that I didn't actually have to experience the frustration of owning a V50. The mini Guzzi was said to be an especially sloppily built Wop when it came to electrics, oil seals and starting. But it offered a comforting truth that motorcycling nirvana could be found here and there, and it didn't require six cylinders or a cubic capacity measured in four figures.

One summer's evening I led the GS out to Buckinghamshire and swapped it for a 1980 Honda XR500A, the one with shocks as long as your arm and a twenty-three-inch front wheel. The XR5 had little use for a front wheel of any size, skimming as it did a few inches above the road surface most of the time, as it leapt from corner to corner. On public roads the XR demonstrated the wisdom that would become Super Moto. Light, agile but nippier than a V50, it produced a grin as wide as a slack washing line.

By then I was back at SD because our man Mario had left Grosvenor and, sensing another sinking ship, we left with him. At one point Lawrence the boss had tried to raise the company's profile by insisting we all wore a company outfit. Only, being Lawrence, he had some cheap nylon cags printed up with 'Grosvenor' and a phone number on the back. Just as before, this was taken as an affront to our independence. Didn't he get it? We were a band of street-fighting messenger-mercenaries, van-slayers beholden to no one as we fought through traffic for whoever paid the best waiting time. With the back of *MCN* full of despatch companies advertising for riders, there was little risk in changing companies on the slightest pretext.

At Security Despatch the anarchic glamour of the early days was on the wane. Whatever happened to... Christian's racer... Shane's Z1B... and Sancho Panza? We'd largely grown up and got over it, settling for a quiet life and steady earnings aboard licence-preserving middleweight twins and a Rukka outfit. But not every day. One time I rode the XR in for a bit of fun as handheld radios didn't rely on a bike having a 12-volt battery. I could sense the disapproval from the managers' front office, but came up with some excuse about the Hondamatic having one of its periodic migraines.

Security had a daily wait-and-return contract with Mitsui, the Yamaha importers. At 3pm documents were collected from their offices in Queen Victoria Street for delivery to Mitsui's UK headquarters in Chessington on the way to Guildford. There was no compulsion to get the job done at breakneck speed, but as we weren't allowed any other jobs going that way, it had become an informal office challenge to cover the sixteen miles to Chessington in less than thirty minutes.

'One Oh Six POB Queen Victoria Street.'

'Rrrroger, Wanasx, call me when you're coming back.'

With an effortless stomp on the kickstarter, the slim-hipped, big-hearted XR hitched up its piston skirt and sprinted for the lights at Blackfriars Bridge. Well suited to the task, it rapidly ticked off the eight miles along the South Bank and through Battersea to the halfway point at the top of Wandsworth's West Hill. Here, the taps on the OHC motor could be opened up along the A3 raceway. The next eight miles passed by in a lot less than eight minutes, with the XR touching 100mph at one point. I know because my nose was about four inches from the speedo dial and I didn't dare move a muscle for fear of setting off a catastrophic tank slapper. Then it was head up, lock arms and down the slip road. Hard on the brakes while dropping gears, the back wheel waggled into the roundabout before turning up the side road for Mitsui. As I flicked down the sidestand I grabbed the radio and called in at what I like to think compared well with the office record of some twenty-three minutes. But jeez, that engine's a bit warm.

Inside, they took the postbag but had nothing to go back to the City. I stepped out and kicked over the XR, which responded with a gruesome racket from the top end. I may have smashed my personal best on the Mitsui run, but it had cost my Honda its head. The XR and I clattered back to town at a gentler pace.

I ended up selling the XR to Giro, who'd been impressed with the big Honda on a run we'd taken along the Ridgeway trail. Paralleling the M4 motorway, at all of fifty miles, back then the Ridgeway was the woeful pinnacle of long-distance trail riding in southern England. In US *Dirt Bike* they bleated on about the threat to the Barstow to Vegas desert race and the dirty tricks of the Sierra Club. What were they complaining about? They had more than enough desert trails for everyone. By fair means or foul, trail biking was becoming demonised in the UK and opportunities were shrinking year by year. The best moment on that Ridgeway ride had been an outrageous, knobbly-assisted power slide coming out of Membury Services on the M4 motorway, but it could as easily have been the BP on the Clerkenwell Road.

One day a court order dropped into Muswell Hill with an eviction date a few weeks away. We had no intention of contesting it or setting up barricades. Instead, I got word of another occupied squat south of the river, a grand, 200-year-old Georgian terrace on Kennington Road, close to the Imperial War Museum and Supreme Motorcycles, a friendly hole-in-the-wall run by two Italian brothers.

Wind the Kennington clock back eight hundred years and you'll see that Edward the Black Prince built a residence nearby at Kennington Cross. It was later demolished on the orders of Henry VIII to help expand the huge royal palace that became Whitehall. Then in 1750 Westminster Bridge and its extension, Kennington Road, were built. By the time I moved in, Kennington was a formerly poor Victorian suburb creeping towards gentrification. The infant Charlie Chaplin had lived in a workhouse round the back of our squat once his mother had been committed to Cane Hill asylum in Surrey. I remember 'Cane Hill' being our playground slang for being sent to the loony bin.

'Your mum's going to Cane Hill, she is!'

'No she ain't. Your mum smells!'

'Your mum...' And so it would continue until the bell rang or hostilities escalated into Chinese burns.

There was a new crowd in the Kennington squat's warren of rooms, which had probably once comprised two huge houses. Residents included the druggies and misfits associated with squatting – thirtysomething addict Rita and her ten-year-old daughter among them, as well as the slightly disturbed

Simon, fleeing a posh background. Charlene and Dirk were siblings from Durban on a working holiday and Charlene's ex, Steve, hung out with a creepy, skeletal guy called Baffy who was a fair bit further down the junk highway than Rita.

Eddie, a dark-eyed Brummie hippy lived upstairs. He'd already flown too high and resembled a combination of Charles Manson and Danny the Camberwell Carroteer from *Withnail & I*. Occasionally smoky salons would convene in Eddie's dimmed boudoir and talk would turn to the possibility of nuclear war. It was Eddie who acquainted me with the newly coined term 'nuclear dread' and it struck a chord. Ronald Reagan had recently been sworn in as US president and was determined to crush the Soviet bloc once and for all. The Second Cold War was intensifying. Believing that the Warsaw Pact's SS-20 missiles were too close for comfort, NATO elected to install American Pershing and cruise missiles in Europe. In the UK, cruise missiles were to be located at the US air base at Greenham Common, just west of London. This either made that part of the UK an even greater target for Soviet SS-20s, or rebalanced things safely in line with the deterrent policy of 'mutually assured destruction', appropriately known as 'MAD'. Those despicable Reds doubtless had a brace of missiles ticking away in some Silesian silo, carefully trained on the Houses of Parliament. And us, we lived by the river, just 1100 yards from Parliament. It spawned a certain fatalism.

The MAD doctrine was based on both sides being capable of unleashing equally destructive retaliation before their enemy's missiles detonated. As one side edged ahead, so the other sought to catch up. The expenditure was astronomical: a breathless addiction that was satirised with great prescience in the 1964 film *Dr Strangelove*. As Frankie Goes to Hollywood put it in *Two Tribes*, you could only score one point before the game was over. Little wonder that nearly half the UK population believed the world would turn dayglo some time soon.

I hadn't been in Kennington long when, one Saturday, riot vans started tearing down Kennington Road from the nearby police station. Hours later they returned, all smashed up. It was the Brixton riot of April 1981. Racial tension had been building following a fire in nearby New Cross in which thirteen black partygoers had died. Accident or racially motivated arson, we were never told, but '13 Dead and Nothing Said' went the song by Johnny Osbourne. Soon after, Operation Swamp 81 was actioned, an intensification of the hated Stop-and-Search 'sus law' that was meant to address Brixton's rising crime rate. Mere suspicion of intent to cause an offence was enough to warrant a Stop and Search by the police: all it took was two patrolling officers to agree, as young black males knew all too well. Then came a stabbing on Brixton's Railton Road, which, depending on what paper you read, was either mishandled by the police or misinterpreted by onlookers. Whichever it was, it kicked off the first of England's 1981 summer of riots. That Saturday, there were said to have been 2500 police battling with up to twice as many rioters, and over fifty police cars got trashed.

The word was that Brixton's rioters had spared locally owned shops, but other stores were looted and trashed. Even then, I didn't understand why rioting against injustices so often degenerated into looting. Throwing petrol bombs and bricks at your tormentors made sense, as in *Assault on Precinct 13*, John Carpenter's 1976 film about a besieged south LA police station. But acting as if you were on Brucie's *Generation Game*, smashing and grabbing a food mixer, a steam iron and a cuddly toy before torching the place? That was just opportunist pillaging.

A few days later, once the burned-out shops had been boarded up and the streets swept clean, the Brixton police came round to our squat for a raid. But if they hoped to recover looted stereos and microwaves, they were out of luck.

No need for the Black Maria – though someone downstairs had their half-lit bong confiscated.

Following several more riots in the UK, the notorious sus law (a spurious interpretation of the 150-year-old Vagrancy Act) got speedily repealed in August 1981. But by then the damage had been done and the practice would return under other names over the years. It all provided material for satirical sketches on TV shows like *Not the Nine O'Clock News*. One sketch had the thuggish Constable Savage being reprimanded for being 'over zealous' in repeatedly charging a 'coloured gentleman' for 'loitering with intent to use a pedestrian crossing, urinating in a public convenience, coughing without due care and attention' and 'walking on the cracks in the pavement'. Savage's punishment? Transfer to the infamous Special Patrol Group, aka the riot squad.

Even us two-wheelers got some rioting in that summer. A retired police officer remembers a rainy weekend in Keswick in the Lake District when a 'mob of youngsters on scooters tried to take over the town'. Somehow, the proclamation of a Wing Mirror Republic by sharply dressed Mods raising a fur-trimmed parka up a Lakeland flagpole doesn't compare with the smouldering ruins of Toxteth or Chapeltown. But the scooterists were angry, as a blogging member of the Norwich Broadsmen club recalls. Their thousand-strong rally found themselves locked out of the pubs and chip shops on the Saturday evening, so they taunted the shuttered frontages of Keswick, yelling, 'There's gonna be a riot!' – a safe bet in July 1981. At the campsite a police car was turned over and torched, and part of the mob went on the rampage while others tried to pacify them. The blogger recalls watching all this in horror, then confessed to being rescued by the police, who cut an escape route through the campsite fence before telling her and her friends to 'Fuck off and never come back.'

That summer, Nick announced his intention to ride his newly acquired Gold Wing to Kenya, where he'd been brought up and which probably held better prospects for him than the UK. Did I want to come with? Kenya sounded a bit of a trek, but it would be fun to cross the Sahara and end up somewhere sunny like the Ivory Coast. By then I'd discovered Stanfords Map Shop in Covent Garden, an Aladdin's cave of travel literature and charts. I'd already forgotten *Jupiter's Travels*, but a couple of other books had caught my eye. *Stay Alive in the Desert* by WEM Melville sounded like a good strategy, while Simon and Jan Glen's *Sahara Handbook* was to become much thumbed over the next decade.

Nick subsequently backed out of the African ride, but I was captivated by the idea of pitting my trail-biking skills against the mighty Sahara. The best machine for the task? Another XT500. The way I saw it, overlanding required a proven, lightweight and expendable hack. Despite BMWs' reputation as world travel bikes even back then, the new R80 G/S was never a contender for me.

I reasoned that if I was going to ride across the Sahara, perhaps I ought to have a peep at life on the other side of the English Channel first. *Bike* had long raved about riding in France and 'the south of France' evoked the same glittering exoticism as the Ivory Coast. So that September I set off for the 24-hour Bol D'Or endurance race held at Circuit Paul Ricard in the lavender-scented hills just east of Marseille, the very port from where boats left for Algeria and the Sahara.

As a family we'd never ventured abroad in a car, so my first overseas adventure had the thrill of the new and the anxiety of the unknown. How would I manage riding on the right and coping with the dreaded *priorité à droite* rule? Some deluded medieval statute still gave priority to traffic pulling out onto a busy road, turning the 'Sorry mate, I didn't see you' excuse into 'Tough titty, mon ami, I 'av zi raght of weh.'

An irresistible, dead-of-night ferry bargain saw me disembarking in Boulogne around dawn and I proceeded warily, primed for some chubby bereted bumpkin to put his rights to the test. But an hour or two in, the biggest drama was nothing more than a tedious roadside puncture. Whatever was needed to fix this unanticipated calamity, I didn't have it, so I paddled into a small town and waited for a garage to open. Once on my way, I steered around the roulette wheel of Paris and headed south into the Massif Central. Here, serpentine back roads led to the Ardèche Gorge, which dropped back off the highlands towards Montélimar, one of my favourites from the Black Magic chocolate box.

As I drooled over the mouth-watering aroma that surely wafted along Montélimar's almond-lined boulevards, I swung merrily down the Ardèche's switchbacks, watching the vegetation shrivel into a Provençal scrub as the warming sun eased my aching limbs. Near the end of the descent it really was getting quite warm, too much it seemed for the right-angled edge of a Speedmaster tyre pitched a few degrees from vertical. On a harmless curve I got dumped hard and sat for a while under a tree, rocking in pain.

My chief memory of the Bol is lying in my Vango tent with a throbbing hip amid a sea of other tents and bikes. A few yards away, twin-lamped Total Hondas, Kvas Kool Kawas and the experimental ELFe screamed through the night, flat-out down the Mistral straight towards Signes. It had been an inauspicious start to my overseas travels and, not really bothered who won, I left before the chequered flag and limped back home.

The perils of *priorité à droite* had come to nothing, but one evening soon after I got back, Nick had exercised his *priorité de l'arrière* while getting us a takeaway, and rammed my XT into the back of a bus. Reparations added up to a new wheel and a pair of forks from an RM370, probably the only part of that widow-making motocrosser suited to road use. Whether the XT was improved once it was shod with the RM forks and a nineteen-inch front rim was doubtful, but I figured the smaller diameter rim meant a rear eighteen-inch inner tube could be stretched over it at a push. It did indeed pay off later in the desert when I was up the creek with a flat.

The summer ended with marching orders at Kennington Road. This time there was nowhere to go, so I teamed up with Charlene, Dirk and Simple Simon to find a new squat. I did my bit trying to get into an empty over a shop, opposite Kennington police station. Breaking and entering was new on me and actually quite a thrill. In my mind it wasn't illegal, but I imagine a pumped-up rioter finding themselves by an off-licence with no front window probably felt the same way. I got in via a back alley and over a couple of walls, but once inside could only access a corridor behind the street door, from where I peeped at the police station through the letterbox. Unable to get further without excessive damage or noise, I backed out. Now it was Dirk and Simon's turn. Entry strategies were much discussed by squatters. Being confrontation averse, I liked the 3am stealth approach, but aided by a spell in the pub, Dirk and Simon favoured the 10pm brazen tactic. It was considered preferable as everyone was either in the boozer or engrossed in the last episode of *It Ain't Half Hot Mum*.

They got into a place round the corner in Hayles Street, a much less grand, late-Victorian terrace built not long after Kennington became incorporated into metropolitan London. Basic houses of that era had a frontage just ten feet wide but went back and up a long way, like Corn Flakes boxes on edge, packing in more dwellings per street. The only thing that had changed here since the war were the cars. A lot of unbombed old Kennington looked the same and a couple of years later Dexys Midnight Runners sought to recapture that untroubled 'gobstopper and conker' era by shooting the video for 'Come on Eileen' at the end of our road.

At the Town Hall the place had checked out as a council property so we were in the clear, and once the two had established 'sole access', Charlene and I slipped back in for a closer look. The electricity meter was missing but joining up the protruding cables fixed that. They'd poured concrete down the toilet bowl too, but they should have tried a bit harder. Half an hour's work with a chisel fixed that as well and with the water on, we were in business. We moved in late one evening, trying to keep a low profile, but in a narrow street of narrow houses our presence was obviously noticed by the neighbours. Anticipating a hostile reception, we kept the corrugated iron on the front windows until the local kids got bored of throwing stones.

Charlene had a secretarial job in Victoria, Simon was on the dole and Dirk spent the days grooming his moustache, power-lifting bricks and smoking the odd bit of *dagga*. Dirk was unapologetically coarse Dutch Afrikaner white trash who'd lost his virginity to his *ousie* (maid) at his father's instruction. He taught me several Afrikaner slang expressions and also had this sage tip – his old man's bombproof remedy for erectile dysfunction: 'I tell ya, Kris, take ma father's advice. You ever av trouble getting' yer peil to pop with a kiff bokkie [attractive young lady], take a sniff up her armpet. Mark ma words, bru, shove yer snoz in her 'pit and BAM!' He clapped his hands. 'Works for me every fokn' time, ek sê!'

Once we'd all settled in, Dirk proposed we adopt a purifying eating regime of carefully boiled brown rice, occasionally embellished with an egg or a lone vegetable. Over the weeks our taste buds fell into disuse as Dirk prepared our modest nightly bowls of chow. The detox meals ended with Dirk rolling a perfect joint, which he and Simon shared. Charlene occasionally took a puff.

In Dirk's parlance, shaven-headed Simon was a bit of a *mompie*, or 'too long in the womb', as they still say down in Cornwall. But along with a heraldic surname, you could tell Simon had received an expensive education before he'd flipped. One morning we came downstairs to find a couple of cosy armchairs – just what the place needed. While he'd been tripping out by the Elephant, like mythical Sirens, the dumped furniture had called out to Simon and persuaded him to re-house them. Other domestic essentials were retrieved from skips and our new squat evolved into a *lekker pozzie*: a nice place. My bikes even helped win over the brats down the road. We got the usual shot of urchins wearing oversized helmets astride my Honda making 'brooom-brooom' noises.

By now I'd left SD for Apollo Despatch behind Charing Cross Station. With my XT500 taking shape, I was busy trying to earn enough money to get me to West Africa before the wet season began. Unfortunately one day I was 'let go' by the boss after losing a large piece of artwork on the way to Putney. I'd arrived at the drop-off, reached back and thought, 'Oh fuck…' Thing was, once you got tangled up in heavy traffic or engaged in speedy episodes, it wasn't uncommon to forget you had a fridge door strapped across the topbox. Knowing that oily tyre prints could be explained away, and might even add a dangerous frisson to a successful delivery, I shot back through the Wandsworth one-way system, certain that was where it had got knocked off. But by the time I backtracked all the way to Vauxhall, I knew I was out of luck. The owner suggested I lie low for a while on a kind of unpaid leave. Perhaps exhaust fumes had dulled my reasoning, but after a while his meaning became clear.

So I spent my time finishing the XT for a January departure. A bloke in Kent took weeks to beat out a twenty-litre alloy tank that didn't quite fit right. And seeing as this was the Sahara we were talking about, I mounted an oil cooler over the headlight, and then unrolled some wire mesh over that and the headlamp to act as a stone guard. This headlight grill is still a common piece of adventure-bike bling, a motorcycle's version of a bull bar advising onlookers that this machine is built for *tough* conditions. The chicken-wire grill never proved useful and the XT was the first and last of my desert bikes to have one.

I got someone to make a couple of load-carrying L-frames to bolt to a Craven rack on the back. I then screwed plywood planks to the frame's horizontal sections to make a platform, not forgetting a span of Dexion 'Meccano' shelving to stop the loaded rack sides flexing in towards the wheel. In principle it was a sound design. In practice, once loaded, the whole arrangement swayed around like a hula-hula grass skirt.

As the big day approached, several inches of snow fell across the south of England, but there was no turning back. I didn't feel at all confident, but what could I do? Set off and hope I'd catch up with myself down the road. Like so many first-time adventurers before and since, I left for the Sahara massively overloaded but hugely under-equipped.

13

GOWER STREET

Honda CD185, BMW R100T

My first Sahara trip was not a triumph, and five weeks later the desert hawked up a weighty glob of phlegm and spat it onto a chilly Portsmouth quay. Like something out of *Alien*, the XT and I emerged from the cloying snot and wiped ourselves down. With no working lights, I was forced to spend the night in a doorway, then rode up the freezing A3 next morning back to London. In Kennington, no one was in, but an eviction order lay on the milk-crate table. Time to move on again.

The Yamaha looked rough. The oscillating pannier racks were thrown back into a skip, the bars – mangled on a first-night crash in Algeria – were replaced and the whole machine liberally sprayed with a can of black satin paint. With a fresh Yamaha speed-block tank decal, I had to admit my tarted-up desert sled was pretty cool, the five-figure urban-scrambler look you'll see posted on BikeEXIF. The cavalier paint job spread to the tyres and other parts, but having claimed a bit of hard-won kudos, I enjoyed tooling around London on the XT for a couple of weeks. It didn't take a headlamp grill to see we'd been somewhere and done something. One night a bloke who'd had a few too many weaved down Hayles Street and rode the XT away for five hundred quid. I bet he didn't feel so good next morning when he peered out the window.

By some miracle my Honda 400AT was still on the scene, eighteen long months after I'd bought it. Maybe, like the Ducati, I'd forgotten I owned it too, though that wasn't to be the theme of recurring sweet dreams. The indestructible Hondamatic was ready for more, but my enthusiasm for radio messengering was fading. Keeping a bike running, the licence clean, the body intact and the spirit upbeat was getting difficult after three and a half years. My curtailed Saharan escapade had opened up a world beyond the Euston Road, beyond even the A5 to Wales. But the way things were, despatching was easy money, so 106 clocked back on again at Security.

Meanwhile, the Argentinians invaded the Falklands, a UK territory no one had ever heard of. A British military response was soon underway, spawning a nasty jingoism stirred up by parts of the media. It also prompted an upswing in Thatcher's hitherto dismal ratings. Without this victory and a few other factors, like North Sea oil revenues and Labour in disarray, things might have turned out differently. The Falklands was a localised conflict in an area so remote that, despite the Cold War tensions of the time, there was little chance of it escalating into World War III. As a member of an ill-informed public, my first adult war initially looked exciting. The daily MoD briefings to the media were guarded, and the full nastiness of actual combat and the inevitable cock-ups only came out years later, when it also transpired that the UK had been secretly negotiating over the Falklands anyway. But when ships on both sides were sunk, not least the *Belgrano* and then the *Sheffield* two days later, it wasn't such a jolly big adventure any more.

The bailiffs duly came to our narrow Kennington squat, but we were ready for the early-morning bash on the door. All our stuff had been moved out and we were packed up and ready to go, but curious to see what would actually transpire. It was fairly civil. Backed up by some police and a council van ready to slap on a steel door, an official proclaimed something like, 'Under Section 23, Clause 4 of the 1855 Housing Act, naff off!!' We filed out with our sleeping bags and said good-bye to Hayles Street.

Down the road, on the far side of Kennington Park, the residents of one of London's longest-occupied squats were made of sterner stuff. They'd been there since the late sixties and went on to resist a series of eviction orders right up to 2007. It helped that they'd got the place designated a Rastafarian temple. Marijuana was tolerated as a Rasta sacrament, but in the end (unproven) charges of crack dealing helped convince the judges that nearly half a century was long enough for a London squat. The building was finally knocked down, sold on and remained an empty plot until house prices took a turn for the better.

Charlene and Dirk went back to Durban, Simon drifted into space like Major Tom, and I was lucky enough to get a room in Gower Street, Bloomsbury with some of the Muswell Hill Kiwis. I never found out who managed to open up a squat in such a desirably central location, but in Fitzrovia, on the other side of Tottenham Court Road, the tradition went back over a century. Famous squatters included the artist Walter Sickert in the early 1900s ('outed' in 2002 by novelist Patricia Cornwell, who believed he was Jack the Ripper), right up to Boy George around our time. George managed to out himself without forensic examination. Even Bob Marley had squatted over the road in Ridgmount Gardens (there's a blue plaque). And in the seventies, fifty long-empty flats in nearby Huntley Street had become the base of the London Squatters Union until, in August 1978, they were kicked out by a squad of 300 police officers, including the SPG, and some bulldozers. No blue plaque commemorates that mass eviction, though it's said Dutch squatters besieged the British Embassy in The Hague in solidarity, and the British embassy in Stockholm was also picketed.

In Gower Street we were innocent of this little-known and occasionally militant 'Bloomsbury Set', thinking ourselves happily isolated amid the academic, artistic and medical institutions around us. Our squat was located between the RADA actors' academy, a bookshop and UCL's halls of residence (the latter overlooked our courtyard), and I moved into a big back room in the basement.

After Kennington I was pleased to be living among a relatively conventional crowd again. The women worked in stores, hospitals or offices, the blokes were despatchers or medical students. Most were visiting Australians or Kiwis, the rest from places like Norfolk, Northumberland or South Wales. I was the only Londoner. Perhaps the fact that they'd all chosen to get up and seek their fortune in London gave our Gower Street squat an upbeat vibe.

Even the couple of in-house junkies were harmless, sad characters, like old drunks. One young Kiwi slowly succumbed to addiction, to the despair of his sister who lived there too. The other was an old hand who subsisted by shoplifting expensive outdoor gear to order from the outfitters in Covent Garden. Many of the King's Cross prostitutes were said to be driven by heroin addiction, and the whole injection business made it all the more unappealing. Then came The Stranglers' 'Golden Brown', which had nearly topped the charts while I'd been in the Sahara. Dirk had explained the not-so-hidden meaning: a dreamy eulogy to a darkly seductive delight that had crept up on us from the East and stolen our souls. It was the best drug song ever, and I didn't even do that shit.

Old-hand junkie had a brother, Graham, who also took the odd fix (once nearly overdosing on purer-than-usual gear) and had recently travelled through distant lands on a Yam XS650 twin. With his mate he was now planning to cross Africa on XT500s, so we had something in common. More than we knew in fact: their first African trip would also end prematurely, but with a near fatal drama.

Graham worked for a typesetter's in Clerkenwell who saw fit to provide him with a 100mph, 35mpg Suzuki X7 for the job of running round the West End. That fuel consumption dropped to 25mpg once he'd siphoned some petrol off for his XT (the fuel was paid for too). His X7 was clamped to a lethal-looking thirty-inch-wide flat metal topbox to carry the artwork. He wouldn't be losing jobs trying to squeeze through the traffic in Wandsworth, though the metal topbox might brain a few school kids who strayed too close to the kerb.

At Security the director with the Guzzi T3 helped me convince myself that the pile of bits in his garage amounting to a BMW R100T could be reassembled and put back on the road with very little work, and maybe even a tidy profit. Just like that Johnny Cash song, one piece at a time found its way into my room, while the rolling chassis got chained to the railings outside.

'Meisterschaft' was another of BMW's self-assured adverts. I wasn't at all convinced but like most bikers was curious to sample the flat twin's mystique. It was well known that BMs were an acquired taste. They weren't like any other bike and they made sure everyone knew that. Smug, bearded old farts rode BMs – there were a couple of those at Security. Christian, back in Security's feral heyday, had done his best to obliterate that image, and of course the smoked paintjob R90S and the silver-blue 100RS were among the iconic machines of the seventies. But who were they kidding, pretending the R80 G/S was any kind of trail bike? A big GS? Mark my words, it will never catch on. As always, however, the best way to confront my prejudices was to dive in and see if there was any water down there.

My basket case had suffered a collision that had mashed the front wheel, the offside pipes and the cylinder head, but otherwise appeared intact. The tank had a red and silver paint job with a depth and lustre I'd never seen before, and one thing I soon discovered was that working on a BMW was as easy as playing with Lego, something I *was* good at. The airbox was above the gearbox that plugged into the back of the engine, out of which stuck the cylinders which were connected back to the airbox via the carbs. There was no need for the rubber fingers of my sixties *Smash* comic hero, Janus Stark, to get to an inner float bowl on a GS750. Not that you'd ever need to, of course.

Several visits to breakers and Gus Kuhn's got the R100T running and I took it for a spin to Colin's down in Cornwall. Maybe there was something in the Rhinewater which gave the boxer the characteristics of a giant MZ, making another ungainly skateboard but at least twice the weight. The narrow bars and long, softly sprung front suspension gave the front end a feel heavy at anything other than steady speeds on wideopen roads. Some said R80s were a better choice, or even the 'new' R65. The slugs on my low-tuned, 65hp version took a lot of momentum to spin up and smooth out. Let out the clutch and it juddered like a traction engine, rose two inches and then launched – but dived twice as far if you braked carelessly. Ironing out these reactions was something I never quite mastered, and in town it felt like trying to pilot a lurching motorboat with the outboard in your hands.

Just as with my short GS750 episode, there were no golden moments on that BMW, no sweeping flashes of motorcycle perfection that made it all worthwhile, or at least that I could remember with a warm glow. The Bonneville, Ducati, the

SP370, 350K4 and not least XR500 had all been one long golden moment, but the R100T was just a well-finished shoe that didn't fit.

By the time the BMW was running, Graham had put me on to a job as a fixed-wage in-house delivery rider for Templar, another typesetter's near Old Street. The hours were long but the load was light, rarely exceeding thirty miles a day and with lots of sitting around in between. The £180 wage was less than I'd earned for real despatching, but the expenses shrank exponentially, as did the risks to the licence now the 'go faster, earn more' element had been eliminated. Obviously there was no holiday pay or other benefits, and as an 8-to-7 salaryman, it was a renunciation of roger-dodging freelance wrangling across the capital's asphalt prairies. But hopefully that would also mean less running over of blind folk while flipping a breakneck U-ey into Chancery Lane during a postal strike. Instead, I could try and calm down and get some reading done while waiting for the next run. Finally, the undefeated two-speed, no-thrills Honda could be retired. In its place came an economical commuter bike costing my first week's wages. Bring on bike #24: the Honda CD185 Benly.

Set against dashing names like Katana and Hayabusa, Benly sounded about as sexy as a budget Argos toaster. No great surprise to learn it was Honda's take on the Japanese word *benri* or 'convenient' – as in nip out to the shops for a packet of noodles. Off and on, there's been a Honda Benly since 1953. It's the same story with Honda's first proper motorcycle from the late forties, the 100cc D-Type Dream. Say what you like, but you have to admire Honda's continuity when it comes to model names.

By the mid-fifties 'Benly' was being stamped into the side panels of a swoopingly handsome 125 single with a fender that could have been a prop in a camp *Flash Gordon* tribute. In typical early Japanese fashion, the J-model Benly was an unsubtle rip-off of the German NSU brand's great-looking 250 Max, only stepping back from copying NSU's novel monoshock back end. As the world's bestselling bike manufacturer at the time, NSU were a worthwhile target for aspirational Honda. They'd been in the game since the start, progressing from sewing machines through bicycles to motorbikes and later cars. In English, 'NSU' translates as 'Neckarsulm Sewing Machine Union', which, like Benly, didn't quite match the cachet of something like Birmingham Small Arms or Vincent HRD. But as the holder of numerous world records, NSU could have called themselves Pingu and still been much admired.

In the late fifties the Honda Benly gained a cylinder but lost those curvy looks, becoming the C92 125cc Benly twin. It cranked out over 11hp at nearly 10,000rpm to reach 75mph, a speed a BSA Bantam could only achieve once it had been melted down and fired from a cannon. As with the Dream, the name was resurrected in 1978 when the ageing and grimly utilitarian CD175 got made over into the comely CD185 Benly. Once fitted with a topbox and a tea cosy, the 185 became the inoffensive commuter bike of choice for the blue-collared Homo Benliticus.

Unless Tom Cruise had ridden one in *Top Gun*, that's about all the excitement you can scrape off the information super highway about a CD185 Benly. The four-speed, single-carb twin had come a long way from the world's first production motorcycle. But not far enough for me, when compared with a hard-decelerating 900SS charging down the Caterham bypass. As I was about to discover, other ways of getting your kicks were also available.

Graham advised me what I had to do on my first day at Templar: set a bad precedent. Like most typesetters, Templar worked round the clock if necessary, and at least twenty hours a day, in two shifts. What the staff output overnight,

I delivered to the advertising agencies in Soho and Fitzrovia by nine the next morning. With nothing to do for a couple of hours once I got back, I would nip home to Gower Street for some breakfast and a lie-down. Then, suitably rested, I'd dash back and run up the stairs into the brightly lit studio as if I'd just left a *Blues Brothers*-like trail of smashed-up chase cars in my wake. If they were on to me, they said nothing, and anyway I had a bleeper.

Aptly enough, Templar was just over the road from Chiswell Street, where former gunsmith William Caslon had established his famous type foundry in 1720. The fonts he designed became popular across the English-speaking world and, two-and-a-half centuries later, one of my jobs was to run around borrowing the modern iterations of Caslon, Garamond (what you're reading) and Bodoni fonts – now supplied on big rolls of film – from other typesetters nearby. I always seemed to be collecting the same small selection of fonts, as if anything else just wouldn't work. 'When in doubt, use Caslon,' went the old printer's saying; it was a font as neutral and pleasing as magnolia house paint.

As new digital technologies changed traditional typesetting forever, so the dark arts of marketing, public relations and advertising began to flex their muscles. The results spoke for themselves: branding and a slickly packaged, well-delivered message could win people over. The new VCRs and TV remotes allowed viewers to skip the adverts, so the ad agencies had to up their game with longer and wittier commercials, the best of which became so-called water-cooler moments at the office the following day. Within a few years, working in PR or advertising would briefly become as glamorous and lucrative as City trading.

This flowering of the advertising industry benefited the despatching industry too, requiring daily shuttles between the City, the broadcast and print media, and agencies like Saatchi,

JWT, McCann and Y&R. Most of the typographical print out-fits which served the agencies were located between the City and the West End, in the still untrendy brown-brick precincts of Clerkenwell and Shoreditch. For a brief period digital pho-totypesetting flourished, then it died as the Apple Mac and WYSIWYG apps like Quark Express revolutionised layout and printing processes once more. It wasn't the only casualty of the era. By the late eighties Saatchi's – the only ad agency that could claim to be a household name in the UK – had col-lapsed under its own weight, and all the Clerkenwell typeset-ters that I knew soon folded too.

But in the early eighties phototypesetting still required a skilled operator to run something like a Quadritek 1200 or the capable Compugraphic 7500, which was only the size of a small piano. With copy from the client sitting like sheet music on a rack, the operator keyed in the text along with some complex code that formatted it all into something slicker than a page of type hammered out on an Olivetti. The humming 7500 would then produce a negative, lay it against photo-sensitive paper and spew out galleys like wet photocopy paper.

These machines could only hold a few fonts of limited size, so straplines like 'The New Hyundai Pony – Full of Western Promise' had to be composed in a darkroom on a different machine. As a negative film reel of, say, Caslon spooled to and fro, the operator would carefully align each letter and press the shutter: 'T...h...e... N...e...w...' Very laborious. All this was then literally cut up with scalpels and pasted down with Spray Mount on to copy all about the new Pony. That got mounted on a board, bagged up and ad-dressed, then I'd saddle up the Benly and gallop off to Soho. Half an hour later, just as I was part way back to the office, the designer would decide he wanted the word 'electrifying' changed to 'affordable' and with less space below the head-line. I'd get bleeped, would find a phone, call in, turn round, collect the marked-up corrections and ride back. The word would be replaced, the spacing adjusted, the galley developed, dried and mounted and back I'd go down the road.

For me, sitting idle in a busy studio took some readjustment. I should have got more involved and taught myself some layout skills, as I did later, but for the moment I spent my spare time reading. I set the bar high and tackled Robert Pirsig's impenetrable *Zen and the Art of Motorcycle Maintenance* but absorbed very little. Perhaps there was nothing there, but it didn't help having BBC Radio Two blaring in my earhole and the disapproving glare of Wilf, an embittered old hot-metal dinosaur who'd been farmed out to some token job and whose cigarette habit was slowly killing him.

'Good, that book, is it?'

'Dunno yet.'

'Much of an art to fixing motorbikes?' prodded Wilf.

I shrugged my shoulders. He coughed and rolled a smoke.

The others in the office were a chummier bunch. Mick and Ron the directors got on like oil and water. Dressed in a sharp suit and gold cufflinks, Mick was the flamboyant one whose job it was to keep the clients from absconding, while tempting others to abscond to Templar. Ron, another hot-metal musketeer, was less flash but had the avuncular charm of ex-PM Callaghan. John, also a director, had a weakness for the ale. After lunch in the pub he'd often get me to nip out and fetch back a couple of bottles of Tinker's Pulp to see him through the afternoon. He had a wry 'ain't this all bollocks?' approach to the business, but his drinking and resultant oversights put him on thin ice with the rest.

Unusually, I was without a trail bike – the Sahara had got that out of my system for the moment – so occasionally I'd nip down to Colin's in Cornwall on the BM, thinking nothing of a 600-mile round-trip down the A303, even if it was spoiled by the lacklustre Beemer. Sitting at a steady eighty, the 100T felt fine, but as soon as you had to do something like change gear, brake or quickly change direction the composure was lost. In that way it reminded me a lot of the MZs, which wasn't part of the plan. Meanwhile, the wages were trickling in as I set all-time slows between Soho and Old Street. The sudden re-tirement from despatching's fast lane, as well as the congenial camaraderie of the squat may explain how I got drawn into the world of mind-altering substances.

Like any curious nine-year-old, I'd slyly sampled capfuls of toxic vodka, sickly Cointreau and other grimace-inducing potions from my parents' drinks cabinet. Occasionally at Sun-day lunch, my dad had encouraged me to take a sip of wine. It looked just like delicious Ribena but tasted as if something had died in there. How could those jet-setting Martini and Cinzano adverts be selling such awful-tasting drinks? 'Any time, any place, anywhere?' Do me a favour. No wonder Cin-zano had to recruit Leonard Rossiter and Joan Collins for their iconic TV promo.

The in-your-face cigarette advertising of my early teens similarly failed to persuade me to inhale. Naturally, had I been tragically struck by a meteor around this time, I'd have wanted the entire series of the raunchy, 'sheer enjoyment' Manikin adverts to flash before my eyes before I pegged out. But even though my parents puffed away, as so many sixties adults did, I'd been in enough foggy train carriages and upper bus decks to not want to add to the fug. You could keep your glamorous images of bronzed cats larking around on speedboats, rugged cowboys and suave pilots with Roger Moore smirks. I could tell my mum only lit up when she was stressed, not when she was relaxing on a palm-ringed atoll with Sacha Distel. That was all the advertising I needed.

As for the illegal drugs, growing up I got the idea that all those rock and roll suicides were down to too much heroin, alcohol and barbiturates. All about as far away as Martini World. At that time, the most used drugs included Moroccan and West Asian hash, speed, LSD, heroin from Southeast Asia and trendy but expensive Colombian coke. There was no skunk, crack, Ecstasy or crystal meth. Laughing gas? We'll come to that later. I must have been around pot since my short-lived college days, but as with beer and cigs, I took no interest. I certainly wasn't going to persevere until I got a taste for it, just to join in.

As in previous squats, the scent of hash wafted around Gower Street. Over the months, I watched my squatmates react to spliffs by merely slumping deeper into the furniture, saying goofy things and best of all, giggling. It didn't get all shouty or slobby as with too much booze, and next morning there were no grey-skinned hangovers. They got up, tidied up the kitchen, in which they'd devoured a midnight fry-up, and went back to work. They didn't take an interest in another spliff for days or weeks. As for the two junkie brothers tied to the mast, it didn't look like they were having half as great a time of it. And so a distinction between junkies and occasional pot smokers emerged: the former morose, feckless addicts mooching round the squat all day, the others enjoying getting bombed once in a while. Clearly pot need not lead to junk, depravity and an early grave, as we'd all been warned.

Most hash smokers told me dope didn't do much for them first time round. With me this was not the case. The night had been planned in advance: 'Normally straight Chris is gonna smoke some hash. You gotta watch this!' To avoid the unhealthy tobacco needed to pad joints, we inhaled neat resin smoke. A pea-sized lump on a bent safety pin was set aflame, then blown out and smothered with an upturned pint glass. Set on a hardback, the glass steadily filled with thick white smoke. When your turn came, you tipped up the glass's edge, took a lungful and held it in as you passed the book on.

181

This was good stuff. Moroccan Double Zero, they said, and when it hit the right parts of the brain your last sensible thought was, 'Oh hello… what's going on here then?' Like the eddying wreaths within the upturned glass, a lightness rolled up from the back of your head, which then seemed to separate and drift off on a warm breeze. The limbs tingled, chattering sounds echoed and perspective became distorted as the room morphed into an elongated chamber. I observed my feet, as distant as an Arizona mountain range rising from the vanishing point of a desert highway. I was intoxicated and enraptured by what a government health warning might describe as 'a feeling of well-being and euphoria'. All the senses were heightened, so that the most banal object or fleeting thought became resonant with significance and meaning. Brilliant ideas popped up and were instantly overrun by others. The room's mango walls shimmered like the aurora borealis – Double Zero was mildly hallucinogenic – and the others were chuckling good-naturedly at the newbie stoner's reactions. Oh no, here came the glass again. Later, I lay on my trusty Crouch End mattress and enjoyed the stream of colourful *Space Odyssey* imagery racing behind my closed eyelids until they turned into actual dreams and sleep.

I didn't know it, but I was part of a growing trend in the UK. In the sixties one in twenty young people had tried illicit drugs. By the eighties I was one in five and by the nineties it was more than half, presumably down to the Ecstasy boom. The cycle peaked around the millennium, after which alcohol had a resurgence, some say because you just couldn't get the good stuff any more.

It's no exaggeration to say that night was a turning point. There was a me before, and a me after. In its wake came a surge of druggy experimentation that matched my bike-buying fervour. Soon I'd discovered hot knives and the burning bin bag game, and within a month or two Colin and I hopped on the R100 and rode along the M4 to Swansea. As narco-journeymen, we were ready to take it to the next level. Our mission: LSD.

Terry and June were old school friends of Colin's who'd moved to Swansea to run a veterinary practice, interspersed by weekends of recreational drug taking. Terry was by then a Grand Master drugsmith and had provisioned his flat with everything we might need: four tabs of acid, refreshing drinks, approved videos plus a half of Moroccan and extra-large Rizlas from the late-night garage over the road.

Following my dopey initiation, I was a little more prepared for how the night might unfold, and it carried an edge of foreboding. This wasn't some skanky weed from the Moroccan Rif, but a mysterious and powerful chemical cooked up in an alchemist's lab where a single droplet had quivered and plopped on to a tiny piece of blotting paper. It might open the Doors of Perception, but there was a small chance it might also lead to a padded cell in Cane Hill.

As the drug took effect, Terry deployed his skills as an accredited hashishin by assembling outrageous joints: foot-long arrangements lit at both ends and drawn from the middle. With the LSD fuse fizzling fast towards its detonator, June gave me my first 'blowback' or 'shotgun', a pothead's equivalent of 'pass the apple', where the provider took a lungful then gently blew the deoxygenated smoke directly into your mouth as you inhaled.

Had you peered through the window that night you'd have seen the four of us ostensibly watching music videos while passing around elaborate spliffs, much like the rest of the neighbourhood. But behind our eyeballs we were caught in the whirlwind of our warped realities. Typically, I couldn't resist trying to step back and make an objective analysis of what the heck was going on, but I'd soon soar off and get lost in the next reverie. Minutes passed like centuries, then I'd touch down with a gentle thud and in a state of near-ordinary consciousness. A slight jolt might flicker across my face and I'd glance around to check my bearings before the next wave picked me up and we were airborne again. These episodes became longer and longer until they seemed to merge.

Like many, I worried that LSD hallucinations would throw me into a completely unrecognisable reality, not unlike the regression hypnotherapy that was popular at the time. I might find myself a Nubian mason in a sweaty loincloth, chiselling blocks of limestone in ancient Egypt, or a foot soldier engaged in some epic medieval battle, or maybe a worm in a pre-Cambrian forest. It was all there in Lewis Carroll's books and the rest. But this wasn't the case and just as well too, as who could be expected to cope with such madness and not make a fool of themselves or need restraining. It was the same with later trips right until the last one. The dose in one blotter or microdot must have been carefully judged to provide a perfect six- to eight-hour trip, during which most users could still catch themselves for long enough to exclaim, 'My oh my, this is a fucking humdinger.'

Little did I know that just a few years earlier, in remote locations to the north of Swansea, an idealistic chemist was said to have cooked up over half the world's acid. When the network was finally busted in 1977, enough LSD crystal was retrieved to produce millions more doses. A year later The Clash eulogised the events of the police's Operation Julie on their *Give 'Em Enough Rope* album and it was likely we were feasting on the remnants of that forbidden Cambrian harvest.

It was a trip all right and as it took hold I experienced the fascinating conviction that I was communicating wordlessly with others in the room – actual telepathic conversations. At one point I was also getting strong vibes from June and became uneasy that the night might turn into a suburban orgy, a delusion that I suspect isn't so unusual with LSD first-timers. Cripes, was I ready for that? Clang! My first serving of paranoia. Like everything on acid, unpleasant thoughts and emotions were also magnified, which is why 'set and setting' – your state of mind and the location – are crucial. But before I could make a fool of myself with June, I was spiralling out through the stratosphere, swept away along another cosmic torrent of consciousness.

After a while I recognised that the urge for a slash wasn't some phantom psychedelic craving but an actual biological necessity. Thankful that there was still a corner of my brain able to oversee such needs, I separated myself from the settee and stood up to carefully walk downstairs to the toilet. At some stage in my pre-departure research I'd picked up the urban myth about avoiding fresh orange juice while tripping. Apparently the sudden dose of vitamin C could snap the psychedelic spell and, like Icarus, you'd crash so fast you might never recover. But on the way to the bog I passed a hall mirror and couldn't resist glancing at myself. Suddenly I felt completely normal – the drug's effects were extinguished. Turn away and the brain raged like a bush fire. Back to the mirror: normal. This game fascinated me for a while. Was I the opposite of a distressed dolphin that supposedly freaks out when presented with its own image in a mirror? Christ! Were those playful porpoises and other higher mammals in a permanent tripped-out state that was brutally shut off when you showed them a mirror? Did androids dream of electric sheep? My Eureka moment was typical of the staggering cosmic certainties exposed to a brilliant half-life when high. Once the drug wore off they'd all shrivel up into pure cobblers, like vampires at daybreak. The night unfurled and eroded a few more layers of innocence and naivety. Did we all end up watching *Deep Throat* down in Terry's den, or was that in my dolphin head too?

The morning after the trip before could be rather subdued. Scrubbed, minced into a meatball then whacked out of the park, your regular daybrain twanged back into its casing with a smack. Settling in, it struggled to digest its bare-arsed streak through the Garden before shutting it all away to return to the prosaic needs of hunting and gathering. But the night held one inexplicable postscript. Colin too was certain that mid-flight we'd all been communicating without words.

One time a well-known actor unexpectedly died of an overdose and in a radio interview a friend had daringly submitted that drug use might be 'the urban equivalent of the call of the wild', which I took to mean an adventure. I'm not sure I'd equate the Prozac-like oblivion of smack with canoeing down the Yukon, but with drugs like Double Zero and acid the correlation rang true. Yes, the hyperactive imagination got overheated, but that was the point. It was tempting to agree with Aldous Huxley's view some thirty years earlier, that we were partaking of a substance widely found in nature and long used by tribal societies (in his case mescaline, taken even on his deathbed). Under its influence like new-born babies, we briefly saw the world in all its raw and agonising beauty before life's necessary filters kicked in.

There was another obvious drug that also demanded evaluation. That Christmas at work they'd given me a couple of bottles of wine. It was a kind gesture and normally I'd have given them away. But in the interests of rigorous research I kept one. Tonight I was going to get rat-arsed. There was no one in the squat so I ran myself a hot bath and with grimacing gulps worked my way through a bottle of red. Slug-swallow-wince, every few minutes until the empty bottle dropped to the floor. By the time I rose from the bath I was actually seeing double, just like they said. I staggered around for a bit and then, once the worst of the nausea had worn off, I went out and did a strange thing: I committed a small act of municipal vandalism.

I'd long coveted one of those stout yellow canvas hoods they padlocked over broken parking meters. There were a few round the back on Malet Street. If I'd been sober I'd have staked out a hideaway days in advance, waiting patiently for a moonless night. Then at 3am as the city slept, I'd have crawled across like a Cherokee to make my snatch. Not that evening. High as a kite, I grabbed the in-house bolt cutters – the squatter's little helper – and marched out bold as brass to snip me what became a handy tool bag for my next desert bike. In fact I got a couple – Graham would appreciate one too. Then, as the evening ended and the drug wore off, another revelation trickled down the vine. By the time the gang returned from the pub I'd become undrunk enough to engage them right at their level of tipsiness, in a gathering of warm camaraderie. So that's what it was all about and how most of the in-house trysts got started (though actual marriages in Gower Street were purely for passport or visa-extension purposes). Smoking tobacco-filled joints wasn't so agreeable, but what a shame you had to go through all that sour-tasting misery and countless smoky, noisy bars to get there.

For a year or two I experimented with drugs in the same spirit as I sampled the world of bikes and explored the Sahara. I had the same urge to go a little further, try something new and, in the case of not-always-so-playful LSD, literally challenge myself to not freak out, not be broken by the drug. With no war to fight for gang or country, such were the risks that animated a millennial road warrior without a cause.

The year drew to a close and I sold the BMW. It had never shaken off its unhealthy top end clatter. But it was a BMW, so I fed the engine a couple of cans of STP – an expensive version of using banana skins (even I wouldn't be that cruel) and made my money back. I left Templar too, sold the little Benly and flew to Australia.

14

A Sunburnt Country

Suzuki DR250S and GSX400

To be catapulted from a wintertime squat in early eighties London into Sydney was like jumping out of a frying pan full of half-set lard into a pile of fluffy down pillows. Pretty girls waved down passing cars by just lifting a finger, peaches the size of cricket balls tasted like peaches not cricket balls, and there really were sandy beaches right around the city. What a difference some sunshine made. It didn't take much time for all this surplus UV to go to my head, and soon after arriving I bought myself a new black Suzuki DR250S. Air-cooled, four-valve, drums all round but with Suzuki's new 'Full Floater' back end. This was when monoshock back ends were novel enough to have names.

But first I needed to grab a quick suntan. That wasn't going to be difficult. The image in the *Sydney Morning Herald* that day revealed a continent that was almost completely cloud-free.

Unfamiliar with the austral sun's intensity and the unassailable local wisdom recommending that you 'Slip, Slap, Slop' (referring to T-shirt, hat and sun cream), I passed a lotion-free morning on Rose Bay beach lying on my front, then flipped over like an ejecting slice of toast to spend the afternoon on my back. That should do it.

I passed the following day in throbbing agony, wafting a damp sheet over my swollen carcass. In a few days I peeled like a bush snake, by which time my 'get suntanned quick' stunt had some effect. Triple J was Sydney's answer to London's Capital Radio and Ozzie band Men at Work were having their big hit with 'Overkill'. I'd done that with my tanning programme so from then on became one of the many men in hats. Everywhere I went in Australia, balding middle-aged blokes who'd ignored the advice wore scalps ravaged like the surface of a crimson planet.

Thrilled to have a dirt bike again, I set out to run the DR in. Up to the Hunter Valley then inland, stopping off at a sun-bleached clapboard settlement called Rylstone, which looked like something out of Hazzard County. Another ride took me into the Blue Mountains and Jenolan Caves. Following a web of dirt roads back in, I pushed the DR's fuel range to the limit and realised I'd want to be more careful out here. Hundreds of miles of deserted gravel tracks cut through rustling gums in all directions, little-used access routes to rural properties, tourist overlooks or natural resources. New South Wales wasn't like congested, rule-struck England – you could ride the dirt for days, not mere hours as on the Ridgeway. And New South Wales covered just a tenth of the country.

Some of the Gower Street crew had come over a few months earlier and were living in a northern suburb called Avalon, near Palm Beach – and those names were not wishful exaggerations. But initially I slotted myself into a backpackers' hostel in Kings Cross, a seedier equivalent of London's Soho where the commerce of sex and drugs was more brazen. The hostel was occupied with fast-acclimatising Poms like myself, hardened local junkies tolerated by the landlords (what was it with all these junkies?), and two-inch cockroaches thriving in the torrid southern summer.

Being a stranger abroad gives you permission to break your own rules, and for a few short weeks I dabbled in scratch-card Lotto, a national craze as yet unknown in the UK. In the Lucky Country, I might just strike it lucky too. I won a fiver here and a tenner there before I came to my senses. Then, one day while flicking through a scuba magazine – diving was on every backpacker's to-do list – I learned there was such a job as commercial diving: risky but highly paid subsea work on oil rigs and similar installations. Could this be the next step from despatching? Something with the same adventure, work ethic and good pay, but which taught skills more useful than knowing the quickest way from Acton to Beckton? I also liked the idea of it being a seasonal job: getting down to it for a few months, then taking off to travel or do my own thing.

First though, I needed to learn how to dive, and in Australia that was easy. The hostel walls were plastered with all sorts of adventure-sports activities and others told me Byron Bay was a great place to get your PADI C-Card. Not surprisingly, the British Sub-Aqua Club didn't recognise the American PADI certification, but I'd snorkel under that bridge when I came to it. I rode the Suzuki 500 miles to Byron Bay and, starting in a paddling pool then progressing out to sea, completed the five-day course. I didn't feel that sprightly after the final big dive down to sixty feet, and was somewhat put off by the ex-Navy instructors, whose teaching methods weren't so suited to us soft-shelled civilians.

Next step would be getting trained up at somewhere like OceanCorp in Houston. All that was missing was several thousand dollars to pay for the six-month course, after which

I could expect to walk into a job anywhere in the world. Except the UK, where, again, lightweight American certification was considered more suited to the balmy Gulf of Mexico than the gale-swept North Sea.

It felt like a good plan and by sheer coincidence I had the right watch. A few months earlier my mum had chipped in to buy me a hefty Rolex Sea Dweller for my twenty-first. Though hardly extravagant, she had a thing for posh watches and had bought me an Omega when I was a teenager. I never really got the whole Rolex thing, though as the eighties progressed, many others did. The self-winding was handy so long as it was kept in motion, but it weighed a ton and wasn't that accurate. Initially I tried to flog it in Sydney, but it soon became clear that Australians also saw little value in overpriced mechanical Swiss watches. Everyone was into digital Casios. Later, after I'd blown all my money and was eating out of the Hari Krishna Centre and a nearby soup kitchen, the Rolex found a steady niche in a Darlinghurst Road pawn shop.

'Ah, it's the rich boy again, come to pawn his Rolex,' the Jewish proprietor would cackle at me. Many years later, once someone told me what the old Rolex was worth, I couldn't sell it quick enough.

Someone in the Kings Cross hostel had a tip: there was construction work going on Fraser Island, eight hundred miles up the coast. That was all I needed to know. Fire up the 'zook: fortune favours the impulsive! I dashed up the Bruce Highway, discovering that Australia's Highway One was no Pacific Coast Highway or even an A5, but a bumpy, ill-maintained two-laner. A few days later I rolled onto the ferry at Inskip Point and rode twenty miles up the beach to Eurong. In a few months this place would be the construction site of a gleaming new resort to rival anything in the Seychelles or Caribbean.

I asked a beardy bloke clasping a beer can in a neoprene sleeve if there was any such work in the offing and got a rather hostile response. It was an early example of an interesting Antipodean reversal I was to experience frequently: unlike in Britain, urban Ozzies were friendlier than rural folk, at least up north.

'There'll be no resort built here, mate. Who told you there was?' he asked with a scowl, looking me up and down, as if the very idea of me in a hard hat was ludicrous. I was yet to learn that, with the exception of the anachronistic Surfers Paradise, Australia was far more conscious of environmental matters than the Spanish costas our family had jetted to in the sixties. Today Fraser Island remains much as it was in 1983.

Oh well, Fraser had been another hare-brained adventure. I spent the rest of the day by the beach, tormented by huge flies, and next morning rode back down the rutted sands, unnerved by the expanse of inky blue Pacific to my left. Was that any sort of place to earn a living as a commercial diver?

Back in Sydney, the Darlinghurst Job Shop offered another promising opportunity: abalone diver. Once I worked out what an abalone was, I went for an interview in a scruffy fish shed in Pyrmont on Sydney Harbour. Unlike in Eurong, here I was warmly welcomed – a bad sign. While the job may have been a form of commercial diving, it wasn't as straightforward as it appeared. I was expected to buy a dinghy with an outboard and a hookah surface-air-supply rig. Then, providing someone tended that, I'd spend the day collecting molluscs off the Victorian sea bed and they'd buy them off me by the kilo.

'We sell the shells to make buttons, see. Your finest shirts from Savile Row will be made with abalone buttons.' He showed me the pearlescent shell which I'd seen used as ashtrays as a kid. I calculated the whole complication of setting myself up as a button diver, but something wasn't right. They may well have used abalone-shell buttons on fancy shirts, but I suspected the hitherto unmentioned meat was where the real money lay. I walked away from that one.

I really needed to get working so figured it was time to fall back on what I knew best: being a postman on a motorbike. I located what looked like a professional outfit, but as at Grosvenor, their fixed radios didn't match my six-volt DR250. So I took a haircut part-exchanging that for a silver Suzuki GSX400, a characterless mini UJM. The plan was to get stuck into a few months' despatching in sunny Sydney and shore up some wonga.

I was given a company-branded bomber jacket, over which there was no discussion, and then spent a few days struggling with radio problems while picking jobs up here and there before I realised despatching downunder wasn't the same fast-paced game it was in London. The lion's share of the work went to the vans, most often heading to the airport at Botany Bay for the quickest link to Australia's other main cities. Melbourne and Brisbane were further from Sydney than Glasgow was from London, and there were no interstate motorways then. In Sydney, bikes took up the slack and it just wasn't that busy. With little will on their part to sort out the radio, within a fortnight I handed it back, along with their poncey jacket.

While the GSX400 languished in the classifieds, I took myself back up the coast on a pilgrimage to Coffs Harbour, halfway to Byron Bay. Coffs was famous for its commercial banana plantations, but also as a place where a chap might score some magic mushrooms. Their effects were similar to LSD, but had the benefit of being a wholesome organic entity, not a blotter or a pill possibly dosed with rat poison or squid hormones. Trying to fund my training as a commercial diver was the day job, but I was still fascinated by my recent discovery of mind-bending psychedelics. If nothing else, they represented excellent value for money.

Soon after I'd arrived in Sydney, a bloke who'd made a pop video for the band Mental as Anything put me on to a series of books by Carlos Castaneda, a California-based anthropologist. Castaneda's books purported to describe his early sixties encounters with a Yaqui shaman in the Sonoran Desert of northern Mexico. The first title, *The Teachings of Don Juan: A Yaqui Way of Knowledge*, had originally been published in 1968 as an anthropological thesis but soon become a cult hit outside the academic community. Along with Castaneda's other books, it was now an essential part of the druggy canon, which also included Tom Wolfe's *The Electric Kool-Aid Acid Test* and Kerouac's *On the Road*. Timothy Leary's *The Psychedelic Experience: A Manual Based on The Tibetan Book of the Dead* was aimed at the scholarly seeker, while for your shameless, drug-fuelled rampage, you couldn't beat Hunter S Thompson's *Fear and Loathing in Las Vegas*. Pretty soon I'd read most of them and more besides.

Castaneda's *Teachings* reported on his paranormal experiences under the influence of psychotropic plants like peyote and datura, prepared by his mentor, the enigmatic Don Juan. Once you accepted the astonishing notion that, not only was your generation not the first to discover sex and rock and roll, but drugs too, it soon became clear that humans had been using mind-altering substances for a long, long time. This was great news as it meant getting out of your head now had a botanical and cultural legitimacy. It also brought up questions as to why ingesting the food of the gods had become illegal at all in Western society, while other equally enjoyable but more harmful drugs were not.

By the time I found Castaneda, he'd already become a controversial figure. Firstly, as a scientist, Castaneda had crossed the line and become involved with his subjects rather than studying them. And secondly, was any of it even true? Soon, equally scholarly works like de Mille's *The Don Juan Papers* attempted to discredit Castaneda. But mumbo jumbo has never stopped people believing what they want to believe. At that time, many were seeking out gurus in India and the ancient wisdom gleaned from Don Juan's mashed-cactus equivalent was swallowed whole as an alternative religion, even if the shaman's apprentice eventually proved to be a charlatan.

Castaneda cashed in and spun out sequels and trequels to his Don Juan adventures, until he boxed himself in with the fourth title, *Tales of Power*, claiming that Don Juan bequeathed his *nagual* or savant powers to the author before transmuting into cosmic dust and heading for the stars. By now perhaps feeling the heat, Castaneda withdrew from public life while the royalties flooded in, and it wasn't until 2006 that a BBC documentary, *Carlos Castaneda, Tales from the Jungle*, revealed how the author had been sucked up the vortex of his own messianic cult. Straight from the pages of the *Cult Leader's Handbook*, he'd surrounded himself with a devoted harem of boyish blondes who'd obediently cut themselves off from their families in exchange for the promise of his immortality. (They, presumably, would have to die like the rest of us). By the nineties he'd resurfaced as the founder of New Age energy channelling workshops, but in 1998 his promise of eternal life failed him and soon after his death, his retinue of brainwashed tomboys all disappeared, possibly in a pre-arranged suicide pact.

All this Yaqui gossip had yet to pass as I rolled into the fuel servo at Coffs Harbour. A guy a bit younger than me came out and was quickly identified as a likely source.

'Howdy, d'you know where I can get some mushrooms round here?' You could do this in Australia. They liked the direct approach.

'What, you mean like gold tops?'

'Yeah.'

'Come back when I lock up around seven and we'll sort you out.'

I rocked up at the allotted time and the guy was waiting in a ute with a couple of mates.

'Follow us. We'll go up to Beacon Hill for a few cones.'

A cone, as I soon I found out, was the pipe part of a home-made bong loaded with local weed which grew on the hippie outstations around Nimbin.

'You've got your "head cone" to get you out of bed in the morning, right up to a "party cone" to knock out the whole room. Don't you have cones in Pommieland?'

An explanation followed about the UK practice of rolling joints with hash and tobacco.

'Never tried hash. They say you can get Leb down in Sydney. Smoking tobacco though – that sounds gross! You up for some 'shrooms then?'

'OK. How many do I need?'

'Oh, I reckon six will do ya.'

'Fuck off,' chipped in another. 'He'll need at least twenty if he wants to get off his face.'

'Don't listen to fuckbrain here. Last time, they found him whacking off inside the Big Banana, howling like a fuckin' dingo. Was on the front of *The Advocate* and all. What a fuckin' dill.'

As another cone was prepared, they handed me the mushy brown caps one by one. I had the feeling they were watching me, waiting for something good to happen, but when I didn't oblige promptly, we all went our separate ways.

'Seeya, mate. Don't do anything I wouldn't do.'

'Thanks, but.'

Night had fallen and, a bit woozy from the dope, I got on the GS and rode slowly back into town, which by now was as deserted as a film set. I was looking for a safe place to ride out the trip, should it happen, when suddenly I was hoisted up by the belt and separated from my body. Breaking away from the group must have unleashed the drug's suppressed effects. The shamen had flung me into the flooded caldera and it was now time to start swimming for my life. With day-to-day reason slipping away fast, I managed to park the bike without causing a scene. Next thing I knew I was prostrate behind a tree at the back of the town park, staked out like an Apache hostage in my psilocybin rapture.

The Suzuki got ditched at another galling loss and that was the end of my biking downunder, but I wasn't finished with Australia. Odd jobs for friends of friends came and went and, as I'd been engaged in a kind of love triangle in which I was the outlying isosceles constituent, it was better for all if I got on the road. A cheap car was the practical solution.

In Australia driving was regarded as a necessity, not a privilege to be discouraged. To take the test you simply booked a date at the nearest motor registry office. No months of waiting like back home, with the certainty you'd fail the first couple of goes. I'd not driven a car since trying Richard's Morris along the Embankment four years earlier, but had access to a Wolsey 24/80 automatic that was nearly as old as me. Borrowing it for the test, I recall the examiner tensing up in her seat and clutching the cracked leather armrest as I slung the six-cylinder around like it was a DR250 instead of the lumbering four-wheeled aquarium it actually was. We stopped at a junction and the unnerved examiner croaked in a pallid voice, 'I don't think you're quite ready to drive, Mr Scott. Do you mind dropping me off here, I can walk back.' And before I could reply, the passenger door slammed shut and a car behind me was tooting. Darn, my cavalier road craft had let me down: perhaps I'd been practising with the wrong sorts of cones. Problem was, legally I could only drive around on L-plates with a licensed passenger.

Back at the Kings Cross hostel I'd made friends with Mullet, a nutty Scottish lowlife who'd tried to sell me a lock-picking kit with an accompanying Xeroxed manual. 'Trust me, bro, best hundred bucks you'll ever spend.'

We scrutinised my UK bike licence, which was identical to a car one but for the key letter codes demarking 'motor car, track-laying vehicle, steam engine'. The categories read like they'd been designated by some stuffy committee soon after the requirement for a red-flag front-walker had been dropped.

'Ah tell ye wha' Mullet'd do. Rough that thing up on a brick wall till ye cannae read the group categories. Then tell the bint at the rego ye fell off yer bike on yer arse, it got all scuffed and the cops told ya to get an NSW licence, quick. Ye don't wanna be caught without a licence, especially up north. It's the fuckin' Deep South up there.'

I followed Mullet's advice, disfigured my licence and limped convincingly into the rego office with my sorry tale of sliding down the street with the thing in my back pocket. The lady behind the counter examined my document, but she was no fool. She assumed I was just some young drongo trying to snatch a motorbike licence on the sly, bikes being seen as frivolous death traps alongside sensible and essential cars. She would, she said, only replace my road-rashed document with a full car licence. Thank you, Mrs!

For a few hundred dollars I bought a Holden Torana, an Australian-built Vauxhall Viva, and early one morning staggered out of the city in fits and starts while getting to grips with the pedals and the stick. By the time I got to northern Queensland I'd mastered this driving lark. I picked up a string of jobs planting sugar cane or picking veg for a fiver an hour and after a couple of months settled down with other pickers and bums at a campsite called Molongle Beach near Ayr.

I spent the evenings chatting with an old commie called Red Ken who lived in his box-bodied 40-series Land Cruiser. Soon Phil turned up, fresh out of jail but long separated from his wife and kids, who he missed. Phil transformed into a charming and funny individual once he got drunk – another interesting life lesson. Catch him sober and he was just another grouchy banana bender. One cicada-chirping night, halfway through a slab of Foster's, Phil gave me a tip about picking up a stash of Thai sticks from a guy out of Townsville.

'Best weed you can get your hands on, son. Nothing like the home-grown Zombie shit you get here. This stuff is pure head. They feed the leaves to the pigs.'

I got as far as meeting the bloke up the coast near Ingham where the stuff came ashore. All I had to do was buy a bail, drive it down south and I'd triple my money. The previous year I'd nearly fallen for a similar proposition on my way back from Morocco, but the idea of me succeeding in this enterprise here seemed even more far-fetched. What was I going to do, set up a stall at Sydney's Paddington Market?

I had a better idea. A middle-aged couple from Victoria, Mal and Denise, had recently turned up at the campsite in a Ford camper. With the kids grown up, they'd sold up, outfitted the F150 and now supplemented their savings by gold prospecting. They'd just spent a few weeks panning on the Palmer River in the ranges behind Cooktown and were now resting up. Most weeks they only found a couple of hundred bucks' worth, but had stories of others who'd struck it rich.

What a great country this was, where an ordinary suburban couple could offload the house, hit the road and pan gold for living. In England they'd be lucky to get a seat at the bingo hall. I'd clearly be as talented at gold digging as I would at abalone fishing, prawn trawling or buffalo hunting, but the very idea that such pioneering opportunities were still out here was thrilling. What a shame I was putting a permanent crick in my back picking peppers – some days red, some days green, some days a bit of both.

I was still set on getting trained as a commercial diver and was gutted I couldn't even afford to dive the fabulous Barrier Reef, which up there was a costly day's journey offshore. My working visa had long since expired, but what was the worse they'd do at the airport – send me to Australia on a convict ship? Still, the longer I stayed the worse it might get, maybe even a fine, so I decided to cut my losses, return to London and do what I knew best. I'd put my head down, despatch for a year then head to Texas for my ticket.

Before I left Molongle Beach I bought an ounce of Palmer River gold off Mal and Denise. It was all kosher, he had proper scales and got the day's price – 450 bucks – from the newspaper. The gold dust slid silently into a 35mm film canister. The very next day news came in that a Korean Air flight had gone down over the Sea of Japan on its way from Anchorage to Seoul. A faulty autopilot had apparently sent it too far north over the Kamchatka peninsula and, with a USAF spy plane also thought to be in the area, KAL 007 got shot down by a Soviet Sukhoi jet. With a bit of luck the shocking incident might give the price of gold a bit of a spike just before the outbreak of WWIII.

Although few knew this at the time, late 1983 was the year when the two tribes came as close to having it out as during the better-known Cuban Missile Crisis of 1962. Reagan had already made his provocative 'evil empire' speech and NASA's space shuttle launch had spooked the Russians into thinking they could be bombed from space. A few weeks after KAL 007, Soviet satellites mistakenly interpreted clouds as five incoming ICBMs launched from silos in Montana. Luckily, the operator in his Siberian bunker hesitated before retaliating as instructed, and so we still breathe today. Now Pershings were heading for Greenham while Soviet General Secretary Andropov lay bed-ridden and on the verge of death.

As the world balanced on a blade of grass, with my ounce of raw gold I'd stumbled on a foolproof money-making scheme, a foot up for my diving ticket. And it didn't require being mauled by sharks in the Bass Strait, crippled by seasonal vegetables, or caught by the notorious Queensland cops with a bootful of pungent Thai weed. I visualised myself smugly walking into a gold dealer's in London's Hatton Garden with my irresistible trove. 'Howdy. Got an ounce of finest Palmer River alluvial from Australia. Interested?' You bet they'd be.

What I hadn't grasped was that, unless I became an overnight master goldsmith, the economic advantage had been made by Mal and Denise in panning the sweltering banks of the Palmer River. The market price for a troy ounce of gold was the same in Molongle Beach, Queensland as it was in Hatton Garden, EC1, New York's 47th Street or the Magnetic North Pole. Maybe that's what they mean by 'gold fever': your reason takes a nap. Unaware of all this, I took down my $20 tent, loaded up the Torana, said goodbye to those I knew and headed back down the Bruce Highway. I'd just enough cash to get to Sydney, the car ought to cover a flight home, and at least I had a glittering souvenir of my sputtering Australian adventure.

A couple of days later, somewhere south of Rockhampton, the Torana coughed a couple of times and died. I wasn't so far from Fraser Island, but that episode was better forgotten too. Steam spewed from under the bonnet where the thing behind the radiator fan was making bad noises. I got a lift into a town and returned in a recovery truck.

'Water pump for a '73 Torana? Dunno if they make 'em any more. Might take a week to get one.'

My banger was becoming a liability. A while back the brakes had gone and replacing the fluid with engine oil had been a costly gaffe. The wipers were on strike and the day before I'd ruined two tyres while giving some loser a lift to visit his estranged family in Dysart. They argued. He stormed off then got kicked out drunk from the town's bar.

The car was supposed to be my plane ticket home. I calculated the cost of hanging around as well as what might break next, then struck the best deal I could with garage man, whose daughter needed a cheap runabout. With just enough money to see me out, there was nothing for it but to cash in my gold. I took one last picture of my stash, then regretfully sent it to the Perth Mint in WA. A cheque would be waiting for me in Sydney. Once their commission was factored in, my gold dealing cost me $50. One final banana skin flung at my feet. It had all been a bit of a disaster, this fortune-seeking caper in the land downunder. But it ended on a high, as well as a sign of things to come.

One time in the west Sydney suburb of Parramatta, I passed Maxim Cycles and there in the spring sunshine shone a white and red XT600Z Yamaha Ténéré. I crouched down and noted the many improvements over my Saharan XT500 shed. The intervening XT550 had been nothing special, even with its monoshock back end, but here on the Ténéré, Yamaha had ticked all the boxes. A huge, thirty-litre tank would easily give a 300-mile range, especially with the 550's two-stage carb. Folding brake and gear levers – check; DID rims – nice; front disc brake – check; plush seat; twelve-volt electrics; big bash plate, the list went on. One day I might just get me one of these and ride it to the actual Ténéré Desert.

Killing time in a south Sydney hostel before the plane home, I got to know a young Dutch couple. Come the evening we'd sit in their room, watching MTV and rolling spliffs. The Ozzie band Icehouse came on: 'Hey little girl'. I liked that one and I realised I quite fancied the pretty Dutch girl too. Actually it was not such a revelation – that's why I was there. The spliff got passed around and a few vids later Billy Idol – a peroxide Eddie Kidd – snarled across the screen with 'White Wedding', which I also liked. Tonight I just liked everything. In the video he rocks up at a church on a Kawasaki 750 Ltd custom. You wouldn't catch Sting riding one of those. A virginal bride arrives in a limo, babes strut around in skin-tight leather, a coffin lid gets hammered shut, the wedding ring draws blood. We get the message. Then a toaster explodes, a kettle explodes – the whole darn kitchen goes up as bridey prances around like a zombie. Message received, Billy-o, five by five. It was all going so well until our man erupted from the stained-glass window above the altar on his Jap cruiser, a preposterous stunt that would almost certainly have got him killed. What next, give the Kawa the soundtrack of an RM125?

Dutch girl's bloke was very shy, almost catatonic in fact. It was just the sort of lucky break my romancing needed. But the reason behind his thousand-yard stupor was no joke. It turned out he too had been a Castanista. One night he'd scored some datura, howled like a dog till the sun came up and was never the same again.

'Hey, Chris, shotgun?' asked Dutch girl with a smile.

'What? Oh, yes, OK then.'

Someone invited me to a warehouse party in Pyrmont. Or should I say, I was told there'd be a girl there selling acid. On arrival I made my way upstairs and mingled with the hipsters chinking glasses against a brickwork backdrop. It wasn't really my scene but when acid girl showed up we spent some time chatting on the fire escape on the off chance there'd be a rapport. It didn't take too long for that notion to shrivel on the vine so I paid up, popped the unusually large ochre-coloured pill and headed into the city of the red night.

By the time I reached Hyde Park in downtown Sydney, the murals there were beginning to shimmer promisingly, but something seemed different. I had a spring in my step and a sense of impending, surging euphoria. I wandered into an all-night cafe on William Street, an act which seemed unusually bold in my state, even if at that time of night I was probably a routinely shitfaced customer. No one served me, which kicked off a flurry of paranoia. Only later, when I happened to glance at myself in a mirror (no reverse-dolphin effects this time) did I jump back from a crimson face fixed with pupils the size of drawing pins.

Around dawn I found myself plugged into my Walkman and leaning against a tree in Rushcutters Bay Park, close to where it had all begun nine months earlier. Despite all the missteps, I was fizzing with elation, a satisfying sense of what they now call closure and self-acceptance. It wasn't until years later that it dawned on me that what I was on that night was MDMA, which in tablet form would become better known as Ecstasy.

That drug had been rediscovered by Californian marriage-guidance counsellors in the seventies, when what was originally called 'Empathy' was found to produce 'the pharmacological equivalent of love'. Shoring up a shaky marriage with a serotonin rush doesn't sound like a permanent solution, but by the end of the eighties, E imitated motorcycles in the UK and also went recreational. The tabloids embraced a new moral panic with open arms as millions of kids got higher than the sun at dance raves across the country.

Twenty years later when the fad had passed, not least due to the proliferation of adulterated pills, a BBC radio documentary bent over backwards to be even-handed about the drug. It dragged up the case of a pothead and former raver whose memory and concentration were completely shot. This guy sounded like a mess and E was the culprit. But then he admitted he'd taken a staggering 40,000 tablets over a nine-year period. Perhaps unintentionally, the programme reinforced the fact that moderation is key and that E was probably the most enjoyable and least harmful drug of all. MDMA is now being considered as an effective remedy against PTSD, although my experience did illustrate the riskiness of buying pills from strangers. It might not have been such a fantastic night had I been in the mood for an E but been sold LSD.

15

OCCASIONAL XS AND FEELING THE PRESSURE

Honda CB250RS, Yamaha XS650

Back in London, the Gower Street squat was still going and there was a room to spare. After dicking about in Australia for most of 1983, I was keen to get back to some proper work, so I signed up at an outfit called Superbear, round the back of Victoria Station. It was run by Hugh, a cocky young entrepreneur who had the use of the whole building and lived upstairs. He had an anorexic-looking wife who helped out but whose nerviness was made worse by the way Hugh treated her.

Reluctant to get bogged down in bike ownership after my losses in Sydney, I was happy to rent one of Superbear's CB250RSs for the time being. Had they loaned out CXs or 400/4s, I'd have gone elsewhere, but the chance to ride one of Honda's cheeky RSs was a big incentive. Giro had had one in Muswell Hill, a light, economical and nimble machine using the four-valve engine from the popular XL-S trail bike. Each exhaust port had its own slender pipe spreading into an elegant megaphone which produced a pleasing blat. The square-profiled alloy rims evoked Akront or Borrani hoops from a sixties cafe racer, and the flat bars and rear-set pegs enhanced that impression. Best of all, the whole rig clocked in some 80lb less than a 250 Super Dream, whose contemporary Eurostyling was about the only thing the two 250s shared. The only swarf in the oil pan was that these original RSs had no button, and swinging the kickstart required folding up the rear-set footrest. Fine for a twice-a-day commute, but a right pain for despatching.

It was great to be on a bike and back at work, doing what I knew well, and with a set goal to cash up and get myself to Houston. The coming winter would as usual thin out the workforce, with a commensurate increase in earnings. I got to rushing about as I had in my early days, scooping up all the work that was going, and occasionally nipping home for a snack and a brew.

As long as you didn't push it too hard, the RS was a great little machine. It was low, slim and light, which in town trans-lated to less fatigue when maintaining momentum. One day I discovered just how light that build was when tearing past Centrepoint into Tottenham Court Road. A taxi did what taxis do, and as I swerved to avoid it, I rode over the twin kerbs of a traffic island, startling a couple of hat-and-coat provincials taking refuge from the melee while trying to reach the Adelphi for a matinee. All in a day's work on an XT5, but although the RS continued up the road with undamaged wheels, the shock of the impact had ripped the front downtube from the head-stock. I'd achieved a career first: writing a bike off without actually falling off or blowing up a motor.

The crippled Honda was returned to base and replaced, but a few weeks later I totalled that one too, this time by ramming a stationary CX500 innocently parked by the roadside in Hyde Park. Its rider, who worked for Dunhill in Mayfair, was having a contractually required fag break when a crashing noise alerted him to a pillock flying backwards over his toppling bike. After months in CX-free Australia, perhaps the sight of a maggot's hindquarters had flipped some kamikaze switch in me. Or maybe it was just a bizarre case of target fixation, not unlike my Capper Street crash or Nick's XT500 bus-plant. I'll never know and indeed it was better not to dwell on the real cause, but my hand and wrist were as mangled as the front of the RS.

I also had a harmless head wound bleeding down my face, which helped catch someone's eye at St Mary's Hospital, nearby. On the ward a short time later, a contented morphine coma laid me out. The dreamy imagery of 'Golden Brown' came to mind, for I was now a connoisseur of all narcotic phenomena. When I awoke, my left arm was in plaster, with metal spikes protruding from fractures in the wrist and another rammed down into the marrow of my middle finger. Each spike was topped with a helpful NHS cork to avoid snagging.

Hugh at Superbear was amazingly understanding about my fleet-wrecking exuberance and gave me a job as a telephone controller, my first taste of life behind the counter, chivvying clients and paging riders. It was while spending all day at the desk that I noticed Hugh frequently nipping upstairs to his flat. Ten minutes later he'd pop back in a state of what can only be described as enhanced agitation, as if he'd just given himself a blowback enema with a Sherbet Fountain. Although I'd not tried that celebrated stunt myself, it dawned on me that his arousal was more probably brought on by a line of coke disappearing up his hooter at twice the speed limit. By the mid-eighties cocaine was becoming a popular drug, but still at around £60 a gram, it was predominantly associated with the rich, famous and upwardly mobile, or those who aspired to being such things. People like Hugh.

'Superbear, canIhelpyou?' he'd blurt into his headset, a nanosecond after the switchboard light had blinked. Simultaneously he'd dart a glance my way and whisper loudly, 'Chris, Chris – line six is going. Is Four Zero POB yet? Line six! Line six!' Then to his headset, 'Yaaah, Persephone, haaaaii. Sure. Yep…yep… yep. Got a rider right round the corner. He'll be there in three minutes. Ciao, bye.'

With the plaster cast removed and following the supposed benefits of ultrasound physiotherapy, my wrist regained some articulation and a few weeks later the off-putting pins were yanked out like sore teeth. My clutch hand was coming back, so my thoughts turned to what bike #27 might be.

Graham at the squat was a long-time fan of Yamaha's XS650 twin, which, when I was seventeen, had been a contender alongside the Bonneville. Now came word of an XS for sale up the Angel. A '75 XS650B for just £100. Even then, that was a good price and we weren't talking about the execrable XS650 Special either. That was another great bike that got lost to the oxymoronic 'factory custom' fad which ruined many a Jap bike from the late seventies onwards. Even the CD200, Benlyman's successor to my previous 185, suffered a sad-arsed mockchop makeover: high bars, fat seat, teardrop tank, short fat pipes and a fat rear tyre. Fat all round, like the 750 Ltd in that Billy Idol pop vid. Oh, hold on a minute. Didn't my gorgeous US-spec Triumph come with high bars and a teardrop tank? Let's move on.

Fact is, to us purist bikers, the Japanese factory customs were a deeply uncool aberration that had seeped across the Atlantic to pollute our virile British biking scene. Mockchops suited credulous wannabes who regarded Harleys as the definitive exposition of bad-ass two-wheeled rebellion, but who lacked the chutzpah to actually ride a Hog.

One reason this XS was going so cheap was that it was incomplete and in two parts: the front end and most of the rest.

One Saturday morning I walked up to the Angel and wheeled the front-end assembly back home. It was all there, complete with an operating brake to stop me running away with myself down the Pentonville Road, garnering smart-arsed yells from gobby van drivers. ''Ere, mate, you lost the back of yer bike!'

Yamaha's original XS1 twin came out in 1969, based on a motor designed by an obscure Japanese manufacturer that had got swallowed up by the expanding Yamaha corporation. Unlike most British twins of the era, the XS was unit construction: motor and gearbox housed in one horizontally split and oil-tight crankcase. In the US the XS motor's potential got quickly spotted as a flat tracker, and in 1974 in the hands of Kenny Roberts it was the only Japanese motor to briefly break the dominance of Harley's XR750 on US ovals. On the dirt mile, though, Roberts was better remembered for his heroic efforts in trying to control the berserker TZ750.

As was the fashion with the Japs, the XS side panels bragged 'OHC' (overhead cam); no antiquated pushrods here, old chap. In its prime the XS650 was regarded as the best Japanese take on the classic British parallel twin, most probably because it came out just as the British era began to fade. For a couple of years in the mid-seventies, Honda squeezed out the anodyne CB500T, then Kawasaki produced a more convincing Z750. But alongside the Bonneville and the Commando, neither of those had the impact of the XS.

By the time I'd got my hands on the XS it was already a relic. Yamaha were producing the XJ650 Turbo and FJ11 cheese-cutters. But with the engine intact and probably running, reassembly was within my Lego-certified capabilities, just like with the BMW the previous year. The front end was reattached to the headstock and Nick suggested a radical rewiring strategy which greatly reduced the spaghetti element. A single live wire ran from the battery to the headlamp and everything fed off that and was earthed to the nearest bit of frame. Or something like that. Whatever, it had the required effect of creating a spark at the plugs and that great moment came when a reassembly of the inert motorcycle gets kicked into life. A meaty growl rose from the beaten-up two-into-one, which filled the room with sweet-tasting fumes.

The XS was still incomplete but there was enough there to take it for a ride. Out on the street it ran like it looked, a rugged twin with a solid feel that suggested it could shrug off being ridden over a double kerb or into the back of a CX500. The original XSs handled terribly, like so many early-seventies Jap bikes, but by the time my B-model cropped up, with a braced frame and proper tyres, they held the road well enough. One of my most cherished biking memories is a ride I took down to Cornwall and then up to North Wales. There was a moment on the way back to London, somewhere in Shropshire or the Chilterns, where a green vale rolled away to the south. I sat behind the wide, flat-track bars as the XS rumbled along, planted on the road like a 'stomach full of stout', as *Bike* once put it (or perhaps that was lunch). Everything felt right – the engine, seating position and weather all combined to create another one of those cherished memories which gets tempered into a rosy, lifelong bond with a given machine.

Much of my time reassembling the XS is associated with speed. Not running the Westway in pre-Gatso revelry, but snorting up powdery crystals with David Byrne or Tom Waits on the cassette. At Superbear I made friends with a guy called ChrisTom, a laid-back guy who didn't take the job so seriously that he smashed up bikes every fortnight. ChrisTom was a regular visitor to our squat and also something of a speed-head and general procurer. With so much more to explore, it seemed a shame not to sample his wares.

Once wired up on amphetamines, most of the Gower Street crew would head out to the West End's nightclubs where they'd dance and drink themselves into a lather. Just a walk away was the Camden Palace, or there was Heaven in Charing Cross. I tried it once but it wasn't for me – the dancing and drinking that is. I wasn't so much a fish out of water as a haddock crawling, fin-over-fin up a sand dune. But on the way up the effects of whizz produced another wonder of the narcotic firmament. This was more than just something to counter fatigue, it also produced a mental buzz and euphoria I associated with cocaine, but for just £15 a gram.

ChrisTom's finest product was some sinister dark orange crystals resembling Demerara sugar. I don't know if there was ever a legendary strain of whizz known as Tangerine Dream, but that's what we called it. It flew up the schnozzle like warm hickory smoke and had us swinging from the trees and babbling for hours. Many other drugs had this effect of course, but speed was unique in that you could tell what utter crap you were talking as the worthless words tumbled from your lips.

Perhaps because he was getting it cheap, ChrisTom became over-partial to the speed. But for me, the 4am comedown was deterrent enough: the body would be exhausted, but the mind still raced at 5300rpm no matter how much blow you smoked. Yes, it was affordable cocaine, but days afterwards, you paid for it with cold sores and other minor ailments, more so than with other drugs. It wasn't healthy and as a way of getting out of it, speed seemed shallow.

In fact, despite the parental anxieties of 'one puff and you're hooked', even after a couple of years, there was no danger of me becoming addicted to any of it. For me at least it was about feeling different, a temporary change of scenery rather than emigrating. A couple of trips a year were as much as my brain could handle and probably enough for a lifetime. It only takes one visit behind the looking glass to modify your world view, plus a few backups to make sure you weren't dreaming. The same went for dope: who wanted to be stoned all the time or even every few days? Moderation with occasional XS.

That December another wave of IRA bombs struck London, but unless you were directly involved, it was usual to shrug off these events as part of London living. Many more people were worried about the nuclear threat. In October, just before the American cruise missiles were due to arrive at Greenham Common, there'd been a million-strong CND march. Around that time the TV movie *The Day After* had been viewed by record audiences across the US. A take on Peter Watkins' uncompromising and long-suppressed 1965 film *The War Game* (said to have inspired John and Yoko's 'bed-in' protest), it depicted an all-too-plausible escalation of events whose inevitable climax was a nuclear strike and immediate counter strike. The consequences were graphically portrayed and chimed with everything we'd been warned about: the collapse of the social order and an unthinkably bleak future for the survivors.

The similar *Threads* set in Sheffield was broadcast in the UK the following year. These weren't your hokey, *Towering Inferno*-type movies or post-apocalyptic revenge fantasies. For all the shortcomings of the period's special effects, these were the real thing and chillingly close to home. And there were no happy endings. The final frame of *Threads* locked on to a girl's horrified face as she saw the presumably deformed baby she'd just given birth to, thirteen years after the nuclear strike. With these horrors now pushed into the open, in July 1985 the BBC finally deemed it safe enough to screen *The War Game*. By then, Gorbachev was on the way in and Reagan's speeches had taken on a more conciliatory tone. It was said that Reagan had also been shocked by *The Day After*. The US had over-estimated the firepower of the Reds and had inadvertently pushed them to breaking point trying to keep up.

In Gower Street we were an apolitical bunch living in our metro-central bubble, vaguely leftish but largely indifferent to contemporary worries and causes. The squat's large

Antipodean element may have had something to do with it. Clearly they'd not crossed half the world to march shoulder to shoulder with the Socialist Workers Party, any more than I'd gone to Australia to fight for Aboriginal land rights.

While I'd not been doing that, the Tories had won a landslide victory on the back of the Falklands effect and a fragmented opposition. Now the Thatcher Machine could really crack on with its agenda, starting with the unions who'd caused so much trouble since the seventies. 'Part of the Union' was the only hit for The Strawbs back in 1973, a satire (or for all I knew, a celebration) of union power, but Thatcher wasn't having any of it. Now, nearly a decade later, her list included abolishing the Labour-controlled Greater London Council (GLC), though you couldn't help feeling this was personal. From his offices in County Hall across the Thames from Parliament, Ken Livingstone, the GLC's mischievously adroit Labour leader, goaded the government with a huge banner enumerating London's unemployed. It was right by the spot where every tourist stopped to snap the classic shot of a double-decker crossing Westminster Bridge with Big Ben in the background. Back in 1978, Ken had made sure that the Huntley Street squatters were rehoused, and in 1981 he'd had the nerve to decline an invitation to the royal wedding, although he'd wished the young couple well. Whether it was just a stunt or he had something better to do that day, it endeared him to those who were similarly indifferent to the spectacle.

With refreshingly plain speech, 'Red Ken' managed to needle the Tories better than most of the Labour windbags, to whom he'd become an embarrassment. The bitterly hostile press found him maddeningly difficult to discredit, so they made scandals up. Even *Private Eye* had to cough up after accusing him of being on the payroll of Gaddafi, the Libyan leader. But what really wound up Livingstone's enemies was his refusal to denounce the political cause of Irish republicanism, while obviously condemning the atrocities the IRA continued to commit. It seems some couldn't see they were two separate things.

By now I'd moved into an empty flat a couple of doors down from the original Gower Street squat, right next to RADA, the drama school. For all of us the benefits of living in the heart of the city were greatly appreciated: the clubbers had their pick of the capital's venues and for me the cinemas of the West End made choosing a film as easy as flicking a TV remote. That year there was plenty to see: *Blade Runner*, *Koyaanisqatsi*, *Fitzcarraldo* and *Countryman*. Many, not least stoner favourite *Countryman*, had soundtracks that lingered long after the popcorn had gone soft. And if there was nothing going in the West End, in the other direction the recently revived Scala Cinema in King's Cross cooked up all sorts of salacious double-bills masquerading as art: *Freaks* with *Eraserhead* was a popular one, along with buxom B-movies from Russ Meyer, zombie trash or avant-garde all-nighters.

There was plenty to enjoy because now my future was wide open. A few weeks after I'd got back from Australia, I'd signed up for a one-day aptitude course at a commercial diving school in Falmouth, Cornwall. I'd learned that British HSE-certified training was costlier and more rigorous than Houston's but would make me more employable in the UK. The timing was good as oil and gas from the North Sea were now on stream. In 1970 the newly discovered Brent and Forties fields became household names as the rush for black gold began. As the BBC drama series *The Troubleshooters* would have it, the oil industry was only a little less exciting than *Stingray* – anything could happen in the next half hour! Its title sequence alone boasted the real-life British techno miracles of the age: Concorde, Harrier jump jets, GP racers, motorboats and hovercraft. None of them got far without oil. The 1973

Oil Crisis and the Iranian Revolution had underlined the need for greater autonomy in energy supply, but exploiting the reserves beneath the treacherous North Sea was costing more than the Apollo space programme. The UK sector alone covered an area bigger than Great Britain and divers were vital to the task of getting and keeping the oil flowing, even if they were hugely expensive.

Down in Falmouth docks I demonstrated my ability to write, add up, turn a wrench and jump twenty feet into a dock and swim it in a drysuit. But when it came to stooping inside a hyperbaric chamber and getting pressurised down to just a hundred feet, I was the only one whose ears wouldn't 'pop' or equalise. With no obvious reason for that, such as a cold, they recommended I get a check-up.

What I found astonishing was that the other young guys on the course weren't adventuresome slackers like me, or even ex-military types attracted to risks for reward. Most were regular blue-collar types who'd lost their jobs in manufacturing or engineering but still had families to feed and mortgages to pay. With the north of England hit hardest by the Tory programme, it proved what dire straits some were in when they had to seriously consider commercial diving as a job.

The best money was in 'saturation diving', which required the diver to remain in a pressurised, nitrogen-free environment for up to four weeks at a time. This was the safest and most economical way of doing things, allowing for a gradual 'desaturation' at the end of the job. Nitrogen, which constitutes about seventy-five per cent of regular breathable air, becomes toxic to humans at pressures in excess of three bar or a hundred feet – the typical limit of recreational scuba at that time. Saturation involved replacing the nitrogen constituent with inert helium, a breathing mixture called 'heliox'. Once pressurised to ten bar or more, the diver's body tissue became saturated with heliox, something it could tolerate without harm.

Sat divers worked in teams of at least three, undertaking basic construction, inspection and maintenance tasks in the subsea environment. Though the oilfields below the North Sea were relatively shallow, they were strung north–south midway between Shetland and Norway, so divers needed suits pumped with hot water to survive. At the end of a day's shift the divers sealed their bell at working pressure and were winched to the surface. Once on the oil rig or ship, the still-pressurised bell was clamped to a more spacious accommodation module at the same working pressure, where the divers could be more easily fed and monitored.

Confined to cramped conditions not unlike a spacecraft, a saturated aquanaut needed a cool head to get by. I thought I could probably manage that, but I wondered if this ear thing was significant. Then, on the train back to London, I came across a small news report while leafing though a discarded *Telegraph*. A day earlier, divers working in the Norwegian sector had been docking onto the deck-top accommodation module where two other divers were resting, when their pressurised bell blew away from the chamber. The result was instant decompression. The four divers' bodies turned to mist and, outside, one of the tenders was also killed. The Byford Dolphin incident turned out to be the worst commercial diving disaster in the North Sea. Twenty-six years later, the initial verdict, of human error by the fatally wounded tender, was reattributed to faulty equipment.

Like space exploration, deep diving was still pushing the limits and urgent commercial demands led to operational flaws and unsafe equipment. I was already aware of the effects of osteonecrosis, the crumbling of joints brought about by the cumulative effects of years of repeated decompression. I knew I had to get rich quick and then get out while my health was still intact.

First though, I booked myself a costly medical with a diving specialist in Harley Street. This revealed everything in order apart from a congenital constriction in the sinuses. I knew
enough about the job to recognise that having dodgy tubes
nixed any hope of my becoming a commercial diver. The diagnosis explained the curtailed hyperbaric test in Falmouth
and, months earlier, the scuba dive in Byron Bay that had left
me headachey and woozy.

Initially I felt affronted that my carefully researched attempt at going straight had been scuppered by a minute
anatomical defect. It was as if the bouncer of destiny had
stepped in front of me and said, 'Sorry, mate, you can't come
in 'ere with those ears.' Up until that point I'd been diligent-
ly working my way through the Submex *Professional Diver's
Handbook*. It now looked like I'd not be exchanging my Bell
Star for one of those cool oral-nasal Kirby Morgan Super-
Lite diving helmets. Instead I resolved to just live day to day
and let dead-end despatching fund the lifestyle, much as I'd
been doing the past few years.

16

HELLO, SUNSHINE?

Honda CD200T

Early in 1984 ChrisTom passed on a tip that a typesetter's in Holborn was looking for an in-house rider. The job's regular hours weren't for him, but recalling Templar's benefits more than the boredom, I popped into Sunshine Typographic off Leather Lane market. There I was interviewed by Bernie, a gruff faux cockney-dun-good who could've doubled for Orson Welles or a portly musketeer. The need to counterbalance his barrel-like belly forced a good posture on Bernie, even if it was combined with breathlessness after the slightest exertion.

'Now look, son. We're not taskmasters 'ere. Just turn up on time and do the job wivaht killin' yerself. We don't wanna be scraping yer brains off the Grays Inn Road, all right? Start Mundy, 8am sharp. See Mo about a bleeper.'

Decoded, that meant, 'Dear boy, I worry for your safety while in our employ but have no way of guaranteeing it. So please be careful. And punctual.'

I had again come up against the despatcher's paradox: boredom, safety and a steady wage versus the swashbuckling adventure of the open circuit with the potential of better earnings as well as all-out carastrophe. Thing was, unless you managed to crack a particularly busy outfit, the safe and boring option was actually more profitable, plus it left time and energy for other activities. It would no longer be a case of flopping exhausted on the bed in all my gear, face caked in filth, to come round at about 11pm and, too tired to cook, shuffling out for a take-away. Sunshine was paying about £300 for an eleven-hour weekday, with up to half of that spent sitting around, either at work or back at the squat.

Bernie was a cheroot-smoking rogue in his mid-forties who'd put in the hours and whatever else was needed to make a success of Sunshine. He was typical of Thatcher's estuarine entrepreneurs, succeeding on his wits and hard work rather than unearned privilege. I never worked out if he was a former criminal and set up Sunshine on the back of that, or if he just had connections in those circles. It was said he kept a shooter under the spare wheel of his Rover SD1, and there was always a steady stream of knocked-off goods coming through the office. For a lot less than they cost at Argos, I got my mum one of those fancy TVs with a built-in VHS slot, and a new-fangled microwave oven.

Once in a while Bernie's brassy wife popped into the studio when on an errand in town. A big-haired, fake-tanned Essex matriarch perched on her white high heels, did she know Bernie was having it off with Mo, the company secretary? Perhaps she did, but then she in turn may well have been having it off with the bloke at the health club.

Bernie's co-director was Gordon, the ruddy-faced, silver-haired creative maestro who sat in the prime corner spot, where natural light flooded in from both windows. Gordon spent his day meticulously cutting and pasting copy with the aid of a scalpel, a steel rule, Spray Mount and Ronson's lighter fuel. With his posh diction, he was not of the East End geezer class, and Bernie appreciated this as it gave Sunshine a little cachet. This was 'cachet' very much not pronounced like 'Datchet' in the Shires west of London, from where Gordon commuted in his Golf GTi convertible. In 1984 the VW was hottest of the hatches and marked out Gordon as a certain type of successful man. He wasn't a bragger, but frequently came in expressing amazement at the GTi's astounding performance down the A40. He lived alone and made regular visits to Thailand, which raised unspoken suspicions. But Gord was Bernie's business partner and mate and therefore under his protection. He could do what he liked on his holidays.

Quarantined in his own annexe at the other end of the studio was Sean, strapped to his humming Computron typesetting machine. If every office has a scapegoat, then poor old Sean was Sunshine's, on account of being scruffy, Irish, henpecked and taking extended lunches at the Hat and Tun pub off Hatton Garden. Around 2.30, a ruddy-cheeked Sean would shuffle back in his saggy-arsed cords, knowing that afternoons were quiet. He knocked off at 3pm anyway. But he handled his Computron like Errol Flynn handled his sword; let them sack him if they dared.

'Oh ho ho, it's the Sean! Thanks for droppin' in, mate. Nice lunch, Sean, wuzzit? Wadja 'ave? Scotch egg 'n' chips?' Gerry the officer manager would taunt.

Keith was Sunshine's rep and, like Mick back at Templar, had that chummy, shoulder-shuffling 'orwite mait' bonhomie born of deep self-admiration. With a windproof perm-and-goatee combo set off by his designer Reactolite Rapide specs, Keith drove his black 5-series BMW the mile and a half to Soho to bring in the work from the agencies. More than Gordon and like most reps, Keith's status and self-image were closely tied to his wheels. Whatever the Beemer cost to run, in his game it was imperative to be seen in the right sort of car, even if it spent most of the day in a traffic jam or a car park. In the mid-eighties a big BMW was the prize every such professional aspired to.

Quiet Dave from Watford manned the darkroom dutifully, but his mind was elsewhere – and not particularly on his Ford Orion. As the months progressed, he let me run off prints and experiment with avant-garde photographic techniques that foresaw the work of the sheep-dipping Young British Artists who'd emerge a couple of years later. One of my most provocative photo-compositions was an A3 sheet on which I'd finger-daubed a trio of flying mallards getting blasted to smithereens by a blunderbuss. It was a punk's tribute to the popular wall ornament that embodied mind-numbing seventies TV sitcoms like *George and Mildred*. Years later, I was amused to see that the cover of Stuart (Angry Brigade) Christie's memoir, *Granny Made Me an Anarchist*, carried a very similar image.

The atmosphere at Sunshine was soured by Gerry, the office manager whose job it was to oversee the day's output, bag it up, and when enough had built up, send me out to deliver it. He exhibited a slimy, awkward insincerity, and his stillborn humour and unrequited enquiries often fell like excess coleslaw on the workplace arena. It wasn't helped by his Brotherhood of Man haircut and dress sense: lapels fit for an aircraft carrier, a sleeveless cardie and close-fitting, high-waisted polyester flares. He was the one I dealt with most but liked least.

There was some pleasure to be had when Gerry had to answer the phone with 'Hello, Sunshine?' Gordon would snigger in the corner, as if the naming of the company had been one big joke. It was an even merrier morning many months later when news broke that Reactolite Keith had caught Gerry shagging his missus. Keith may well have been chucking it about like Bernie (or at least fondly visualising himself doing so), but knocking off a colleague's wife? That was deeply dishonourable conduct, for which Gerry was sacked immediately. For a couple of hundred quid, Bernie could have had Gerry roughed up as well. All Keith had to do was say the word.

Instead of slouching by my desk, picking over *The Sun* or *Puzzler Magazine*, I tormented my monoxide-withered intellect by tackling stimulating but sometimes difficult books by Erich Fromm, Roland Barthes and William Burroughs, or Judith Williamson's *Ideology and Meaning in Advertising*. Fromm went down pretty well, but I was often staggered that an entire page, chapter or even an entire book like Debord's *Society of the Spectacle* could be composed of grammatically correct but still frankly impenetrable sentences. 'The spectacle is capital to such a degree of accumulation that it becomes an image' or, put another way, 'The spectacle does not realise philosophy, it philosophises reality'. This wasn't like the good old days on Molongle Beach, reflexively brushing ants out of my tent while leafing through Castaneda, Martin Amis or JP Donleavy. I was pushing the limits now, unravelling the meaning of meaning, but often finding it meaningless.

'Ass a funny ol' book ya readin' der, Cwis? Thee Ana'omy ov 'Uman Dee-Struktivnis. What, ya gonna turn inta da new Rippa? Ha-ha-ha-ha.' Gerry's staccato chuckle was like having one of Gordon's scalpels pushed under your fingernails, not that anyone in the studio took any notice.

Day by day my mind was pummelled like dough in its quest to unravel existential enigmas. Egged on by the drugs, I explored other uncharted avenues in the name of lifestyle research. I attempted to dye my hair blond like Sting or Debbie Harry. The result was an embarrassing amber resembling Jasper Carrott or an RNLI lifeboat. Meanwhile, my clothing took on a ragged Maxian scowl, but without the dangling ammo, even if under it all was a simple South London boy, sliding down the road alongside his moped.

Right from that early camo-and-duvet era, I was on a mission to find the ultimate motorcycling jacket: one that married biking function with a precise look I tried so carelessly to articulate. Back then I'd bonded with a peeling brown-leather pelt picked up at Camden Market, which a controller once gratifyingly described as resembling a Yugoslav partisan's coat. To me it was very *Ill Met by Moonlight*; to others it was something hauled from a skip after the dogs had finished with it. As the buttons fell off one by one, I customised it with a big wetsuit zip, topped the collar with a nappy pin and fitted the sleeves with bedroll straps to cinch up for high-speed assignments. I loved that coat right up to the day I stuffed it into my squat's fireplace in an unrehearsed bid for sartorial regeneration.

Not all my early clothing choices were so successful. A gentle old hippy called Vince had slipped into one of the Gower Street empties. He was at least a decade older than us and our smart-arsed jibes sometimes hurt, proving that despite his smackhead's nasal whine, a shred of self-esteem survived. To ChrisTom and me, Vince had a highly decorated drug vet's glamour: wounded in action but still up for the fight. Once in a while he'd bat himself a speedball, a mixture of heroin and cocaine which yanked his muddled central nervous system in both directions and left him dangling in the middle, relaxed yet agitated. Or so I imagined. Speedballing sounded a little too depraved for me, too much like getting smashed for the sake of it, rather than exploring the intricate wormholes of the cosmos with LSD or good hash.

Somewhere along the way Vince had acquired what looked like a genuine Wehrmacht officer's black leather greatcoat. Tailored and styled with an elegance for which the Nazis were noted, in a moment of weakness (and before I discovered the Balkan look), I persuaded Vince to part with the coat for a speedball's ransom. Weighing at least twenty pounds, this thing was built to outlast the Reich. A thick rubberised canvas lining kept out the weather and there was even a Luger-shaped holster-pocket on the left breast for brisk return of fire when ambushed by scruffy Yugoslav Resistance fighters. Cunningly too, the separate leg sections could be pinned round each leg, for riding motorcycles, or perhaps astride an officer's cherished Arab stallion while on leave with his mistress at his Baltic villa.

I tried out my new *Überzieher* aboard the XS on a cross-country run; it proved impervious to the weather, even if it was a little like wearing a leather tent. But ambling down to the West End on a chilly evening to see a film, with acres of leather swishing around my ankles, the tang of the Gestapo and the *Hakenkreuz* became too strong. While I was never actually set upon by the Anti Nazi League, neither fancy-dress irony nor functionality was excuse enough. Laurence Corner and other less theatrical surplus outlets may have given us lifestyle despatchers and the likes of Adam Ant an appreciation of ex-military workwear. But pretending that submarine-grade drysuits made superb motorcycling waterproofs, or adopting Waffen-SS greatcoats as natty urban outfits was deluded. I was dressed like an orange-haired Nazi officer when the image I longed to cultivate was Balkan Freedom Fighter.

Before it got incinerated, my brown partisan's coat was topped off by a piece of safety headwear unmatched on London's streets. While browsing the porkpie hats, fishing smocks and Druidic paraphernalia in an Oxfam shop in Camborne, Colin had uncovered an RAF helicopter pilot's helmet. At that time moto lids had yet to knock off the *Top Gun* stealth-fighter look popularised by Roof's lid from the mid-nineties. A decade earlier the real thing was the best you could find, a heavy white helmet with built-in earphones and a DIN radio plug dangling off the back like a Chinese ponytail. Best of all was the inky-black visor which swivelled down on a central rail for those low-sun sorties.

Obviously, MoD procurement protocols pooh-poohed the BSI-approved kite mark required of civilian headwear, though in truth that helmet was too big and uncomfortable. Head-butting the side of a VW van, as I tended to, would have given me quite a headache. It was a fun look, though if any other bikers noticed, they made sure they didn't show it. Only once, when a frustrated cop was trying to find something to pin on me, did he turn on my unusual helmet; but he was easily convinced it was kosher on account of the Letraset BSI coding I'd applied one quiet afternoon at Sunshine.

My hands were clad in crochet-backed driving gloves most easily found in Harrods, and leather trousers remained unbeatable and durable legwear. Depending on my mood – lithe hipster or battle-ready motocrosser – my feet were shod in a pair of charity shop, side-zip Chelsea boots or steel-faced Alpine Stars.

All that was missing was a bike to undertake the tramlining from Holborn to Soho and back. The XS650 was sold to ChrisTom and with a heavy heart I bought myself another sensible Honda CD200T Benly. Now honed out to its full 200cc potential, it was otherwise the same humdrum commuter blob that started daily on the button for months and years on end. Maintenance amounted to a single operation every few days: unscrew the fuel cap, stick the nozzle in and pull the trigger.

'Yor-gonna get-yor fakin' 'ed-kiktin.'

The familiar football hooligans' chant came down the corridor of Sunshine's office.

'Yor-gonna get-yor fakin' 'ed-kiktin. Oright, Christo? Cant uv Mon'y Cristo! Bereft in deafly bloom.'

Make way for Wayne, Bernie's late-teenage son, brought in to learn the ropes ahead of me taking a fact-finding mission to Namibia. Wayne was a chirpy northeast London Jack the Lad, a scaled-down version of his barrel-shaped old man, brimming with youthful, oikey brio. He wouldn't be riding a humble Benly to cover the ten-minute run to the West End. No sirree. Like any teenage blade with well-off parents, he ran a 130mph CB900F and he wasn't dead yet. Far from it.

'Whoar, I tell ya, Chris, I'm well overdue for a shag, a bit of rumpington-pumpington. I got that pressure in me goolies, know what I mean? 'Ave to get me dahn to WellJells in Chingfud or it'll be oozin' aht me fakin' pants!' This was all delivered with a sturdy crotch lift, but with no bragging intended or implied put-down. It was simply an update on Wayne's testosterone levels.

Wayne loved his double-cammed 900F, which his dad must have bought him as a gift for not burning the school down. Once he'd relieved his surplus of pearl jam, Wayne set about doing up the F with belly pans and other badly fitting fibre-glass bodywork that was the fashion of the day. Assuming I might be a good source of advice, I played along with the perky Waynester.

Then, a few months later came some bad news. In trying to establish his villainous reputation, or perhaps just enacting a dutiful rite of passage, Wayne had misread the era's get-rich-at-any-cost zeitgeist, and got himself arrested in Liverpool while robbing a corner shop with a mate. Worse still, they'd beaten up the Asian owner in the process.

'Soppy pair of cunts,' spat Bernie. 'There was no need to beat that Paki up. That'll cost 'em another year in stir.'

But underneath you could sense Bernie's beaming pride.

'That's my boy. Next time, just don't get effing caught!'

Wayne wasn't the only one with criminal intentions. Capital Couriers' Nick turned up at Gower Street one day on a hot CBX – hot but not in the low oil-level sense. We all bent the law with our pot smoking, squat breaking and unapproved

safety wear, but at times Nick took it all a bit too far. Still
– stolen CBX? Don't ask and who cares, I'd never seen one
up close before, so hand over the keys! Though barefoot at
the time, I grabbed my RAF lid and tore off down Gower
Street to get a taste of this late-seventies icon which had had
us all thinking, 'What will these crazy Japs come up with next
– turbo-chargers?'

In fact, once everyone had got over the technical accom-
plishment of cramming a 108hp engine-and-a-half into a
motorcycle frame, and having it turn out to be surprisingly
effective, the CBX was a flop. Only LJK Setright, the culti-
vated engineering guru whose *Bike* magazine columns were
wasted on readers like me, believed we'd all missed the point
with the CBX. He compared the six's appeal to Aphrodite
(goddess, not rare mineral), a megabike which bashful buy-
ers found to be out of their class, only to buy plain Jane
CB900Fs. But just like Wayne, I could see that the 900F was
a much better proportioned machine, went as fast and cost
much less than the 600lb CBX.

Of course all these finer points of bike spotting were far
from my mind as I banked into Bedford Square, changed
gear with a shoeless wince, and then drag raced from light
to light up Tottenham Court Road without getting much
beyond second gear. As I went, the preposterous engine
shoved a bow wave of air northwards, sending crisp packets
fluttering all the way to Mornington Crescent. Barefoot on a
CBX: one for the memoirs.

17

THE EXORCIST

AJS 370 Stormer, Honda XR200R, CD200T and Bénélé

I needed excitement, a project of some sort. At Sunshine, the repetitive drudgery of short-range Benlying, together with the challenging nature of my reading matter, was getting irksome. And we all knew where that had lead. Help was at hand. In Cornwall, Colin put me on to a guy selling a shit bike at a great price – a combination as irresistible as a backstage pass to a Spinal Tap gig. For fifty quid I bought something called an AJS 370 Stormer, an early-seventies Brit scrambler I'd never heard of, and one of the least desirable motorcycles since the disastrous 125 Tadpole, Jawa's short-lived amphibious scooter.

The fact that the AJS wasn't road legal and had as much chance of achieving that status as a twenty-five-foot-long, methanol-fuelled drag racer was only partly due to the 370's abhorrent din. My old IT250G had sounded bad but at least brought some style to the table. The best the Stormer could do was stagger up and hurl a bucket of cold vomit in your face.

The first time I tried to start it, the vile motor kicked back and gouged a six-inch dent in the steel shin-plate of my Alpine Stars. This was not a bike for Italian elk-skin loafers. Once it was running, and before someone called the police, we followed the back lanes out through Redruth on to the wasteland below Carn Brea hill to wrestle with the beast. On the dirt there was no middle way, either the untamed motor bogged like an overloaded cart, or it ripped the grips from the bars.

I'd driven down that time in a car given to me by a mate's dad, a Rover P4, the one that looked like a bowler hat and had suicide doors at the back. Driving the weighty sedan was a novelty: it was made long before I was born and with its walnut dash could be mistaken for an entry-level Bentley. The AJS was de-wheeled, crammed through the suicide doors and transported to London, just the place for a two-stroke 'crosser that sounded like an overheating Gatling gun. Nevertheless, the pictorial evidence does record an AJS Stormer with a hastily taped-on number plate running the bomb holes of Featherbed Lane. It's hard to believe I rode that thing the twelve miles from Gower Street without setting off various early-warning systems right across north Kent.

The devil machine had a catastrophic combination of unusable power, similarly all-or-nothing brakes and indifferent suspension, capped with the most atrocious racket. Should you manage to match the correct gear with the powerband's vicious, ectoplasmic discharge, it could launch you into the lower branches with the force of a Macedonian siege catapult. But there was no realistic prospect of civilising the snorting Stormer. Turn your back on it and it would toss you head first through the window of a casualty ward, with a pair of crucifixes rammed in your eye sockets.

This was not quite the excitement my project was looking for, but all was not lost. I had a cunning plan to castrate the AJS. However, while I looked around for a suitably sharp knife,

I picked up an infinitely more affectionate Honda XR200R Pro-Link. I recalled Giro's brilliant twin-shock XR200 from Muswell Hill and was looking for a similarly lithe trail bike that would do for work as well as the odd enduro. One time in Wales we'd met a local guy on an XR350 and which had impressed me with its bog-surfing abilities. The 200R would be even better at that (if not the long ride there), and was one of the best-looking XRs.

Once home, it got carried up the stairs into my squat and perched on a milk crate for closer inspection. That soon revealed a cracked rear subframe hidden behind some suspiciously redundant insulating tape. Darn, I'd been shafted. I suppose the crack could have been repaired, but given my weight and the use I intended for the bike, it would probably crack again, there or somewhere else. So the tape was reapplied and back it went into the classifieds to snare another impulsive buyer. I was sorry to see that one go.

Still committed to my project, one weekend I unchained the evil AJS from the railings, got it in an arm lock and wrestled it over onto its handlebars by the kerb. Before it woke up to what was happening, I quickly ripped off the phlegm-spitting pipe and disembowelled it of its malignant motor. With the fiend safely eviscerated, what remained was a not-so-shabby full-cradle frame with a top tube like a drainpipe and chain adjustment off eccentric swingarm pivots, like on some Ducatis. What it was crying out for was an affable motor-next-door, and they didn't come more neighbourly than a CD200: Ozzy Osbourne crooning alongside Doris Day during her radiant, 'Move Over, Darling' prime.

I bought myself another Benly, pulled the motor and carted the lot to a bike garage down in Clapham, which, according to the magazines, was *the* place in London to get this sort of transplant done. It was a Saturday and the bloke who ran the place was drunk and disinterested but took on the job; this sort of attitude was normal. Weeks later, my Frankenbike was ready for collection, but the crucial alignment of the Benly and AJS sprockets had been cocked up and the guy couldn't give a toss – also a normal attitude. Another hired van got the bike to a no-name garage in Shepherd's Bush and the bike I christened the Bénélé was finally in business.

The Bénélé was a protest bike conceived in the spirit of Dylan, Lindsay Anderson and Citizen Smith. Any old plonker could buy a brand new Ténéré, bounce up and down on the seat a few times and then cover it in fur. All that took was money, 'Loadsamoney', as we'd all soon chime. I'd had enough of that. I'd been chucking cash at new bikes since I was eighteen – little wonder UK bike sales peaked around that time. The Bénélé was a defiant two fingers to shallow consumerism, while from the other arm rose a clench-fisted '*nein danke*' to acceleration and good brakes. I was going to prove to myself I could literally deconstruct two crap bikes and, in a non-conceptual sense, create a third crap bike with enough change left over to pay the milkman. Incredibly, yet again I'd single-handedly uncovered the fabled terra imbecilica in motorcycling's atlas mirabilis: rat biking. Just six short years after the Pistols had imploded, a punkish 'why not?' sensibility had broken free of my imagination's silty seabed and surfaced with a ripple and a light 'pop'.

The modest horsepower secreted by a CD200 meant the AJS drum brakes might never wear. To match the long forks, on the back I threw on some Kayabas off an XL500S that provided a useful foot of ground clearance. For the pipes I copied an idea off a BMW rider I'd met in Algeria: I junked the yard-long silencers and got some inexpensive VW Beetle tail pipes welded to the exhausts. The weight saving was outstanding, the noise wasn't too bad and the look was commendably lean. All the bike needed now was the donor Benly's headgear clamped to the sharp end, its number plate hung off the back and, with an RD400's handsome speed-block tank decals and five feet of Izumi chain, the Black & White Mongrel Show was on the road. In fact it was the road that led to a show: the BMF Rally, where I proudly entered the Bénélé into the Concourse de Grot. Way ahead of its time, it was roundly trounced by a GT750 covered in black snot and chicken wire. Que sera, sera.

Riding the Bénélé was actually no worse than trying to row a fridge with an umbrella while perched on a stool: awkward but possible, provided you watched your speed. Between them, the masses of the under-damped suspension and the ten-inch silencer tubes helped absorb any errant horsepower to make the Bender substantially slower and less responsive than a standard CD200. Flat-out gave 55mph, which was probably for the best, though it had to be said it looked pretty good for a polished turd.

Losing the BMF's 'Palme de Merde' had been a blow, but Le Bénélé had been built for a mission that lay far beyond a hairy-arsed, East Midlands field. By now I'd forgotten my vow never to return to the Sahara. Still craving a challenge, I calculated that even with its strangled performance, my horse-with-a-name could be ridden a thousand miles down the highway-to-the-danger-zone and back within a fortnight. It would require leaving from work on a Friday evening and getting back on Sunday night two weeks later, with long, long hours in the saddle. But it gave that late summer a focus that lifted me from the grind of the Sunshine trail.

As dystopias go, George Orwell's vision of *1984* was a few decades premature. The inevitable remake of the film of the book felt reassuringly far-fetched, at least for those of us on the sunny side of the Iron Curtain. This good fortune struck both Colin and me when we attended the Stonehenge Free Festival at the end of June. Five years earlier, in 1979, I'd felt

a cap-doffing gratitude to the Establishment for simply allowing the Isle of Man TT – and 'Mad Sunday' in particular. Now,
as we arrived at the famous pagan ruins, the Stonehenge Free
Festival seemed an even less probable event.

It had been founded ten years earlier as a celebration of alternative culture, but even back then it was trying to recapture
the lost late-sixties hippy nirvana of Woodstock. The decade
and a half between Joni Mitchell and Frankie Goes to Hollywood might as well have been measured in light years, and we
were assured the whole hippy ethos had collapsed. It hadn't
of course; it's just that, as with punk, some supporters chose
plain clothes, not headbands. If there were any other types of
bands at Stonehenge '84, we didn't notice.

A little further down the A30, Glastonbury was already a
better-known and better-organised event, which continues to
thrive today. But even with proper acts and famous speakers,
Glasto was another fifty miles away and cost a tenner for the
weekend. Stonehenge was free, unlicensed and with a claimed
70,000 visitors that year, was twice as popular.

Like Union Jack tourists in Amsterdam, we wandered between the lines of tents unsure if we weren't already halluci-
nating. Cardboard menus perched on sticks listed 'Microdots
£2.50; Whizz £12/g; Nepalese Temple Balls £15'. We stopped
at a tent where the brother of Terry, the Swansea shaman,
was selling mushroom tea for a pound. It was notable that no
one was openly selling coke, booze or heroin – they were the
wrong drugs. As we mooched through, we passed from one
soundsphere to the next, which was a free gig in itself. Batty
Arthurian prog rock segued into 'Stir it up', then something
Tubular Bellsy met the ear before giving way to the tom-tom
intro of 'Sympathy for the Devil'.

By dusk we were out over the Sargasso Sea, vibrating on
primeval frequencies, while around us the flying circus had
taken on the aura of a medieval camp before battle, gravid

with tension. Except that here, in the pre-dawn Beanfield, most of the yeomen wouldn't be invoking Harry, England or Saint George. This lot were higher than a giraffe's eyebrows.

Stonehenge '84 was to be the last event of its kind. That year the government and much of the police force had been busy with the miners' strike, a bitter battle of wills between union leader Arthur Scargill and PM Thatcher. A year after we'd ridden back from the sarsen ring dazed and defused, the police deployed tactics honed during that strike to crush the New Age pilgrims as they made their way towards Stonehenge '85. Thatcher proclaimed that she was all too eager 'to make life difficult for hippy convoys' and if new laws were needed to crush this menace, so much the better. What became the 1986 Public Order Act made trespass a criminal offence, something that had ramifications for the future of squatting too. The new law even stated that 'two people proceeding in a given direction can constitute a procession and can be arrested as a threat to civil order'. Perhaps Orwell hadn't been so far off the mark after all.

18

PRESIDENT GAS

Yamaha XS650 NO², XT600Z Ténéré, XT350
Kawasaki Z250 and Yamaha IT250J

One day I found a note tucked into the Bénélé's saddle. Roger Willis, editor of *Which Bike?* magazine, was curious about my contraption and wanted to do a feature. It just so happened that over the winter I'd discovered a new form of mind-expansion made possible by a device called a typewriter. Something about the activity or pace of typing unleashed a creative surge that I never got from scribbling. Although most of this output was achingly inane slurry, I had banged out accounts of my 1982 XT500 Sahara trip as well as the 900SS experience and they were ready to go.

Roger Willis soon moved on to *Bike* and a few times I dropped in to the office of the magazine I'd read so avidly as a teenager. Any glamorous notions about the frontline of British bike journalism were quickly suffocated: a cramped office contained a bunch of stressed individuals trying to produce the next issue with the same cumbersome technology used at Sunshine. Like Mark Williams many years before, Roger Willis was unusual for the time in that he was a Brit bike mag editor who was more into trail bikes than out-and-out GP replicas. Running a flashy, custom-painted Hilux, he certainly looked to be enjoying *Bike's* brief relocation in central London, before the magazine got sucked back into EMAP's media hub in Peterborough.

One day in March 1985 I was scanning the bike mags in a Mortimer Street newsagent's and found both my articles in print: Ducati in *Bike* and Sahara in *Which Bike?* Over the next year or two I contributed and participated in a few features for *Bike*, including watching Roland Brown wring a paltry 88mph from my XT600 down the famous MIRA test track I'd read so much about. But I also came to understand the nature of freelance journalism, at least for a novice. It had more to do with capitalising on being briefly in someone's favour than buzzing from magazine to newspaper like a pollenating hummingbird.

I bought myself another XS650. This one was intact but puffing a bit of smoke, for which the best cure was a rebore to 750, and while I was at it, some nitrous-oxide injection. Clearly that scene at the end of *Mad Max 2* when Humungus unleashes his triple-bottle set-up had made an impression on me. The recent spate of factory turbo bikes giving one-litre performance from a 750 may also have given me ideas. Most probably, though, I figured it would make a fun feature for *Bike*.

Turbos work by using the pressure of exhaust gases to spin a compressor or turbine like a watermill wheel. The spinning energy is then used to suck in and cram more air into the induction charge. A supercharger is a similar compressor, but powered via a belt off the crank rather than by exhaust pressure. In both cases the added air in the induction mixture means more oxygen, which means better combustion and more power, providing fuel levels are increased proportionately. With nitrous oxide the 'oxide' does the same job, only delivered at much higher pressure from a bottle of compressed gas like those clamped to the side of Humungus' six-wheeled chariot.

I found a bloke down in Epsom who imported the American NOS kits for cars and who was happy to get me gassed up in return for some exposure in a bike mag. I left the XS by his garden shed and when I came back, a two-pound bottle of gas compressed to 800psi was clamped over the tail light. Nitrous oxide worked rather like crack-cocaine: it would be either 'Goodnight Vienna' or dipping a stale Viennese Whirl in a mug of cold tea. Once the tap on the bottle was opened, the tiny, high-pressure tubing plumbed into the inlet tract became charged. But the vital solenoid that opened the floodgates on the gas was primed to activate just before the throttle hit the stop. My '76 XS may have been a doddering pensioner alongside the current turbocharged pocket rockets, but 400 pounds of bored-out 750 twin running with the throttle pinned would ruffle the roadside leaves all right. Inject at least fifty per cent more horsepower just as you reach that point, and you want to be sure someone's remembered to hang out the safety net.

But, just like crack, the hit doesn't last long. At full bore the nitrous oxide bottle was spent in a couple minutes – perfect for a drag strip, less handy for the Uxbridge Road on a wet Friday night. Graham and I had some fun taking moody burn-out shots for the *Bike* article at the gasworks behind St Pancras. But once my gas ran out, it was too much hassle to visit the BOC plant near Greenwich for a refill. Instead, I got my kicks simply leaving the NOS-stickered bottle on the back.

'What the fuck is that, mate?' Some van driver leant out of his window, nodding at the bottle.

'Oh, it's just a fire extinguisher. These 650s run a bit hot in town.'

One day at the lights on Southampton Row, the usual scrum of despatch hacks pulled up past the bumpers. I had bikes either side of me and one behind, one of them an agitated bloke on a 350LC, glancing in his mirror at the back of my bike while whang-danging his throttle. With one eye on the lights, I reached back with my left hand and unscrewed the valve on the bottle, then fiddled mysteriously near the carbs and blipped the throttle a couple of times. The big twin juddered, and with both hands back on the bars, I snicked the Yam into gear, leant forward and angled my legs back for a clean launch. Elsie man and GT550 on the right were up for it and adopted similar stances. The cross lights turned orange – our turn soon. We primed our engines to 4000rpm and... wait for it... the cross lights turned red, ours went orange and the LC was away on one wheel with the GT hard after him. Me, I trundled off on my mid-seventies fossil with its depleted fire extinguisher on board.

Funnily enough, my launch prank had been right opposite the Royal College of Anaesthetists, where the gas had its uses in surgery. Nitrous oxide was the same as the 'laughing gas' I remembered being given as a kid at the dentist. Back then, I'm pretty sure they gave you enough to pass right out. In the early nineteenth century, travelling shows would administer these 'Factitious Airs' to those who dared; Romantic poet Robert Southey, friend of lifelong addict Coleridge, was certain 'the air in heaven must be this wonder working gas of delight'. In modern times, mini cartridges of the sweet-tasting gas also propelled soda and whipped-cream dispensers. When out of cream (or nitrous oxide for his XS), the indigent *Rattus narcoticus* could suck out the dregs and cackle like the Joker, while brain cells fell like ripe corn before the scythe.

The summer of 1985 concluded with eviction notices finally reaching Gower Street. It was the end of an era: for me, well over two years at the same address, not including the spell in Australia. We'd all got attached to the place: ravenous, red-eyed trips to the late-night supermarket on Tottenham Court Road, searching for a working phone box to pull off the free overseas calls scam, bringing bikes indoors and cultivating a look to our rooms with little more than planks and milk crates.

Some might have claimed there were similarities between our way of life and the 'anarchic antics' of TV's *The Young Ones*, but we didn't really rate that show. It was said that Alexei Sayle, who played one of the show's characters, also lived in Bloomsbury. It probably wasn't a squat, so we assumed it was a whitewashed Georgian townhouse, which rather clashed with his right-on image.

The Gower Street gang broke up, spinning off to rooms in other squats, or in most cases leaving London altogether. That was easier than trying to crack the rental scene in the capital. To be in with a chance required snatching a still-warm copy of either the *Evening Standard* or the new, weekly free-ads paper, *Loot*, the Gumtree of its day.

Eviction day drew close and my steel-door-spotting antennae were tuned to a high frequency. I was looking for the standard-issue grey steel door that denoted a Labour council empty. Tooled up, I took myself into Fitzrovia in the dead of night to check out potential places, but close up either they looked unlikely or the risk of getting caught was too great. I heard of an empty in Peto Place, a lovely Georgian mews alongside Regent's Park that had been squatted by Graham's friends in the seventies. I'd ridden past Peto hundreds of times but never noticed it, one of those hidden, sanctuary-like enclaves you stumble across in London from time to time. It would be a great place to live, even for just a few months, but the front edifice looked impenetrable.

Like the master criminal in the sixties heist movie *Topkapi*, I realised the only way in was through the roof. I shinned up the drainpipe and after a couple of nights had dislodged enough tiles to slip through. Inside the roof, I inched my way across the rafters to an attic door, lowered myself down and looked around with the torch shining through my fingers. After all that effort, it was a sorry scene: the electrics had been ripped out, the sinks and toilet smashed down to their stumps, and behind the steel guards the windows were missing. Whoever owned this place – it probably wasn't Camden Council – had done a good job of dissuading someone like me from moving in.

Time was running out. In the end, Graham, a few others and myself got in to an empty hotel in Mabledon Place near St Pancras. We knew this wasn't a promising long-termer, but it gave us some breathing time. Sure enough, the police did a mini harassment-raid, walking off with my bolt cutters because they could. We were told to move on in a few weeks.

I was now finding it quite easy to wake myself up in the wee hours and go on the prowl. I'd noticed an empty just down the road, near the Brunswick Centre, the modernist bank of flats arrayed either side of an underused shopping centre and the art house Renoir cinema I knew well.

My target was next door, the top floor of Medway Court, an eight-storey block. With regular council tenants on all sides, stealth was the key. That meant getting in through a window on the outside of the building and separating the steel door only once inside the flat. Achieving that would be like something out of a seventies 'Man from Milk Tray' commercial, but without the jet boat, cliff diving and racy score. Once on the roof, I used a rock-climbing trick and braced myself off a concrete screen that ringed the roof about a foot or so off the walls. Clinging on thirty yards up, I could just get a foot onto a window ledge, from where I managed to open a small hopper window. That done, I was able to reach in, open the larger window and step inside. Everything was in good shape, so I worked out what I needed, then spent the next couple of nights quietly separating the steel door from the door frame until it was just resting there; my replacement Yale lock already fitted to the front door. We moved in swiftly the next night, trying to minimise the commotion against the usual grumbles and threats from the neighbours. Once they realised we weren't slavering junkies or Marxist revolutionaries, they were soon appeased.

For me the accommodation problem was soon to be less of a long-term issue. I'd had my fun with the silly Bénélé that had been featured in *Bike*, but I'd recently moved on to the very bike it parodied: an XT600Z Ténéré, which I'd admired two years earlier at that bike shop in west Sydney. It was time to get serious and take the Dakar clone out into the desert. This time I was planning a longer trip to West Africa, so couldn't expect to get a mate to cover me at Sunshine. The money had been great and the creepy Gerry had got the boot, plus maybe a light beating. But nearly two years of being on call eleven hours a day had made me hungry for an adventure that didn't involve squat-breaking or self-medicating on industrial gases.

The Bénélé got flogged to a bloke from the studio below Sunshine where they regularly photographed Page Three girls for *The Sun*. The ex-nitrous XS had gone too. That left the XT-Z, desert-ready out of the crate, so needing little more than a black paint job, a block of firmer foam in the seat and a cunning repositioning of the oil cooler out over the handlebars. Once there I felt it was a shame to see all that engine heat going to waste so, always ready to make a dog's dinner from a sow's ear, I crafted a cardboard-and-duct-tape cowling to catch the oil cooler's surplus warmth. From the cowling, one-inch hoses ran off to either side. This time, when I set off for my mid-winter ride to Marseille, I'd stuff those hoses up my sleeves, strap up and enjoy the balmy drift of the oil cooler's heat wafting towards my armpits.

That trip across the New Year into 1986 turned out to be quite an adventure, one that benefited greatly from a new go-with-the-flow attitude which the locals called *ainsh Allah*. As I passed through Mali, Thierry Sabine, the founder of the Dakar Rally, got killed in a helicopter crash along with several others; they'd been flying around in a sandstorm looking for stragglers on one of the Rally's monumental 1000-kilometre days. I'd also scraped through to Dakar by the skin of my inner tubes, then shipped back to Valencia and rode home to find Medway Court still occupied two months on.

The trusty Ténéré bore the scars of a small fire I'd picked up midway across the Sahara, but that didn't stop someone nicking it soon after. And within a month probably the same mob pinched the new XT350 I bought to replace it. Before they nabbed it, I did manage to enter the 350 into an enduro near Banbury, but I found it lacked the pleasing grunt of the 600, so I didn't mind too much. I now needed to downsize to a theft-proof ratbike, so picked up a nice blue '82 Kawasaki Z250A3 for 250 quid from *Loot*. Bike #36.

I was back on the open circuit, earning my courier's crust at Streetwise, behind the *MCN* office off Clerkenwell Road where I used to regularly fill out my bike adverts, one letter per box. Streetwise was run by an ex-Security Despatch rider who'd hired in some bleepers and, being a cycle racer, was among the first in London to employ pushbike couriers. That should have meant we bikers got longer-distance work, but it mainly just put us out in the suburban Outer Zone, one job at a time.

The little Zed was a fun hack, a proper small motorbike, not a pressed-steel pony like a Benly. Alloy wheels with twin discs and a two-into-one painted black by the previous owner, with some welcome overspray on the chrome mudguards. With black duct tape peeling off the seat, not even a junkie would bother nicking this.

But something was missing from our Medway Court bike park, and after a bit of thought I realised what that was: a Yamaha IT250J. You'd hope I'd have learned my lesson with the cracked-out G model I'd bought new four years earlier, but I'd either forgotten or forgiven. It's not always easy to explain my erratic purchasing patterns, but the J proved you should never give up on a series of bikes. A competition enduro bike in the heart of Bloomsbury might appear to be about as much use as a combine harvester, but at least I managed to stand it up in the lift and get it to our eighth-floor landing, beyond the claws of the bike-stealing filth.

It seemed the message about the difficulty of riding two-stroke racing motors with powerbands as wide as a gnat's pecker was getting through. While that might work on a forty-minute motocross race, in a typical enduro of several hours, a rider would be beaten to a pulp. The key to making the J compliant was in attaching a canister to the inlet tract via a short hose. Foretelling *When Harry Met Sally*, Yamaha called it YEIS, or Yamaha Energy Induction System. But this was no fake 'bell mouth' trick like the one Honda had tried to pull on a CB750 one time. The can worked a bit like a two-stroke reed valve, smoothing out induction pulses which could get out of phase at lower rpm. The canister's exact volume and tube length were presumably carefully calibrated – the reservoir collected the errant induction charge, which would otherwise have backed up and over-richened the carb, and then fed it back later. Or so I read in *Dirt Bike* and pretended to understand.

Graham and I took the IT-J to our usual wasteland haunts in south Essex and north Kent, where, compared with the G of 1980, I was amazed at what I could now manage on the bike. The boost bottle had subdued the Hyde element while giving a perkier Jekyll full rein. We pulled all sorts of dumb stunts on that IT, carving one-eighties off grassy banks, blasting up ramps for low-flying passes, and doing any number of brain-out wheelies.

Road or trail, any bike that enables you to ride better or get away with moves you'd never normally dare gets a backstage pass into your Hall of Fame. Sure, the piercing racket remained unchanged – a marble inside a paint shaker with inbuilt amplifiers. Plus it wouldn't manage sixty miles on a tank or a thousand miles on a top end. But from my know-all's pedestal I was able to absolve the sins of two-stroke dirt racers as long as they sat at the back and kept the noise down.

When Medway Court was disbanded, there was just nowhere to go. I'd already spent months scanning the immediate neighbourhood, but, spoiled by years of metropolitan living, I wasn't yet prepared to head for the outlands of Hackney, London's squatting homeland. Instead, I ended up camped like a vagrant in a derelict house in Kentish Town, worried that one night a real death's-head vagrant might steal in and grind my bones to make his bread. But as luck would have it, the riding lessons I'd been giving a spunky cycle courier at Streetwise bore fruit and the green-haired girl invited me to shack up with her and her chums, squatting not far from my derelict bolthole.

19

A Tourist in Anarchadia

The house in Lady Margaret Road was another solid, semi-detached Victorian villa with no visible reason for being unoccupied by rent-paying council tenants. But like thousands of properties in London and most of the squats I lived in, that's the way it was. 'Lady Margaret' presumably referred to Henry VII's mother, who'd given birth to her first and only child at the tender age of thirteen, and not to Thatcher's inevitable ennoblement.

It was unlikely the occupants of the squat had any affection for either, because I'd fallen in with supporters of the anarchist group Class War. For all I knew they may even have been associated with its shadowy subsidiary: the Tufnell Park Militia, North London's sinister red-on-black panthers. If not, then the LMR crowd certainly hung out with them at the boozer.

Along with green-haired Marie, my latest squatmates included Tim, a nice chap from Surrey who looked considerably less anarcho than me. He worked in lighting but was much more devoted to Class War's administration, preparing articles for their notorious newspaper and dealing with the ever-growing postbag it generated. Tim seemed like a docile bloke and didn't wear his black flag on his sleeve; when I turned up at LMR he was hooked on *Back in the DHSS* by the Liverpool band Half Man Half Biscuit. New people always meant new music. Tim also put me on to Linton Kwesi Johnson's 'Fite Dem Back'. I'd heard it here and there over the years but had never listened to it properly. Smash their brains in: it could have been a Class War anthem.

Black-clad and red haired, Fiona was our mandatory in-house angry feminist; a staunch vegan, she required an electric shock to flip her scowl into a smile. She occasionally debased herself by submitting to visits from a nice boyfriend, something which tarnished her ideological cred. However much you tiptoed around her, even the mildest of ill-judged quips would see you getting jabbed in the balls with a red-hot glare. I was to encounter a few like her in the coming years.

Also in residence were Mathew, a bright, middle-class Jewish Marxist paying a visit to the wild side but popping home on weekends, and Greek Emil, a demo- and Class War regular. Emil hung out with other surly, comb-dodging punks who could often be found on a street corner, surrounded by a few bottles of screw-top booze and brandishing a placard for the latest cause: 'Homes for All' one week, 'Boycott Barclays Bank' the next.

The *Class War* newspaper had been co-founded in Swansea a couple of years earlier by a chap called Ian Bone. He'd got into anarchism at university in 1968 and spent the intervening years in a rowdy struggle against the rich elite, while also supporting members of the Angry Brigade during their trial. (The Angries were an anarchist troop of disenchanted graduates, famed for their shockingly extensive but actually harmless bombing campaign in the early seventies). Ian's class antagonism must have been at least partly rooted in his upbringing as a socialist butler's son among the grand houses of the English aristocracy's dwindling ranks.

Vowing to make the *Class War* paper as 'fucking funny as fucking fuck!' (barely a page of his unrepentant autobiography, *Bash the Rich*, escapes an F-word), he pitched it as 'Britain's most unruly tabloid'. Scrappily montaged covers featured incendiary headlines like 'Another Fucking Royal Parasite', on the birth of Prince William in 1984, or an image of a Flanders cemetery with 'We've Found New Homes for the Rich'. It sold for pennies at marches and demos and shifted up to 15,000 copies per edition, using a language and layout that poked two fingers at serious anarchist periodicals like *Freedom*, which in 1986 had been going for a hundred years.

Besides the obvious targets, Class War the movement also scoffed at ineffectual pacifists and spineless lefties linking hands around US airbases singing 'We shall overcome'. Fuck that! CW was engaged in a fierce 'if you want peace, prepare for war' brawl, lifting that slogan from an Angry Brigade pamphlet, although certainly not endorsing all of AB's methods. Instead, on a good day, the pattern seemed to be: get drunk, mess up a right-on demo (perhaps by storming a stage from which CND leader Bruce Kent or the Labour Party leader 'Kinnochio' might be bleating on), lay into some despicable fascist scum, have a punch-up with the pigs, evade arrest, then finish up with a window-smashing high-street rampage. With that done, it was time to retire to a pub.

All this was a long way from my understanding of anarchism. In an era of riots and football hooliganism, CW's actions came across as just more yobby fodder to get the tabloids in a froth. That media attention-seeking ambition worked rather too well for CW in the end.

Class War were not in the same league as the Angry Brigade, who by then had become romanticised by everyone who wasn't actually involved. By comparison, Class War were a mixture of hooligans, misfits, rabid animal rights activists and counter-cultural dropouts for whom being 'an anarchist' was cooler than being a Trot or Marxist in a jaunty beret. After all, Johnny Rotten never snarled 'Iy-yam a sociaLIST, Iy-yam a commuNIST'.

It wasn't just dropouts who thought anarchism was edgy. One time on a train I spotted a young student-type reading something which he held up like a hymn book to make sure all could see. It could have been *The Wasp Factory*, *A Hundred Years of Solitude* or *So Long, and Thanks for All the Fish*, but I quickly recognised the black and red cover, which boldly announced, 'People of Carriage H. Take note that I am reading George Woodcock's *The Anarchist Reader*. Power to the People!' I smiled to myself. That might have been me, ostentatiously parading my flirtation with dangerous ideas.

Despite 'anarchy' being a common synonym for chaos and disorder, anarchism the movement was and is a serious ideology based on anti-state lefty libertarianism. The crew at LMR got me to question things like the origins of ruling elites. Why was a royal family royal – because William the Conqueror's Norse ancestors had wielded bigger clubs than other warlords? By whose consent did the police act or Customs levy taxes? And so on. Like student-on-a-train, we looked at these long-established institutions and wondered why things had turned out as they had. Given the history of the 20th century so far, youthful idealism couldn't resist harbouring an allied sense of moral outrage as well as possible alternatives.

What exactly would happen if authority lost currency? Would it go all *Lord of the Flies* – William Golding's 1954 dystopian vision in which kids stranded on a desert island descend into savagery? Or, with less anarchy and more anarchism, might it be more like parts of Spain during the revolution, or less convincingly, Tristan da Cunha before WWII. This was the ideology's predicament: could a group of people really sublimate their own desires for long enough to make it work, or did society work best under a hierarchy of authority?

Exploring such sanguine visions of social harmony was given added piquancy by Britons' love-hate attitude towards Thatcher's steadfast government. By 1986 some were beginning to reap the rewards of her policies, but many were not. Ian Bone admits openly that 'without Thatcher, there wouldn't have been Class War… You couldn't have felt that level of bitterness, anger, loathing, hate, violence towards Ted Heath or Callaghan. Thatcher was a Class Warrior – just on the other side of us.'

It may have been galling to acknowledge, but she was as much a rebel within the Tory establishment as she was a nemesis to socialism. She'd eventually clawed out a period of economic growth which led to unprecedented social mobility, including people like Sunshine's Bernie and your braying Bill-ericay Dickie with a gold Rolex at the wheel of his Porsche. A million had grabbed the chance to buy their council homes cheap, house prices soared anyway and in London people sold up and moved across the street to gain a garden that was two feet longer. The Stock Exchange was opened up and nationalised industries were sold off. Everyone was invited to make a quick buck, and soon share-holders outnumbered union members. High fives all round at Number 10.

Despite my lifestyle, I was a beneficiary of this belated economic prosperity in a job that until then had surfed over recessions. But it didn't mean I bought into the whole aspirational, consumerist merry-go-round. If anything, the desert riding and my urban nomadism proved how little was needed to get by comfortably. Anarchy in the UK was absurd of course, but that's because in the UK we were fortunate enough to be able to turn on, drop out and live in our own way. And doing so didn't mean hunkering down in a rain-sodden wigwam up a remote Welsh valley.

Saturday evenings, the house would saddle up and gallop off to Wapping near Tower Bridge to hook up with similar groups protesting outside the News International compound where *The Sun* and *The Times* were printed. Now owned by Australian media baron Rupert Murdoch, *The Sun* was Britain's bestselling newspaper and a strong supporter of Thatcher and her policies. Murdoch had furtively equipped the new Wapping compound with modern printing technology which would do away with the need for bolshie print-workers. They'd had it their way since before the year-long *Times* strike of 1979 over similar issues. In 1986 negotiations over the relocation collapsed and six thousand newspaper employees went on strike; they were immediately sacked, to be replaced by a much smaller workforce that straightaway moved into Wapping. The crafty Murdoch had pulled a fast one, even anticipating possible hostility of the rail unions by organising a road haulage fleet to deliver his papers. It all looked like another dreary union dispute, unless you took the anarchist line in the comic spoof *The Scum*, that union bosses were as complicit as the rest. Either way, obstructing Murdoch's operation became a weekly appointment for Class War and some Saturdays it got pretty nasty.

Me, I found that despatch riding was a more than adequate means of releasing tension, meeting policemen and risking injury. So I skipped Saturday Nights Live from Wapping, but started attending Class War meetings with the rest of the house and the nearby TP Militia. Sunday evenings, twenty or thirty ragged-trousered radicals convened in a room over a pub in King's Cross under the nom de guerre 'The St Pancras Woodpecker Impersonation Society', or some such. This was the latest pub the group used as there were rumours of bugging, although once the beer flowed discretion soon fell away with talk of planned demos and other confrontations.

There'd been more riots across the UK the previous year and, as we'd found in Kennington in 1981, when Babylon was burning, squatters were thought to be among the trouble-makers, perhaps because the once-feared Angry Brigade had been apprehended in a Hackney squat. Class War were seen as much as militant brick throwers as supporters of workers' rights (though that too was considered suspect), so surveillance by Special Branch was quite likely.

In September 1985 a 'Bash the Rich' CW march to the wealthy London suburb of Hampstead had been blocked by a solid wall of battle-ready cops. A couple of warriors, one of whom was Bone, took on the law and the law won. Left alone in a cell after everyone else had been bailed, Ian Bone recalls in his autobiography how he suddenly understood that the comeback could be a lot worse than just another round of cautions and fines.

As *Bash the Rich* puts it, looking to restore their trashed post-Hampstead reputation, a week later a CW posse rushed over to Brixton to join in the rioting and looting that followed the police shooting of a black woman, Cherry Groce, in her home. A week after that, when another black woman, Cynthia Jarrett, died while police searched her home in north London, the resulting Broadwater Farm riot ended with policeman Keith Blakelock getting hacked to death by a mob. Suddenly *Class War*'s regular 'Hospitalised Copper' feature didn't look so funny. This may have explained why, even nine months on, the meetings I attended felt subdued.

Although it wasn't quite like the scene in Monty Python's *Life of Brian* where Reg (John Cleese) and a few others discuss fighting their oppressors for men's theoretical right to have babies, the meetings were still pretty dull. I was, however, struck by how, despite anarchism's avowed opposition to hierarchy, it was the same few who spoke most. Tim, Spike and Angie and Andy the Hackney gardeners contributed most, along with

Mad Mark, a fervent animal libber who could barely contain his craving to attack vivisectionists, something for which he'd already done time. But the meetings would soon have imploded without the charismatic and articulate Ian Bone.

For weeks and months I sat wordlessly, an impartial but attentive observer. I was Marie's boyfriend, the flash git with three motorbikes. Then one evening I found a way to take some indirect action for the cause. The gang was planning to counter-demo some fascists in Liverpool. Anti-fascist groups from across the land were going to show their support and CW didn't want to be left out. The problem was, in the entire congregation of revolutionaries, only one person had a driving licence and was old enough to hire a van. From the back I raised my hand and offered to drive the other van.

One way or another, someone was gonna get their 'ead kicked in, but I had no intention of getting involved in a bundle with thugs, with or without pointy hats. Once in Liverpool, I watched my placard-bearing comrades marching off to war at the court house, while I stretched out in the van with some of Kropotkin's unpublished poems. After all, if I got locked up, they'd be stranded. Also, Giro had recently put me on to the chilling 'Beasley Street' by John Cooper Clarke. It did for industrial northern cities what *Midnight Express* had done for Turkish jails and I wasn't taking any chances. So it was that I avoided the sharp end of the Struggle until a few hours later when someone rushed up to the van: a group of Warriors were isolated and needed rescuing from bloodthirsty Nazis. 'We gotta get over there quick!'

OK then. This was much more my thing – like tackling a Mitsui run or sailing through all the reds with someone's chilled kidneys in the topbox. With a crunch of gears and a lurch, Class War Search and Rescue launched Thunderbird 2.

'Right here. Right. RIGHT!'

I cut across an oncoming car with a mouthed, 'Sorry mate,

I saw you but ignored you. Class War emergency,' and swung the Transit into a bleak terraced street, half boarded up and scattered with trollies and wrecked cars.

'There. There! Stop!'

A knot of anxious Class Warriors emerged from behind a low wall, where they'd given their swine-like attackers the slip. They bundled into the van and we roared off back to the agreed rendezvous. It seemed the demo had got too fiery for some, but nobody had been nabbed and if there'd been a fight, no one looked any the worse for it. As we headed out to the M6 for London, we were trailed by a police van to make sure we pissed off and never came back.

A couple of years earlier, the *Sunday People* tabloid had identified Ian as 'Britain's most dangerous man'. Perhaps Ken Livingstone was on holiday at the time. In *Bash the Rich*, Ian admits that the sudden unwanted attention from the national press succeeded in penetrating his rhino-like hide. Well, for about a week at least, until he realised that surely any anarchist worth his dripping Molotov should celebrate such a prestigious accolade – the revolutionary's equivalent of an OBE.

Dangerous maybe, but some bourgeois pursuits must have contaminated Ian's childhood as he frolicked in the meadows among southern England's filthy rich. He and I met up one morning in Finsbury Park for a bout of tennis. If I'd been someone else, I'd have arranged for a *People* photographer to shoot our game with a long lens. 'Exposed! Britain's Most Dangerous Man Likes a Nice Game of Tennis!' I knew my moves and had even reached some *Evening News* tournament in school, but Ian thrashed me anyway and seemed irritated I hadn't put up a better fight. What could you expect of a lifestyle anarchist?

Ill read and ambivalent, I was hardly a contender, and there was a lot more than a threadbare tennis net between us. We were on opposite sides of the divide identified by Murray Bookchin in *Social Anarchism or Lifestyle Anarchy: An Unbridgeable Chasm*. There were those of us that dabbled in a 'harmless personalistic, yuppie ideology' that presented no threat to the existing powers that be, and there were those that genuinely felt part of a revolutionary movement working for the annihilation of the class system.

'Have we got the balls?' asked a sweaty but victorious Bonehead.

Have we indeed.

20

OUTLANDS

BMW R100S, Yamaha XT600ZE

Giving IT250s a second chance had been worthwhile so it must have been that kind of thinking, or perhaps an offer I couldn't refuse, which explained why I bought another boxer, a lush green R100S with delicate gold pinstriping, a nose fairing and Krauser racks. There was nothing wrong with that bike except that it was a BMW R100S, although it was at least in better shape than that T model I'd reassembled before going to Australia. Still, the lack of rapport was undeniable: I just couldn't get on with these lumbering leviathans. Something closer to Gaston Rahier's HPN Marlboro desert racer might have done the trick. I'd seen it close up in Dakar earlier in the year and it looked so much more focussed and fun than my awkward green brick. I sold it to Giro a fortnight later.

After a few months, time was also called on Lady Margaret Road and my exodus from cushy, city-centre squatting continued. Class War Tim had meanwhile sorted out his own

accommodation needs: a cell in Wormwood Scrubs for brick-
ing a bank window one drunken night. For the rest of us, the
usual period of steel-door hunting saw us touch down in the
pus-riddled badlands of west 'Acne.

Among London's poorer boroughs, Hackney's long history of incomers gave it a distinctive and unrepentant working
class vibe. Here, immigrants – once, long ago, Huguenot; now,
Kurdish and Vietnamese – mixed with delinquents and dissenters, artists and activists, bent police and drug dealers, cor-
rupt councillors and entrepreneurs, plus a few anarcho-squatty
punks, all in one messy, inner-city mash-up. This whole 'caw
blimee, guvnor' cockney commotion had lately struck a chord
with the nation – at least when filtered through a TV screen.
After just two years on telly, *EastEnders* had become so popular
that a staggering thirty million viewers tuned in for the Christmas Special; that was well over half the country and the larg-
est British TV audience of all time. Was someone shot in the
shower or the whole cast absorbed in a to-the-death ballroom
dancing contest? Not quite. Dirty Den told Ange their marriage was over. Doof-doof, doof, doof-doof-doof.

The Blitz had razed some of Hackney's dilapidated Victorian slums, but as elsewhere in British cities, the well-in-
tentioned but misguided high-rise regeneration schemes had
backfired. The borough continued to fester in poverty, depri-
vation and the crime that came with it. The Labour-run borough was the poorest in the land, in part because the Tory
government was ill-disposed to support them. At the same
time, what might charitably be called 'inefficiency and poor
management' by the housing department meant that change
and improvement came slowly for the most needy tenants.

Hackney hadn't always been 'Acne. In the Tudor era, pal-
aces had sprung up on open ground, and later Pepys would
escape there to 'take the air' and try his first home-grown
orange, perhaps plucked from a teenage Nell Gwynne. Well-

to-do eighteenth-century merchants went on to built elegant townhouses in the district and entertained themselves in beery sessions spent watching pig-swinging contests in London Fields. With nineteenth-century industrialisation came new canals, railways and light industry that ate away at the meadows; the rural jobless surged in and Hackney dropped its aitch and grew in notoriety.

Away from the crack-blighted outlands of Lower Clapton, one of the grottiest corners was said to be the Holly Street Estate on Queensbridge Road in Dalston, notorious for its drugs and prostitution, dereliction and vandalism. The sprawling estate was a mix of snaking five-storey low-rises and a few twenty-floor towers. In other words, another monumental testament to the failure of post-war mass housing. Future PM Tony Blair lived in a charming Victorian terrace just over the road and later recalled 'how Holly Street [estate] represented everything... we needed to change in inner-city life'. While trying to share in the good news that things might one day get better, he was shocked at 'the tremendous fear people had of living on the estate... You had to speak to them through their letter boxes'. Maybe it was him they were unsure about.

In our case, the letterbox of one of the ground-floor low-rises in Laurel Court spoke to us, and four of us from Kentish Town moved in. Like the estate itself, all the blocks were cheerily named after trees, because obviously that's all it took to convince you that you were living inside a gilt-edged Constable painting and not a John Carpenter movie. Completed in the early seventies, it must have looked nice at the architect's presentation, but within little more than a decade the estate was in steep decline. Parts were so badly made that burglars could actually punch their way through top-floor roofs or even outside walls. Hopefully the asbestos would get them a few years down the line. Just two decades after it was built, the wretched Holly Street development would be deemed the worse of 'Acne's sunken estates. Even with the Tories' right-to-buy scheme, no one was going to waste a penny here. When asked, eighty per cent of tenants voted for it to be regenerated with extreme prejudice, some TNT and a wrecking ball. A few years after we'd gone, they got their wish.

Right around the time we relocated to Hackney, Sutton House, which dated back to Henry VIII's reign, was also a squat. Known as 'The Blue House' it hosted bands with names like the Warm Dough Babies and Sons of Bad Breath who later became Spear of Dentistry. All had just missed out on auditions for the Eurovision Song Contest. Astoundingly, once the Blue House ratbags had been evicted and the National Trust had got hold of the prized building, they saw fit to retain and preserve some of the squatters' artwork during their renovations.

Laurel Court was never going to earn such an honour, but as is often the case, living on the frontline wasn't so bad. You adapted to your environment and behaved accordingly. Either that, or we didn't stay there long enough to get targeted, or even have our bikes maltreated. The worst thing about our flat was that the centrally controlled heating was on 24/7 and couldn't be shut off – but leaving windows open any longer than it took to throw out a bed pan was asking for a burglary, even with someone inside.

I'd taken back the job at Templar typesetter's, flipping again to the benefits of having both a steady wage and time to sit around, reading. Part of the reason for going steady again was that I had another Sahara trip in the works. Year by year my adventuresome urges were steadily being transplanted from the Westway's rain-soaked cambers to the pistes of the Tassili N'Ajjer. Just three trips in the desert and I thought myself ready to tackle the trackless 350-mile crossing into the remote Ténéré Desert. Following a story in *SuperBike* describing my eventful Dakar trip of 1986, Pete from Liverpool had got in touch to ask about joining me on a future adventure. *SuperBike* even offered me a job. I'd turned that down, but proposed to Pete we each buy one of Yamaha's second-generation 1VJ Ténérés and ride them to the Ténéré Desert. The 1VJ had a cool look based on the blue Sonauto-Gauloise rally bikes, as well as firmer suspension, a better-positioned oil cooler and a smaller but still handy twenty-three-litre tank. My fourth Sahara bike was going to be an 'Acne-built acme of functional desert touring.

As was the form in those days, Pete set about tracking down one of the few fabricators in the UK who could hand-make him some alloy boxes and a steel rack. I followed with what I thought was a superbly engineered platform rack, a weight-bearing design based on old army-despatch-rider BSAs and an improvement on my Saharan XT500. A blacksmith in Stoke Newington took on that job. Meanwhile I wheeled the XT into the squat to perform surgery on its annoying safety rims that made tyre removal difficult.

It was in Laurel Court that I had the brainwave to write a guidebook about desert biking. Like any aspiring author of the period, I bought myself the latest edition of the *Writers' and Artists' Yearbook* from Foyles, then meticulously identified the publishers who'd slap their foreheads in astonishment at my compelling proposal. I prepared my submission by the book: double-spaced, covering letter, synopsis, maps and return envelope. Thirty envelopes were released to the Royal Mail, like a flock of doves from a papal balcony. Over the coming weeks a bloom of polite, pre-printed rejection slips crept across our bedroom wall, until twenty-nine notes reached from floor to ceiling. One publisher just kept the stamps.

Undeterred, my creative juices would not be stymied and I decided to experiment with film. One Sunday morning while mooching around for knick-knacks at Brick Lane market, I'd unearthed some complete Standard 8 filming outfits going for twenty or thirty quid. This was for the whole kit: projectors, editing viewers and any number of rugged clockwork cine-cameras from the fifties and early sixties, before the slicker Super 8 cassettes came in.

Standard 8 film came on mini spools of 'professional' 16mm stock. Operating at a jerky sixteen frames per second, you ran one edge of the film through the camera for two minutes, then flipped the spools (out of the light) to expose the other edge. When processed, cut down the centre and spliced, this gave you a longer reel of 8mm film. I tracked down a place off Baker Street selling out-of-date monochrome Kodak surveillance film for a fiver including processing, and it was '[no] Lights – [crude] Camera – Action!'

Standard 8's modest duration and relative expense at over a pound a minute ought to have been a good lesson in not squandering shots. But I went ahead and wasted film anyway. I subscribed to the chimps-with-typewriters theory that if I just swung the camera around for long enough, I'd eventually capture a fascinating and spontaneous cine slice of the world around me: something that could never be achieved with forethought and composition. After all, none other than Truffaut himself had asserted that 'cinematic success is not necessarily the result of good brain work… but of a harmony of existing elements in ourselves that we may not have even been conscious of… an accidental coincidence'.

That would do me, so in the spirit of Godard, Rohmer and La Nouvelle Vague, and long before the word 'Go' became fused with 'Pro', I riveted a 3/8th thread to the top of my crash helmet and rode around London with a 2lb clockwork Eumig whirring on my head. This freestyle shooting technique was complemented by the Burroughs-esque cut-up technique I adopted when editing the rubbish I'd filmed. The postie would deliver my exposed footage from the Kodak labs, at which point I chopped up and mixed the slithers of film like salad in a bowl, then stitched it all together randomly, fully expecting the result to be an avant-garde despatcher's take on *The Naked Lunch*. After weeks of work, I gathered my squatmates together one night in our perpetually sweltering lounge to watch twenty minutes of shaky, badly exposed and unwatchable drivel.

Early 1987 brought the call to move on, the fourth time in a year. I'd tried all the usual housing associations and co-ops, many of which had been founded by squatters in the sixties and seventies. Problem was, I was too white, male and able-bodied to even get on a waiting list, which anyway might take years to come good. So instead I began sleeping light again and riding off in the dead of night to investigate the promise that lay behind a steel door. A few recces like this led us back into a nice terraced brick house on Tancred Road on the north side of Finsbury Park.

Not one among us knew that the street was named after a Crusader knight who in 1099 had helped wrest Jerusalem back from the Muslim Saracens. Nine hundred years later, post-war Turkish immigrants had reversed Tancred's trail from the British colony of Cyprus all the way to Haringey, N4. Now the Green Lanes high street round the corner was thick with smoky backgammon clubs and general stores that sold a then-unheard-of range of olives, Mediterranean breads and fresh herbs. Turkish gangs were also getting into the heroin trade and many of those shops were paying for protection, but to us it was all just another colourful London suburb with a big park on our doorstep. Next door lived the bloke who did the horoscopes for one of the tabloids and he let us in on a secret: it was all bollocks but paid his bills.

For something to do, one Sunday Marie and I took ourselves to an enduro near Louth in Lincolnshire. I removed the XT's pillion pegs to save weight and improve my chances of a podium finish. She suffered quietly on the back, feet dangling in the breeze. I don't know what I was expecting, certainly not Plynlimon in the Fens, but on arrival I set off on another one of those round-and-round-a-small-field events, like my first enduro near Orpington in 1980. So round and round I went, like slow-motion motocross, shaking my head once in a while to avoid getting dizzy. The Louth enduro was another anti climax, but I received a small credit when contestant #34 was pictured later in *Dirt Bike Rider*, commended on having gone for the 'bravery award' while snatching some pretty decent air for a 600 Yam. My conscientious pillion-footrest weight-saving had paid off after all.

Some weeks later I found myself in Warren Street with a pick-up in Charlotte Street. Without thinking, I nipped over the pedestrianised cobbles of Fitzroy Square – straight into a police ambush. Drat, this might cost me some licence points and fifty quid.

'Documents please, sunshine.'

I handed over what I had on me, while the other one called in to check me out, even going so far as to read the bike's chassis number.

'This vehicle has been registered as lost or stolen in South Yorkshire in September 1982, sir.'

'Really? It's a C reg. They didn't even make them until 1986.' But such smart-arsed logic fell on deaf ears.

'Please get in the car, sir. We'll arrange to have your – sorry – *the* motorcycle collected.'

Sitting in the back of a police car, I tried to recall the seller, who'd said he'd bought it new. It had all seemed kosher. Down at Theobald's Road nick, I gave the same replies to the same questions, they relieved me of my possessions, allowed someone to come and pick up my jobs and then locked me up 'just until we sort this thing out'. Neither cautioned nor arrested, I was getting my first belated exposure to the supposedly repealed 'detain first – establish facts later' sus law.

South Yorkshire police confirmed that a Yamaha YZ465 motocrosser had indeed been pinched back in 1982. Unregistered dirt bikes were commonly stolen and recycled as parts, or flogged off to become a field bike behind some edge-of-town estate. The fact that my bike was also a Yamaha had produced a five when adding two with two. After some persistence, they admitted the Police Traffic Computer only read the numerical part of the Ténéré's long VIN or chassis number, which by coincidence matched the stolen YZ's. The 1VJ prefix was not read, which was a bit like identifying someone by their surname or year of birth. They let me out within an hour or two and handed back my stuff. Obviously no apology was offered, but I wasn't done for crossing Fitzroy Square.

A couple of months later, I could probably have looped a few loops round Fitzroy Square, no questions asked. It was the morning after the Great Storm of 1987, which had laid waste to southern England. The mini natural disaster made my usual ride to work in Old Street great fun, as rules were off. Feet up, I gingerly Benlyed round an obstacle course of stationary cars, fallen trees and other debris, but once at the office found the door locked; no one had made it in to work yet. With a touching devotion to the despatch rider's duty of deliverance, I deployed my squat-breaking skills and nipped up a fire escape, got in via the roof, got back out with the night-shift's artwork, delivered the jobs and was back at the office just as Mick and the rest were turning up.

Around New Year I got someone to cover me at Templar. Pete arrived from Liverpool on his fully laden XT and we set off for Dover and across freezing France to Paris, from where the overnight Motorail whooshed us to Marseille for a ship to Algiers. Ahead of us lay a 5000-mile round-trip through the heart of the Sahara. Two Ténérés to the Ténéré, Desert of Deserts: surely a Mitsui marketing dream.

21

ONE MORE WINTER

KTM GS600, Suzuki GS450 and GS550

I was back from the desert. The trip hadn't gone as planned, but what's new. I found a job at a place called Speed Couriers in Whitechapel, still on the old Ténéré, which by now had racked up 20,000 miles, including a few thousand on Algerian two-star. It didn't sound so good any more. One Saturday morning I woke up to find the previous night's last job still in the bag and panicked. Tearing down the Kingsland Road to Stepney in my pyjamas may have amused passers-by, but it was harsh on an engine still in its oil-starved overnight stupor. A rebore at Sondel Sport on Highbury Corner turned out to be the usual overpriced and unsatisfactory experience, so the well-used Yamaha, the only bike I'd bought in 1987, was released into the pages of *Loot*.

I was part of a national trend: new bike sales fell sharply that year. The UK's biking frenzy was beginning to wane. Were we all getting bored of bikes? Given the range of fabulous machines, the mid-eighties should have seen biking prosper, but within a year or two, bike registrations had dropped to nearly a quarter of their 1980 peak and eventually bottomed out at a low unseen since the end of the war. One reason must have been the motorcycle test, which had finally become more difficult than a two-piece Rubik's Cube. Other pundits put it down to the changing priorities of a maturing generational wave, passing unseen like a mid-ocean tsunami. Or perhaps there was simply such a huge pool of pretty darn good used machines from the boom years that the instant depreciation that came with buying a new VF1000F, GSX-R or an FJ12 didn't make sense, even in the eighties' whirl of ostentatious consumerism. I downgraded to my final Benly. It didn't bark, it didn't bite and it was all I needed to get the job done.

I flipped from Speed to Templar and back to the circuits, ending up working at a crumby minicab outfit in sleazy King's Cross, opposite the Scala cinema. Coming from Grays Inn Road, you could reach the office from the back via a bike-wide pedestrian alleyway. It saved negotiating the one-way system and felt satisfyingly subversive, if not quite anarchic. But this back alley was also a place where some prostitutes brought their clients for a bunk-up. More than once the Benly trotted by, its headlamp illuminating a punter's pale arse pummelling away across the passenger seat.

That wasn't my only encounter with the seedier side of King's Cross. I was putting in long hours to buy a 4x4 for my inaugural 'Sahara Motorcycle Tour' and was slumped in the office one evening, working my way through a succulent shish kebab, when Baz, the chubby night controller, picked up a phone.

'Cross Cabs… 'Old onaminit.'

He barked through the Plexiglas at me and Derek, a Jamaican driver. 'Either of you two got a big chap?'

We both turned towards him, nonplussed.

'How big's yer chap? Yer knob? Derek, ain't you black gee-
zers supposed to be hung like the fakin' Mull of Kintyre?'

'Was da fokin' Mola Kin Tyre?' replied Derek.

'Got the porno studio up Copenhagen Street on the blow-
er. Damsel in distress. Apparently their new stud's porksword
has turned out to be a bit of a chipolata. They need the full
salami. Forty quid in it for ya.'

"S'not fur me, Baz. I don' wanna end up wiwana dem sek-
shaly trans mitted diseases.'

'Oi, biker. Four Zero. 'Ows yer piston rod shape up?'

I did think about it for a few seconds, then came to my
senses. I mean, what if I didn't fancy her?

Turning my back on a career in porn, I found myself at
Security Despatch again. But a decade on, SD was just another despatching outfit, struggling to keep ahead of the cut-
price competition. To extend their client base and presumably
increase their market value, despatch companies were busy
buying up smaller outfits. They'd then trim off the slack and
reduce rates in the name of competitiveness. Suddenly the
money wasn't so easy any more; every two-wheeled jock was
in the game. Despatching's heyday was coming to an end and I
was just another mule with another load of deliveries to drop
along the same old streets. Newer activities like exploring the
Sahara were what inspired me now, not impulsive bike buying,
tearing through a multi-drop press release just for the thrill, or
psychedelic voyaging.

After a series of short-lived squats back in Bloomsbury,
then all over Stokey and Dalston, Marie and I found ourselves
a room in an already occupied place in Bethune Road, Stamford Hill. Before that I'd investigated an 'empty' near the top
of a thirty-storey tower block in Rotherhithe, south of the
river. No levering of steel doors or Milk Tray Man abseiling
required. I just walked in and had my pick of several flats on
the twenty-somethingth floor, all in good-enough shape and

with a view across the river to the forest of cranes where Canary Wharf was steadily rising out of the Isle of Dogs. But despite having at least a dozen flats to a floor, the entire tower was served by just two heavily armoured, dimly lit, piss-tainted lifts. Actually, I base that description on only one lift; the other was out of order. Had I moved in, I could have watched helplessly as far down below, my bike got dismantled and remanufactured into crack pipes.

Bethune Road was another solid and spacious three-storey Victorian house of the type we squatters liked. Solid, that is, apart from the screw props supporting the ground-floor doorways and the damage caused by a recent fire, which had cleaned out the sitting room and heavily charred the bedroom above. Someone had dozed off drunk with a fag in hand. The local paper had led with 'Naked Couple Burst Through Window' and then claimed everyone had been rehoused – it was bollocks in both cases.

Such a headline would have scandalised the ultra-orthodox Lubavitch Hasidim who lived in Stamford Hill. Over the years, I'd seen plenty of Jewish men in their Homburg hats and dark frock coats around Hatton Garden, where they worked in the gem trade. But I never saw orthodox Jews on public transport, in Sainsbury's or at Ridley Road market. This made locating their Stamford Hill community all the more striking. They'd been there since the twenties; patronised their own shops, schools and clinics and looked after their own, too. Families were large, close-knit and avoided all eye contact with outsiders. They held deeply conservative values and were far from wealthy. Ratty, overloaded Transit vans carried kids to their schools, which were located in private houses. There, the boys studied their holy books by rote; this was said to be one reason why the men ended up so unemployable and poor.

Hasidic Jews almost always drove Volvo estates, and for years I'd puzzled over this. In 1980s London, the driver of any Volvo estate was almost always a dark- or ginger-bearded bloke wearing glasses, a dark coat and a 1930s hat. The Swedish marque had coincidentally long been notorious among motorcyclists, who regarded their drivers as arrogant and inconsiderate. Volvos were the SUV 4x4s of their day, built to survive a crash and so attracting a certain type of unsporting driver who sought an advantage in the event of a lethal pile-up. It was certainly true that the Hasidim were engaged in energetic repopulation following their near-extinction at the hands of the Nazis, but could that explain their uncanny devotion to the super-safe Swedish cars? It seems that's all there was to it. In that pre-people-carrier era, Volvos were simply valued for their solidly built, family-carrying attributes.

With their retro outfits and dangling sidelocks, the men and boys were an incongruous sight, rushing about nervously like hunched Mad Hatters, and always bespectacled. At the squat we'd assumed their poor eyesight was a product of an inadequately stirred gene pool. Our knowledge of the sect's peculiarities were based on many such rumours: shaven-headed wives in wigs; their supposed vulnerability to burglaries on the Sabbath when they couldn't lift a finger. In fact, a study has since suggested that, as in Islamic madrasas, the *shucklen* or rocking forward and back while memorising the holy texts plays havoc with the eye's ability to focus and causes myopia.

One day a shy boy in sidelocks and skullcap appeared, gazing at me from a distance as I worked on my Tonka-like Land Rover in preparation for the desert tour. Any other kid might have asked, 'Can I 'ave a sit in your van, mister?' but he didn't dare speak and when I noticed him, he soon hurried away before someone reported his transgression. It was the only contact I ever had with the Hasidim of Stamford Hill.

My last desert bike, the 1VJ Ténéré, had been good, but now that I was getting a taste for the Sahara, I began wondering if there might be something more suited to the dirt – something lighter and with better suspension. At that time Honda's XR600R would have fitted the bill, but though I'd loved my XR500 twin-shocker, word was the 600's rear chassis was too skimpy for load carrying. Instead, one chilly autumn night in Rochester, I picked up a 1986 KTM 600GS.

By the late eighties, just like Ducati or Triumph, KTM were some way from the renaissance that's given us the vibrant, bright orange output of today's KTM Sportmotorcycle. Back then, KTM was just another small European dirt-bike factory like Husqvarna, CZ or the now dormant Bultaco, Ossa and Maico, banging out trials bikes, ISDT racers or bandy-legged two-stroke motocrossers not unlike my Stormer.

My 600 came with white plastics, gold rims, these newfangled USD forks, a 'Pro-Lever' back end and a finned slab covering the 558cc Rotax engine's timing belt. That belt turned a camshaft with the profile of a Dairylea cheese triangle. Once you'd mastered the left-side kickstart, the thing barked into life and took off like a banshee right up to 65mph. By then the close-ratio box had given its all and your eardrums were being pummelled by a stampede of rampant decibels.

When I got it back home I was already prepared to concede that I might have made another of my periodic procurement errors. I tried despatching on the KTM but, even if the kick had been on the normal side, the carb looked like it came off my 900SS and made starting the bike tiresome once the thing got hot. Starting aggro was normal with some big singles, but the limitations of a close-ratio box began to dawn on me. It hadn't been an issue with my similarly race-oriented ITs – I never went anywhere far on those – but preparing the KTM for a desert trip wasn't simply a question of fitting a smaller back sprocket and tying a knot in the chain to take up the slack. The internal gearbox ratios would still be close, just with taller overall gearing. That, and the bike's general fire-breathing nature, put it out of contention for me. It would be a decade before the out-of-a-crate desert-ready KTM 640 Adventure came on the scene.

My Benly was fed to the goats and I set off on a new type of adventure, leading my first tour to the Sahara, accompanying half a dozen bikers in a Land Rover 101. It was to be about as successful as the Charge of the Light Brigade; *Desert Travels* covers that story. Once back in Bethune Road, it was adios GS600, hello GS450, a sensible work bike on which I could pay off the debts incurred by my costly desert venture.

The eight-year-old Suzuki was of the previous, two-valve generation to the GSX I'd had in Australia and brought back memories of my Honda 350K4. Sadly, our bonding was cut short when it was nicked in Pall Mall. Helmet on the bars, keys in the ignition may have had something to do with it, but I'd been doing that for years. A mate from Bethune Road flogged me his GS550 for £350, before heading back to university. The 550 – bike #43 – wouldn't have been my first choice, but it got me back on the road without delay.

'Bethune Road, your time is up. Please leave the area.' And so was my time with Marie. She went abroad, the others dispersed, and I found an empty in a block of flats in Shoreditch, just off Old Street roundabout. The great location should have been seen as a warning, but inside the place was a tip. In fact it was worse than a tip. In my mind's eye the previous occupant had got progressively sicker until they'd keeled over, died and started decomposing. Even with the windows open, the stench inside suggested they may have remained in the flat for some time before their passing had been noted. I spent an entire weekend scrubbing the smallest bedroom and filthy bathroom with sugar soap, then repainting to freshen them up. The rest of the place would have to wait, not least the kitchen, where weeks of dirty dishes and mould-covered food lay piled in the sink like a scene from a Cronenberg movie. The fact that I was prepared to put all this effort into cleaning it up, where previously I'd turned my nose up at a tower block in Rotherhithe, showed that squatting was going the way of despatching.

After the tour fiasco, for the first time in years I owed money, which I didn't like. So I took everything going at Security. One morning, a few days after moving into the Shoreditch squat, I was coming back into town from Radlett along the A5. Charging downhill and into a spacious roundabout near Elstree, I became aware of a car cutting in from my left. 'Hesitation is death!' is the despatcher's hearty motto. Unfortunately the driver lived by the same motto. A minute later I was resting against a bollard with a broken shin and a huge gouge below my left knee where the side of the engine had ground my leg against the driver's door. It was to become the latest in my scar collection. Like just about every other big biking crash I'd had, this one was my fault: a combination of too much speed, poor anticipation and slow reactions. But never mind that, my first thought was: what pretty nurse will I meet this time?

In fact she was a brown-eyed, olive-skinned honey – a dark-haired Sharron Macready clone from *The Champions* TV show. Once I realised we were getting somewhere, it was well worth the broken bones. That, and the fact that I'd helped tidy another boring transverse four off the UK road network. The bailiffs evicted me while I was laid up in hospital. Jeez, not even a fortnight this time. As I'd guessed, the squat had been too central to be a runner. Clive, a mate from Canterbury, came up and collected my stuff. The hospital staff were just great. The chaplain even came round offering solace, as did a lady from social services who'd heard I was of no fixed abode. She told me I was due either some sort of benefit or even rehousing. I thanked her but explained I'd find somewhere to recuperate, probably in Canterbury.

As it happened, once out of hospital, I shacked up with someone else. Let me tell you, crutches can be excellent seduction aids. Must be something to do with vulnerability. Just as that brief affair came to an end, the police announced they'd located my GS450 from the depths of the Lee Valley, running and intact apart from a packet of chips in the topbox. It was great to have the 450 back, and soon I was back on the job, though wary of damaging my recently plated leg.

I had a big trip lined up with Steve, who I'd met in Algeria the previous year: an epic 4WD trek across Algeria, Mali, deep into the Fouta Djallon mountains of northern Guinea, then out through Mauritania. With just a month to go before we left, on weekdays I'd work late then sleep in the back of my latest Land Rover. Weekends, I'd leave the bike in town and drive down to Canterbury for a bath.

However, away from brief encounters and recovered bikes, things weren't all going my way that year. One Friday evening I picked up a multi-drop job with deliveries right across the southeast of England that would take half the night but would swing me towards Canterbury in time for an early breakfast. Somewhere near Crowborough, the Land Rover's reconditioned engine threw a rod and took the whole thing down. Now I was deprived of my urban caravan and the expedition itself was on the rocks. It was just a couple of weeks until we set off but I would not be beaten. Steve offered me his Ténéré to ride alongside his Toyota. Because of my leg, I was hesitant, but figured I'd give it a whirl. I took to working as late as they wanted, then sleeping discreetly in the office. Just one more winter. Once I got back from the trip, I'd do a couple of months then get out of this game for good.

An overnight job came in for Bristol. I had to hang around till midnight until it was ready and then get it there as soon as possible. It was the sort of well-paid reward you picked up when working round the clock. Back in town the next day and with a few jobs already under my belt, I was heading in from Notting Hill along the Bayswater Road. As I passed the Soviet Embassy a black Sierra pulled out on me from the side street opposite. It was a perfect morning for a small accident.

During a decade of riding London's streets I'd dealt with countless such incidents, and on a good day could anticipate them even before the driver had made up their mind. But the overnight job had slowed my reflexes. The impact was only a fork-bending, knee-grazing affair, but after the year I'd just had, on top of my current situation, it was the final straw. It was all becoming too much like life during wartime.

That November evening I hauled the front-ended GS off the recovery van, grabbed the crooked bars and shoved it up the drive to Clive's place, then simply let it drop to the ground. The others in the house came out and observed, a little disturbed, as I pulled out my dog-eared *Nicholson*'s and stuffed it into my helmet.

'Anyone got any petrol or something?' I sighed.

'There's some leaking out your tank.'

'Oh yes. So there is.'

I let some trickle on to the *Streetfinder* and the helmet's grease-caked lining, then yanked off the fuel hose and gave them both a proper dousing.

'Here.' Someone passed a box of matches.

With the satisfying finality of a priest sprinkling a coffin with holy water, I threw in a match and *whump*, up it all went. We stepped back a bit and with hands in pockets like pickets round a brazier, gazed at the pretty flames as the *Nicholson*'s pages curled into ash. The helmet's foam lining turned to sludge and soon the polycarbonate shell lit up, deformed and sagged into a pool of bubbling tar.

No lid. Bent bike. No *Streetfinder*. There was no going back for 106. How fitting that my last big job had been to Bristol, the very city I'd planned to move to when I started out on that brief summer's messengering back in 1978, aboard my gleaming Bonneville. Whatever adventures my motorcycling future held, the days of despatching were done.

Acknowledgements

©Anthony Bourdain, 2000, 'Kitchen Confidential' by kind permission of Bloomsbury Publishing Inc.

Thanks to Richard Kemplay and Glenn Burtenshaw for help with the front cover. Thanks too to Nicky Slade for proof-reading, Bryn T for guidance, Colin R for recollections and ideas, and above all Lucy Ridout for more suggestions and forensic editing services.

I also appreciate the information I received from the original directors of Security Despatch, Mark C on typesetting in the 1980s, Gerry B on saturation diving in the same era, and the MCIA for UK motorcycle sales figures through the ages.

See the book's webpage: adventure-motorcycling.com/the-street-riding-years/ for imagery from the period, including some of the bikes and places described in this book.

Some names have been changed.